To my wife, Helen,
and our sons:
James, Gary, and David

DR. IRVING L. KOSOW, EDITOR
CHARLES M. THOMSON, JOSEPH J. GERSHON, AND JOSEPH A. LABOK, CONSULTING EDITORS
PRENTICE-HALL SERIES IN ELECTRONIC TECHNOLOGY

FUNDAMENTALS OF ANALOG COMPUTERS

PRENTICE-HALL, INCORPORATED
ENGLEWOOD CLIFFS, NEW JERSEY

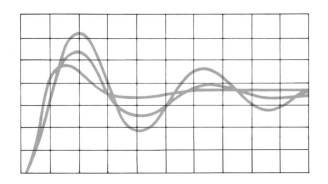

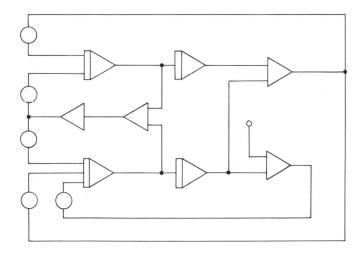

ROBERT C. WEYRICK
ASSOCIATE PROFESSOR
UNIVERSITY OF AKRON
AKRON, OHIO

PRENTICE-HALL INTERNATIONAL, INC., London
PRENTCE-HALL OF AUSTRALIA, PTY. LTD., Sydney
PRENTICE-HALL OF CANADA, LTD., Toronto
PRENTICE-HALL OF INDIA PRIVATE LTD., New Dehli
PRENTICE-HALL OF JAPAN, INC., Tokyo

Current printing (last digit):
10 9 8 7 6 5 4 3 2

13–334318–9

Library of Congress Catalog Card Number 70–81767

Printed in the United States of America

ROBERT C. WEYRICK
**FUNDAMENTALS
OF ANALOG COMPUTERS**

Analog computers are well established as devices for the solution of engineering and scientific problems. Large analog computing facilities have existed for a number of years, and small desk-top computers now provide the individual with means for analyzing problems of a dynamic nature. In addition, analog computing equipment finds wide application in instrumentation and control, where its uses range from simple computations to maintaining control of a complete process or system.

To the engineer, the analog computer is primarily a tool which aids in the analysis and design of dynamic systems. To the technician, the computer is basically an item of equipment to be installed, operated, and maintained. Consequently, although their objectives differ, it is desirable that both engineering and engineering technology students become familiar with analog computation.

For the past several years I have taught a one-semester course in analog computers to electronic technology students. Although a number of excellent analog computer texts are available, those with which I am acquainted are primarily written for the engineering student and emphasize the application of the computer to the solution of engineering problems. Thus, a working knowledge of differential equations is necessarily assumed. Since the engineering technology student rarely has this mathematical background, existing books have generally proved inappropriate for this course.

PREFACE

Consequently, I developed a series of course notes which I believe are consistent with the objectives and level of engineering technology training, and these notes form the basis of this book. The aim of the book is twofold: (1) to describe the design and operation of the equipment and circuits used in electronic analog computers, and (2) to provide an introduction to the application of analog computers in the solution of problems involving differential equations.

Regarding the second intent, I have included introductory material on differential equations which should provide adequate mathematical background. Although some knowledge of the calculus is prerequisite to this material, this need not be extensive. An understanding of the concepts of differentiation and integration and a familiarity with simple derivatives and integrals should prove sufficient.

Although this book is specifically intended for the technical institute student pursuing a curriculum in electronic technology, it should also prove useful to the practicing technician or engineer who wishes to obtain an introduction to analog computers.

Chapter 1 of this book provides a descriptive introduction to electronic analog computers and their application. Chapter 2 discusses linear computing elements. The uses of operational amplifiers, which are regarded as the heart of an electronic analog computer, are emphasized. Chapter 3 describes in detail the characteristics and design of solid-state operational amplifiers.

Chapter 4 is concerned with the application of computing servomechanisms to multiplication and other nonlinear operations. Chapter 5 deals with electronic multipliers and function generators. Chapter 6 describes the complete general-purpose analog computer including its modes of operation and problem setup equipment. Readout equipment used with the computer is also discussed.

Chapter 7 is an introduction to linear differential equations and their methods of solution. Chapter 8 discusses programming the computer to solve differential equations. The procedures for developing a computer setup diagram and scaling the problem equations are explained. The background necessary for this discussion is provided in Chapter 7.

In Chapter 9 we apply the analog computer to several representative problems involving electrical, mechanical, and chemical systems. An appendix presents several useful tables including basic derivatives and integrals, computer symbology, and special computer circuits.

I firmly believe that one's education in analog computation is greatly enhanced through seeing and doing. Consequently, I recommend that some laboratory experience be part of a course in analog computers. Several inexpensive analog computers are available which are well suited to educational purposes. It is my experience that the student acquires a more thorough insight into the application and solution of differential equations as he observes the simulated behavior of systems on the analog computer.

The originality of an elementary text lies not in its contents *per se*, but in the attempt to present the subject in terms appropriate to a certain group of readers. For the subject matter of this book I am generally indebted to those many individuals who have contributed to analog computation. In particular, I would like to single out my former co-workers at Goodyear Aerospace Corporation: our long-time association in the design and use of analog computers provides much of the inspiration and background for this text. I should also like to thank both my colleagues and students at the University of Akron for their many helpful comments and suggestions.

Finally, a great deal of appreciation must be expressed for the painstaking task of converting the manuscript to typed form. My most sincere personal thanks to my aunt, Miss Helen Hassler, for her indispensable help in this respect.

Akron, Ohio   ***Robert C. Weyrick***

CONTENTS

1-1 EVOLUTION OF COMPUTING DEVICES

In beginning a study of analog computers, one might first ask the question "What is a computer?" Perhaps the most simple answer is to say that a computer is a problem solving device or tool. In this sense a computer might be regarded as a device able to receive information and process it in a predetermined manner to provide useable results. With this introductory definition, our interest might turn to the history of computers and computing devices. What manner of evolution has provided us with the powerful computing tools which are now an integral part of virtually every segment of our society?

Undoubtedly man's earliest computing device consisted of the five fingers of each hand, tools that are still used by every child learning to count. These ten fingers enabled man to communicate numbers by holding up fingers and to perform simple addition or subtraction by adding to or reducing the number of fingers displayed. At some point in human development, pebbles superseded man's fingers as a basic counting device. A convenient container for counting purposes was a clay board with grooves in which the pebbles were placed. About 600 B. C. a counting device appeared in the Far East in the form of a rectangular frame with beads strung on parallel wires. This device in somewhat more sophisticated form is known today as the *abacus*. Each column of beads

1

INTRODUCTION

1

represents a place in the decimal system such as units, tens, etc. The location of the beads in a column determines the value of the corresponding order. Addition is accomplished by displacing the beads upward from their normally "down" position on the appropriate wire. Subtraction is accomplished by reversing the addition process while multiplication and division are performed by successive additions and subtractions. The abacus is still widely used in some parts of the world and can be manipulated by skilled individuals to provide remarkably rapid calculations.

More than two thousand years elapsed before the next significant development in computing devices took place. In 1642 Blaise Pascal, a Franch mathematician and physicist, constructed the first mechanical calculator, the forerunner of our modern desk calculator. Pascal's invention replaced the wires and beads of the abacus with toothed wheels divided into 10 parts. The wheels, representing units, tens, etc., were placed next to one another in a manner similar to the wires of the abacus. The positions of these wheels could be observed and sums read through windows in their covers. The primary feature of this machine was the mechanization of the transfer of tens or "carry" operation. As one wheel completed a revolution and moved from 9 to 0, a ratchet caused the wheel on its immediate left to move forward one unit.

Pascal's machine was essentially limited to performing the operations of addition and subtraction. Multiplication and division could only be accomplished by repeated addition or subtraction of numbers. Several years after Pascal's invention, Baron von Leibnitz, a German mathematician and philosopher, constructed a machine that could multiply directly by means of additional gears. Unfortunately Leibnitz's designs were handicapped by the industrial technology of his day, and mechanical flaws limited their reliability. However, his calculator embodied almost all of the principles now used in desk calculators. The significant difference is that electric motors now cause the wheels to turn at a rapid rate rather than the slow hand action of Leibnitz's machine.

The first attempt to develop a universal automatic calculator (or analytical engine as it was then known) was by Charles Babbage, an English mathematician, in 1833. Babbage's design had all the elements of a modern digital computer, namely: memory, control, and a calculating or arithmetic unit. The very important ability to modify the course of a calculation according to the intermediate results was to be incorporated. As with Leibnitz, the ideas of Babbage were too far advanced for nineteenth century practice and, although Babbage worked on it for about 20 years, his machine was never completed. However his project proved to be the seed for the subsequent development of our present digital computers.

The computing devices which we have so far considered are essentially extensions of the ten-finger counting system. Since they work with discrete numbers or digits, these devices are broadly classified as *digital* in nature. In addition to the counting or digital principle, a second principle of computing has evolved over the years. This is the *analog principle*, which is based on computing by measurement or analogy. The distinguishing feature of this principle is that numbers are represented by continuous physical quantities such as lengths, shaft rotations, or electrical voltages or currents. By "continuous quantities" we mean that there are an infinite number of points on the measurement scale. For example, integer numbers can be represented by corresponding voltage levels. Since a range of voltage is a continuous quantity, intermediate mixed numbers are identifiable so long as they are within the resolution of our measurement equipment. We might simulate the addition of two or more numbers by adding the voltages which represent the numbers.

A familiar computing device which illustrates the analog principle is another seventeenth century invention, the *slide rule*. Here the distances along two sticks are analogous to the logarithms of two numbers which are to be multiplied (or divided). The sum of the distances is then analogous to the sum of the logarithms which, of course, represents the product of the numbers.

Another familiar computing device is the *planimeter*, which measures the area bounded by a curve by passing a stylus along the perimeter line. That the planimeter is an analog computing device is evident when we consider that the area bounded by a curve is the value of the definite integral of the mathematical function represented by the curve.

Another integrating device of historical significance was invented by James Thomson, the brother of Lord Kelvin, about 1875. The features of this device, the *ball and disc integrator*, are illustrated in Fig. 1-1. In the ball and disc integrator, means are provided to move the ball across the flat disc in such a way that the distance x is proportional to the quantity to be integrated. When the disc is rotated the ball will spin at a speed proportional to its distance from the center of the disc, and this motion is transmitted to the output shaft. If the angular rotation y of the disc is proportional to the variable of integration, then the total rotation of the output shaft is given by

$$\theta = Kxy = K \int xdy \qquad (1\text{-}1)$$

where K is a proportionality constant determined by the physical dimensions of the device.

Several years after Thomson's invention, Kelvin connected a number of his mechanical integrators together in such a way that equations involving integrations could be solved. Kelvin's efforts proved to be the groundwork for research by Dr. Vannevar Bush of Massachusetts Institute of Technology (M.I.T.). In 1931 Bush completed the first large-scale computing machine incorporating mechanical integrators similar to those of Thomson. Using a

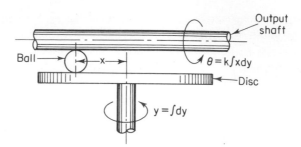

FIGURE 1–1   Ball and disc integrator.

variety of mechanical devices, such as gear assemblies and special linkages, Thomson's machine was able to solve complex equations arising out of physical problems. Bush's computing assembly was termed a *differential analyzer* and is regarded as the predecessor of the modern analog computer.

The beginning of the modern computer era coincided with World War II. The rapid development of electronic technology during and after this period made possible the transformation of computers from bulky, slow mechanical machines to the compact, high-speed devices of today.

In the digital field, the first large-scale computer utilizing twentieth-century engineering advances was built jointly by Harvard University and International Business Machines Corporation (I.B.M.) between 1939 and 1944. This computer, known as the Harvard Mark I, brought the ideas of Babbage into existence. It was electromechanical in nature and contained large numbers of switches, relays, counter wheels, etc. Although having all the functional components of a digital computer, the Mark I was extremely slow by today's standards. For example, division required about one minute, as compared to present times in the microsecond range.

The first electronic digital computer, the ENIAC, was developed and built at the University of Pennsylvania beginning in 1943 and completed in 1946. As evidenced by its full name, "*E*lectronic *N*umerical *I*ntegrator *a*nd *C*omputer," it was not intended to be a general-purpose digital computer but was designed for computing ballistic tables. The ENIAC contained over 18,000 vacuum tubes, required 130 kW of power, and occupied a space 30 by 50 feet. Nonetheless, it represented a significant step in computer technology, since it provided an increase in speed of over ten thousand times as compared to the relay computer.

During this same time period comparable advances were made in the field of analog computers.

The first electrical analog computers appeared in the 1920's and were used for studying the behavior of electrical power networks. These devices, known as *network analyzers*, are used to investigate problems such as voltage drops along transmission lines, current flows in lines, etc.

The first differential analyzer of an electromechanical nature was completed at M.I.T. in 1942. Essentially an extension and refinement of Bush's earlier computer, it incorporated numerous vacuum tubes, relays, and motors, and provided much greater versatility than its predecessors. Other analog computing devices, similar in nature, were also developed during this period for military applications such as gun direction computers.

A significant development at this time was the introduction of electronic amplifiers to perform precise mathematical operations. The use of such amplifiers has been perfected to a high degree, and they now form the basic element of electronic analog computers.

Two pioneering large-scale analog computers of the late 1940's are worthy of mention. These are the Cyclone computer, built by Reeves Instrument Corporation, and the Typhoon computer, constructed by the Radio Corporation of America.

The last two decades have seen an almost explosive growth in computer development and utilization. The advent of transistors and, more recently, of integrated circuits, has made possible computers of both greatly reduced size and power consumption and high reliability. Both analog and digital computers have reached a high degree of sophistication and are now applied to the solution of problems in virtually every field of endeavor.

Although this brief historical review is intended to provide an introduction to the subject of analog computers, a second purpose is to impress upon the reader the relatively short time between the construction of the first large-scale computers and their wide-spread acceptance as scientific, engineering, and business tools.

1-2 DIGITAL COMPUTERS

In the preceding section, it was pointed out that computing equipment may be divided into two major classifications: *analog* and *digital*.

A *digital* device operates directly upon numbers. Its basic operation is counting, whether it be the counting of beads, of gear teeth, or of electrical pulses. All of the mathematical operations are performed by counting or addition; for example, subtraction is accomplished by adding the complement of the subtrahend to the minuend. In digital computation, a problem is broken down into a series of arithmetic steps which are completed in sequence to arrive at the solution. This method is known as *sequential operation* and is basically the same as if pencil and paper were used to carry out the arithmetic operations. The difference, of course, is that the tremendous speed and memory capacity of the digital computer permit complex calculations to be made in a fraction of a second. A point to emphasize is that the mathematical operations and the method by which the computer derives a final result have little if any resemblance to the actions of the physical problem under study.

The accuracy of digital computer solutions is theoretically unlimited. The precision of a digital computer is readily increased by providing additional decimal places in the numbers throughout the equipment. However this both increases the cost of the equipment and decreases the speed of computation.

Because of its numerical nature, the digital computer is well suited to problems involving the processing of large masses of data where simple calculations are repeated over and over again. Consequently, digital machines find their widest use in business applications such as accounting, record keeping, and billing, as well as in scientific problems involving statistical analysis and data reduction.

Digital computers are also being applied to the control of industrial processes. The computer generally performs a supervisory function by evaluating process conditions against desired performance criteria and determining changes to provide optimum operation. More recently, digital computers have been used to provide *direct digital control* (DDC) of individual process variables.

1-3 SOLVING ENGINEERING PROBLEMS

In general, one objective of engineering is to apply scientific knowledge in the design of some device or system. Frequently, the engineer attempts to evaluate the performance of a proposed design before time and money are invested in its construction. In almost all cases modifications will be made to the initial design before the system requirements are considered to be satisfied.

Traditionally, engineers have applied both mathematical analysis and experimentation to the solution of engineering design problems. Wherever possible, mathematical equations are derived which express the relationships between the variable quantities in the system. A set of such equations is known as a *mathematical model* of the system. The solution of these equations may be used to evaluate a proposed design in order to develop a system which will provide optimum performance.

In some problems, the system variables are related by algebraic equations. In this case mathematical expressions for the variables can be obtained using the algebraic operations of addition and multiplication. More frequently, though, the system variables change with time, and the designer is interested in determining the *time-behavior* of these variables. The mathematical model then relates the variables as well as the rates of change or *derivatives* of the variables. Equations of this type are known as *differential equations* and their solution requires the calculus operations of integration and differentiation.

As systems become larger and more complex, analytical solution of the mathematical model becomes overly difficult, if not impossible. In some instances, a problem may be simplified to permit solution by analytical means. However this is done at the risk of introducing significant errors into the solution.

By contrast, an experimental approach employs a minimum of analysis, and the design proceeds largely on the basis of experimental data. In some situations, direct experimentation with a prototype of the system is feasible. This approach is commonly used in the design of electronic circuits. However, direct physical experimentation is frequently inconvenient, expensive, or even dangerous. One can readily visualize the difficulty of direct experimentation in the design of a nuclear reactor or a manned space vehicle.

To overcome these difficulties, a physical *scale model* of the proposed device may be constructed and its behavior observed. Such a model has the same basic form, structure, and proportion as the original, but is scaled to a different size. For example, a scale model of an airplane may be tested in a practical wind tunnel, a model of a ship hull may be evaluated in a small basin or channel, or a pilot plant may be used to develop new chemical operations. However, scale model experimentation also has limitations. It may prove to be overly expensive, the model may not be easily altered to improve its performance, and the characteristics in which we are interested may not closely resemble those of the original. Finally, observing the behavior of a model may not provide sufficient understanding for design purposes.

A scale model can be described as being *analogous to the object which it represents;* that is, the original and the model exhibit a correspondence or likeness in a number of respects. Consequently, a scale model is often referred to as an *analog* of the original device.

In addition to the scale model, or *physical* analog, a second type of analog may also be used in studying a system. Where a mathematical model of the system is available, an analog may be constructed of elements which have no similarity in form but do have the same mathematical characteristics as elements of the actual system. Such a model represents a *mathematical* analog of the system. When its elements are connected together in an appropriate manner, the model will exhibit behavior of the same form as that of the system itself. Thus, we say that *the behavior of the analog simulates the behavior of the system.* Since the mathematical analog simulates the system behavior, it is referred to as an *analog simulation* or, more commonly, as an *analog computer.*

The mathematical analog overcomes several of the limitations of a scale model. Since it is simulating behavior rather than physical characteristics, it provides the performance information required for engineering design. Secondly, since the analog elements may be interconnected in any desired way, a simulation is easily modified to improve the system design.

1-4 ANALOG SIMULATION

In the previous section it was pointed out that the behavior of a physical device or system can conveniently be studied by analog simulation. Analog simulation or computation works by representing the system or problem variables by some set of physical quantities that are easily generated and controlled. Mechanical, fluid, and electrical quantities have been successfully employed in analog simulators. For example, the analog quantities in Bush's early analyzer were shaft rotations.

This book is concerned with the design and operation of a specific kind of analog computer in which electrical voltages represent the variables of the physical system being studied. The electrical voltages are known as the *computer or machine variable*. Their behavior with time corresponds directly to the variation with time of the original problem variables. Thus, if the vertical position of the center of gravity of an automobile oscillates with time because of an uneven road surface, then the voltage representing the height of the center of gravity will also oscillate. If the temperature of a fluid rises with the application of heat, then so will the voltage representing temperature in the computer. Hence, we see that for every action that occurs in the original system, there is a corresponding action of the computer variables.

As an illustration of analog simulation, assume that we wish to study the flight of a rocket fired vertically upward as shown in Fig. 1-2. We might wish to know the height, velocity, and acceleration of the rocket at any instant of time. These three quantities are the problem variables and, as such, our analog computer simulation would contain a voltage proportional to each of them. By observing these voltages, we would effectively be observing the behavior of the rocket.

To carry out our simulation, we would need to know the equations governing the rocket's flight. We would then set up in the analog computer an electrical circuit whose voltages behave in the same way as the variables in the problem. This step is known as *programming the computer*. During actual operation of the computer, the information about the problem exists in the form of continuously varying voltages. The solution from the computer is a series of plots or curves of these voltages as a function of time. This is illustrated in Fig. 1-2, which shows voltage curves representing the behavior of the three variables in our rocket simulation.

An important aspect of analog simulation should be noted from this example. Although we did need to know the equations which describe the system's behavior, it was *not* necessary for us to solve the equations for the problem variables, or to even know a method of solution. The analog computer provides the solution for us.

Although solutions in the form of curves are generally convenient for

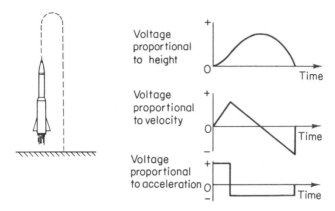

FIGURE 1-2   Simulation of rocket flight.

engineering use, results in this form have another important aspect. It is easy for the computer operator to visualize the results as the actual response of the system under investigation. Since he can simultaneously observe the actions of all parts of the system, the operator cultivates a "feel" for what is happening. Changes made in the simulation are meaningful in terms of the actual system, and the effects of these changes can be immediately evaluated. For example, in the rocket illustration, we might wish to vary the time-of-burn in order to obtain different trajectories. Thus, a trial and correction process can be followed in modifying the simulation to obtain the desired, or even the optimum, performance from the system.

1-5 ELECTRONIC ANALOG COMPUTERS

The type of analog computer with which we shall be concerned is generally known as an *electronic analog computer*. This name is derived from the fact that the voltages which represent the problem variables are largely generated and controlled by electronic circuitry. This computer is sometimes identified as a *dc analog computer*, since the voltages are dc in nature, although of course they vary in magnitude as the problem variables change. Almost all general-purpose analog computers are of the dc type. "General-purpose" refers to the ability of a computer to handle a variety of problems.

A second type of analog computer using electrical voltages is known as an *ac analog computer*. The machine variables in this computer are ac voltages whose fundamental frequency is commonly either 60 or 400 Hz. Although the basic principles and method of problem solution are the same as for the dc computer, the ac computer circuits are somewhat different and there is a large reliance upon electromechanical computing devices. The ac computer has not found wide acceptance as a general-purpose computer. Its use is largely confined to special-purpose military and aircraft applications including flight simulators, navigation computers, and gun direction computers. We will not discuss the design of ac computers in this book; information on this subject may be obtained from references listed in the Bibliography.

The electronic analog computer consists of basic elements or building blocks which perform specific mathematical operations. The operations commonly available are:

1. Summation of two or more variables,
2. Multiplication of a variable by a constant,
3. Multiplication of a variable by a variable,
4. Integration of a variable with respect to time, and
5. Generation of a function of a variable.

In simulating a system, various computing elements are connected together in conformance to the system equations. Thus, in addition to the computing elements themselves, the computer must incorporate means for their interconnection. In a special-purpose computer to be used in solving one specific problem, the elements may be permanently wired. For the general-purpose computer, provision for flexible wiring must be made. This almost always consists of a *patch board* with terminations for the computing elements and removable wires or leads called *patch cords* which provide the interconnections.

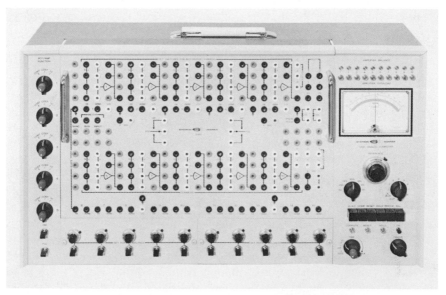

FIGURE 1–3   Small analog computer for individual desk-top use. (Systron Donner Corporation)

A separate analog computing *element* is used for each individual mathematical operation required in the solution of a problem. Since all of the elements operate simultaneously on continuous variables, the problem solution may be obtained quite rapidly. As problem complexity increases, a larger number of analog elements are required. However, the solution time does not increase. Thus, speed of computation is one of the advantages of the analog computer; in fact, systems are usually simulated so that the time of computation corresponds directly to the *actual* time of response of the system.

In addition to the computing elements and means of interconnection, a complete analog computer requires several other parts. Regulated power supplies are necessary for operation of the electronic equipment, as well as for providing precise voltages for the computer variables. The latter are known as the *computer reference voltages.* For convenience, values of either $+10$ volts or $+100$ volts are usually selected for the computer reference. A *control unit* is necessary for operating the computer in its various modes. *Read-out devices* such as recorders, plotting boards, oscilloscopes, and voltmeters are used to indicate and record the results of the simulation.

Although all general-purpose analog computers employ the same basic items, computers differ greatly in capacity, capability, and operator convenience. Their physical size ranges from desk-top units to racks of equipment which may fill an entire room. Figure 1-3 shows a representative small analog computer for individual use. Computers of this size typically provide from 20 to 40 computing elements and can handle problems having perhaps as many as 10 variables. Several computers of this type may be interconnected and operated together for increased capability. A large analog computer

FIGURE 1-4   Large analog computer with display unit at left. (Electronic Associates, Inc.)

installation, as shown in Fig. 1-4, contains hundreds of computing units and is used for simulating systems involving many variables.

1-6 ACCURACY OF ANALOG COMPUTATION

It was previously pointed out that the computation accuracy of a digital computer is theoretically unlimited. This is not the case with the analog computer and, in general, problems requiring high accuracy are not solved on an analog machine.

Before discussing analog computer accuracy, it will be helpful to define several terms. *Accuracy* is a broad term, but the general connotation is freedom from error. Thus the word denotes how closely a result or measurement conforms to fact. Hence it should not be used to describe physical devices such as computer elements, but should rather be applied to the results of a computation or measurement.

The word *precision* is used to describe the exactness of computing components. It takes into account factors such as the resolution (fineness of operation) and stability of the component or device. Precision is indicated by a *percentage*, such as 0.1 %, or by a *ratio*, such as one part in 1000. The reference scale in either case is taken as the full scale range of the computer variable. For example, the precision of an analog summing unit may be specified as 0.01 % of full scale. If the unit has an output range of ± 10 volts, then the full scale is 20 volts, and the output will be within ± 2 millivolts of the exact value (independent of any errors in the input voltages).

This inherent difference in accuracy between digital and analog computers may be illustrated by considering the multiplication of two numbers. Using a desk calculator, the accuracy of the result is determined by the number of significant places in the display, which is generally ten or more. On the other hand, with a slide rule the accuracy is determined by the precision with which linear distances can be established and measured. This is typically three significant figures for the common ten-inch slide rule. Of course, the precision of the analog device can be increased by increasing the range of the device variable (on the slide rule, length). However there are obviously practical limits to this approach (we would need a 1000-inch slide rule to obtain five significant figures).

The precision of electronic analog components is typically between 0.01 % and 0.1 % of full scale. However, the accuracy of solution is generally much less, for several reasons. In solving a problem, a number of analog elements are interconnected, and their individual errors combine in some fashion. Noise, which is always present in an electrical signal, also degrades accuracy. Another factor is the accuracy with which the computer output voltages are recorded and read. It is important for us to note that solution accuracy is related to the selection of *scales* for the computer variables. For best accuracy, the range of each computer variable in the problem should correspond as closely as possible to the full scale voltage range of the computer.

Under ordinary circumstances, an analog computer solution is accurate to about 0.1% to 0.5% for small simulations and to about 1% or higher for very large simulations. Accuracies of these magnitudes are quite acceptable in the solution of most engineering problems, since input data are usually not known to any greater accuracy. It is obviously of no avail to calculate solutions to accuracies beyond those to which the problem parameters are known. Consequently, analog computer accuracy is usually not a limitation in practice.

1-7 HYBRID COMPUTERS

If we should attempt to compare analog and digital computers, the characteristics inherent in each might be summarized as follows.

Digital computer:
Variables are discrete numbers.
Operations are performed sequentially.
Extremely high accuracy.

Analog computer:
Variables are continuous quantities.
Operations are performed simultaneously (high solution speed).
Limited accuracy.

To take advantage of digital computer accuracy and analog computer speed, another type of computer has been developed in recent years. This is the *hybrid computer*, which is so named because it incorporates both digital and analog techniques and equipment. Figure 1-5 shows a large-scale hybrid computer.

The hybrid concept might be described by considering the application to which it was first applied in the late 1950's. The simulation of a space mission involves computing the dynamic behavior of the space vehicle as well as its trajectory or path. Since these computational requirements differ, combined digital and analog methods are advantageous. A block diagram of a hybrid simulation of a space mission is shown in Fig. 1-6. A digital computer is used to accurately compute the trajectory of the vehicle in three dimensional coordinates as well as to simulate the digital navigation system. An analog computer simulates the motion of the vehicle and its control surfaces where greater bandwidth and less accuracy are required. Thus, each computer is used for the

FIGURE 1–5   Large-scale hybrid computing system. (Electronic Associates, Inc.)

type of problem to which it is best suited. Since the analog and digital variables differ in form, equipment must be provided to convert analog voltages to digital form, and vice versa. Devices of this type are known as *analog to digital* (A/D) and *digital to analog* (D/A) converters, respectively.

Another area in which hybrid computers find wide use is the design of

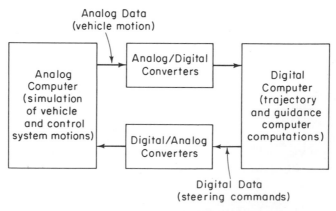

FIGURE 1–6   Block diagram of hybrid simulation.

industrial control systems. In these applications, the analog portion of the computer simulates the continuous process and control equipment and the digital computer determines overall control functions to optimize the operation of the entire process.

In solving complex problems, hybrid computers have generally proved to be faster and more economical than either analog or digital computers alone. Hybrid computation has been able to resolve many complex problems which it was impractical to approach by either analog or digital techniques alone. It is expected that computers of the future will more and more incorporate both analog and digital features, and the characteristics of each may become so completely merged that they will no longer be separately identifiable.

PROBLEMS FOR CHAPTER 1

1. What is meant by the discrete nature of a digital device? By the continuous nature of an analog device?

2. What are the basic differences between digital and analog computers?

3. What is a mathematical model of a system?

4. What is an "analog"? Identify two kinds of analogs.

5. Identify the basic parts of an electronic analog computer.

6. What mathematical operations may be performed by the elements of an analog computer?

7. What limits the precision of analog devices?

8. What limits the accuracy of analog computer results?

9. What is a hybrid computer?

10. The equation of motion of a body thrown vertically upward is
$$h = v_o t - 1/2gt^2$$
where h = height in feet, t = time in seconds, and g = 32 ft/sec². If v_o = 100 ft/sec, plot curves showing height and velocity as a function of time.

11. An analog computer is to be used to simulate the motion of a pendulum which is pulled away from its equilibrium point and released. What are the variables in the problem? Sketch curves showing the way in which the variables might behave as a function of time.

12. Analog computer simulation is used in all branches of engineering. Suggest a problem which could be studied by means of simulation in (a) civil, (b) chemical, (c) electrical, and (d) mechanical engineering.

A large number of physical systems are made up of components whose output is closely proportional to their input over the range of operation. Such components are known as *linear elements*. Their input-output relationship may be graphed by a straight line. This is illustrated in Fig. 2-1, which shows the linear characteristic of such components as a resistor, a coil spring, a motor, and a generator. Furthermore, if linear elements are *cascaded* so that the output of the first provides the input to the second, the overall input-output relationship is also linear.

When linear elements are interconnected in some manner to form a linear system, the principle of *superposition* is applicable. The superposition principle states that the total response of a linear system having two or more inputs is identical to that found by separately considering the response of each input with all other inputs removed, and then summing the individual responses. The implication of this statement is that the effects due to each input will *superimpose* as a simple sum and that no interaction exists between the inputs. This principle is always true in a system made up of linear elements.

From a mathematical standpoint, a linear system is described by linear equations in which none of the terms are higher than first degree. For example, consider a simple electrical circuit having input voltages e_1 and e_2 and an output voltage e_o

2

LINEAR COMPUTING CIRCUITS

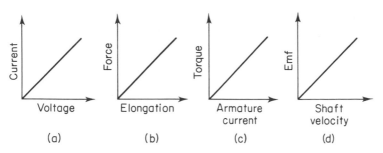

FIGURE 2–1   Linearity in (a) resistor, (b) coil spring, (c) dc motor, (d) dc generator.

as shown in Fig. 2-2. If this circuit were linear and the variables were unchanging, the equation for the output would be an algebraic equation of the general form

$$e_o = Ae_1 + Be_2 + C$$

where A, B, and C are constants or parameters which define the system. If this system were non-linear, the equation would contain terms higher than first degree, as for example

$$e_o = Ae_1^2 + Be_1e_2 + C$$

From the above discussion, we note that the equations describing a linear system involve the mathematical operations of addition, subtraction, and multiplication by a constant. These operations are, therefore, identified as *linear operations*. It is important to point out that these operations are inherent in the linear elements which make up the system.

Rather than assume only fixed values, the variables in a physical system will more likely change as a function of some independent variable such as time. In this case, the equations describing the system are *differential* equations. The formulation and solution of simple differential equations will be discussed in Chapter 7. We will not consider them further at this point, other than to note that such equations are also linear or non-linear, depending on whether terms are first degree or higher.

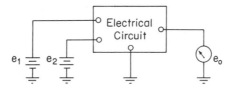

FIGURE 2–2   Illustrative circuit.

Therefore, in addition to the algebraic operations which were previously identified as linear, we will consider the calculus operations of differentiation and integration to be linear operations which occur within linear elements and systems.

2-2 ELECTRICAL NETWORKS

In an analog computer, a mathematical analog of some physical system is constructed of elements such that some set of computer variables is substituted for the set of variables contained in the actual system. Since the equations describing both the system and its analog are of the same form, the behavior of the computer will be analogous to that of the system which it simulates.

As we mentioned in Chapter 1, one set of variables which may be conveniently substituted consists of the voltages and currents of an electrical network. A network may contain only resistors, capacitors, and inductors connected together in some way. A network of this type that contains no power sources, and is capable only of dissipating power applied to it, is referred to as a *passive network*. On the other hand, if power sources or amplifiers of some type are included in the network, it is an *active network*, and the power losses in the passive elements are compensated for by the active devices.

Let us examine the linear properties of passive network elements. In the case of resistors, linearity is defined by the well-known Ohm's law

$$e = Ri \tag{2-1}$$

Equation 2-1 states that the voltage across a resistor is directly proportional to the current through the resistor and is equal to the current multiplied by a proportionality constant, the resistance R.

For pure inductors, voltage is proportional to the time rate of change, or derivative, of current and is expressed mathematically as

$$e = L \frac{di}{dt} \tag{2-2}$$

In the case the proportionality constant (or parameter) is the inductance L.

The voltage drop across a capacitor is proportional to the total charge q which is built up on the capacitor. This relationship is stated as

$$e = \frac{q}{C} \tag{2-3}$$

where the capacitance C represents the element parameter. Total charge q is the summation, or integral, of infinitesimal charge increments dq and may be expressed by $q = \int dq$. By substitution, Eq. (2-3) may be written

$$e = \frac{1}{C} \int dq \qquad (2\text{-}4)$$

By definition, current is the time rate of change of charge and is expressed as $i = dq/dt$. Equation (2-4) then becomes

$$e = \frac{1}{C} \int i dt \qquad (2\text{-}5)$$

Thus, capacitor voltage is linearly related to the integral of the current charging the capacitor.

Superposition (Sec. 2-1) applied to linear networks states that if several voltage sources are present, the currents and voltage drops due to each source may be computed separately as though all other voltage sources were absent, and the resultant currents and voltage drops may then be combined to arrive at the overall effect.

This principle is frequently applied in the solution of linear multi-loop networks containing several voltage sources. The various loop currents due to each source are solved for independently, and the total current in each loop found by summing the individual components.

A second principle applicable to linear networks consists of two laws known as *Kirchhoff's voltage and current laws*. These laws may be stated as:

1. In any closed loop of an electric circuit, the algebraic sum of the emf's must equal the algebraic sum of the voltage drops;
2. At any junction point or node in an electric circuit, the algebraic sum of the currents entering the point must equal the sum of the currents leaving the point. In other words, the algebraic sum of all the currents at a node is zero.

2-3 PASSIVE COMPUTING NETWORKS

A passive network composed solely of resistors can perform the operation of addition or summation. Consider the circuit shown in Fig. 2-3 where e_1 and e_2 are taken as input voltages and e_o represents an output voltage developed across a load resistance R_L. The voltages are referenced to a common or ground line and might represent variables in a system which the network is simulating.

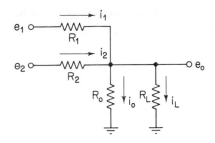

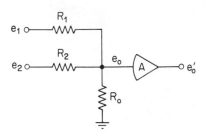

FIGURE 2–3   Resistor network for
voltage summation.

FIGURE 2–4   Summing network
with followup amplifier.

Summing the currents at the common node, we have

$$i_L + i_o = i_1 + i_2 \tag{2-6}$$

The currents may be written in terms of the voltage drops across the resistors, in which case Eq. (2-6) becomes

$$\frac{e_o}{R_L} + \frac{e_o}{R_o} = \frac{e_1 - e_o}{R_1} + \frac{e_2 - e_o}{R_2} \tag{2-7}$$

The parallel combination of R_L and R_o may be replaced by an equivalent resistor R_p. Equation (2-7) may be solved for the output voltage e_o giving

$$e_o = \frac{(R_p/R_1)e_1 + (R_p/R_2)e_2}{1 + R_p/R_1 + R_p/R_2} \tag{2-8}$$

Thus, we see that the output voltage is the weighted algebraic sum of the input voltages.

The above analysis may be extended to networks having more than two inputs. For the general case of n inputs to the network, the equation for the output is

$$e_0 = \frac{(R_p/R_1)e_1 + (R_p/R_2)e_2 + \cdots + (R_p/R_n)e_n}{1 + R_p/R_1 + R_p/R_2 + \cdots R_p/R_n} \tag{2-9}$$

The resistor network can perform the operation of subtraction rather than addition by simply reversing the polarity of the input voltage to be subtracted. For example, if e_2 in Fig. 2-3 were a negative voltage, then the output as given by Eq. (2-8) would be the weighted difference between the inputs e_1 and e_2.

For the output of the resistor network to be proportional to the sum of the weighted input voltages, the load resistance R_L must be fixed. However, in analog computing practice, it is customary for summing networks to drive other computing circuits so that R_L may *not* be constant or, for that matter, may not be well-defined. In order for e_o to be independent of R_L we may choose a value of R_o which is much less than R_L. Unfortunately, the improvement is obtained at the expense of greater losses or attenuation through the network. The output voltage will now be quite small in comparison with the input voltages and, if several summing networks are cascaded, the final output may actually be lost in circuit noise.

This signal attenuation could be overcome by connecting an electronic amplifier to the output of the summing network as shown in Fig. 2-4. The gain A of the amplifier compensates for the network losses and the circuit output is now

$$e_o' = Ae_o \qquad (2\text{-}10)$$

Since the output given by Eq. (2-10) is proportional to A, the gain of the amplifier must be both well-defined and stable to ensure computing accuracy. Because amplifier gain is affected by supply voltage variations, component aging, ambient temperature, and other factors, these requirements are not simply met. This is especially true if a dc amplifier is required as is the case with inputs which are either dc voltages or slowly varying ac voltages. Although the use of a passive resistor network and followup amplifier is possible in theory, it does not prove practical for accomplishing the operation of addition.

EXAMPLE 2-1

The circuit shown in Fig. 2-5 is used to sum the voltages e_1, e_2, and e_3. Determine (a) the output voltage e_o, and (b) the change in output if the 10kΩ load resistor is removed.

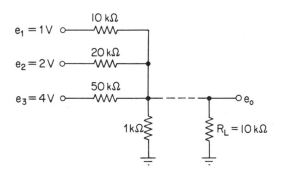

FIGURE 2–5   Circuit for Example 2-1.

SOLUTION:

(a) The equivalent resistance R_p is $(1 \times 10)/(1 + 10)$ kΩ or 910 ohms. From Eq. (2-9), the output is

$$e_0 = \frac{(910/10k\Omega)1 + (910/20k\Omega)2 + (910/50k\Omega)4}{1 + 910/10k\Omega + 910/20k\Omega + 910/50k\Omega} = \frac{0.255}{1.155} = 0.221V$$

(b) If R_L is removed, then

$$e_0 = \frac{(1k\Omega/10k\Omega)1 + (1k\Omega/20k\Omega)2 + (1k\Omega/50k\Omega)4}{1 + 1k\Omega/10k\Omega + 1k\Omega/20k\Omega + 1k\Omega/50k\Omega} = 0.239V$$

The percentage change in output is

$$\Delta e_0 = \frac{0.239 - 0.221}{0.221} \times 100 = 8.1\%$$

Integration with respect to time can be accomplished by a passive resistor-capacitor (RC) network as shown in Fig. 2-6. The input voltage e_i represents the variable to be integrated, and its integral is the voltage e_o developed across the capacitor and load resistor.

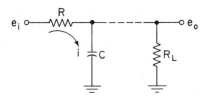

FIGURE 2–6 RC integrating network.

To simplify our analysis, consider R_L sufficiently large to have a negli-gible shunting effect on the capacitor so that load current may be assumed to be zero. From Eq. (2-5), the voltage across a capacitor is proportional to the integral of the capacitor current. Hence

$$v_c = \frac{1}{C} \int i\,dt = e_o \tag{2-11}$$

The capacitor charging current may be expressed in terms of the voltage drop across R so that

$$i = \frac{e_i - e_o}{R} \tag{2-12}$$

Substituting for i in Eq. (2-11), we have the result

$$e_o = \frac{1}{RC} \int (e_i - e_o)\,dt \tag{2-13}$$

When $e_o \ll e_i$, we can say with reasonable accuracy that

$$e_o = \frac{1}{RC} \int e_i \, dt \qquad (2\text{-}14)$$

Equation (2-14) expresses the ideal output voltage of the circuit as the time integral of the input voltage multiplied by a constant $1/RC$.

To illustrate the operation of the RC integrating circuit shown in Fig. 2-6, consider an input in the form of a voltage of magnitude E applied at time $t = 0$ seconds. For simplicity, assume that the capacitor has no initial charge. Using Eq. (2-14), the output of the circuit is

$$e_o = \frac{1}{RC} \int E \, dt = \frac{Et}{RC} \qquad (2\text{-}15)$$

A graph of the ideal output is shown in Fig. 2-7. The output voltage increases linearly with time and, when time equals the circuit time constant (RC product), the output voltage is equal to the input voltage.

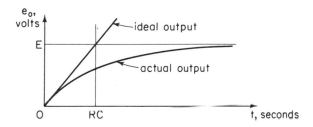

FIGURE 2–7   Ideal and actual outputs of RC integrating network with dc input.

From elementary circuit theory, we know that the actual capacitor voltage in a series RC circuit with a dc input voltage is given by the exponential equation

$$v_c = E(1 - e^{-t/RC}) \qquad (2\text{-}16)$$

This actual output is also shown in Fig. 2-7 and is the familiar charging curve of a capacitor with series resistance. Note that the ideal and actual curves are nearly alike for values of time much less than the circuit time constant ($t \ll RC$) or, correspondingly, for the output voltage much less than the input voltage ($e_o \ll e_i$). For $t = 0.1 \, RC$, the difference between the ideal and actual curves is approximately 5 per cent.

Hence, a series RC circuit can function as an integrator if e_o is restricted to values significantly less than e_i. This imposes the same limitation on the use of a passive integrating network as was previously noted for the summing network. The signal attenuation which is necessary to achieve accuracy of integration results in output voltages which, again, are too small for practical use.

EXAMPLE 2-2

A sinusoidal input voltage $e_i = 10 \sin 100t$ volts is applied to the integrating circuit in Fig. 2-8. Determine (a) the ideal and (b) the actual outputs of the circuit.

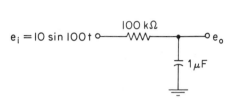

FIGURE 2-8   Circuit for Example 2-2.

SOLUTION:

(a) The ideal output of the integrating circuit may be determined using Eq. (2-14). Thus

$$e_o = \frac{1}{RC} \int e_i \, dt = \frac{1}{0.1} \int 10 \sin 100t \, dt$$

Performing the indicated integration, we have

$$e_o = -\cos 100t$$

(b) For a sinusoidal input voltage, the actual output voltage may be exactly determined using ac reactance and impedance, and rms voltages E_o and E_i. In this case

$$E_o = \frac{-jX_c}{R - jX_c} E_i = \frac{E_i}{1 + R/(-jX_c)} = \frac{E_i}{1 + j\omega RC}$$

$$= \frac{10\sqrt{2}}{1 + j10} = 0.704 \, \angle \, -84.3° \text{ volts(rms)}$$

This output may be expressed as a sine wave

$$e_o = \sqrt{2} \, E_o \sin (\omega t - \phi) = 0.995 \sin (100t - 1.47) \text{ volts}$$

where 1.47 is the phase angle in radians corresponding to 84.3°. Alternatively, the output may be given as a cosine function

$$e_o = -0.995 \cos (100t + 0.099) \text{ volts}$$

where 0.099 is a leading phase angle equal to 5.7°. Comparing the actual and ideal outputs, we note that errors exist in both phase and magnitude.

The amplitude error is

$$\epsilon(\%) = \frac{1.0 - 0.995}{1.0} \times 100 = 0.5\%$$

and the phase difference is 5.7 degrees.

Differentiation is the inverse operation of integration and, as such, can be performed by interchanging the elements of the resistor–capacitor network of Fig. 2-6. The output voltage is now taken across the resistor R as shown in Fig. 2-9. If we differentiate both sides of Eq. (2-5) with respect to

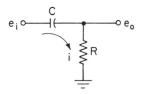

FIGURE 2–9 RC differentiating network.

time, the current through the capacitor is expressed as a function of the rate of change of voltage across the capacitor. Thus

$$\frac{de_c}{dt} = \frac{i}{C}$$

or

$$i = C \frac{d(e_i - e_o)}{dt} \tag{2-17}$$

The output voltage is given by

$$e_o = iR \tag{2-18}$$

Substituting Eq. (2-17) in (2-18) gives

$$e_o = RC \frac{d(e_i - e_o)}{dt} \tag{2-19}$$

If e_o is very small compared to $e_i (e_o \ll e_i)$, then Eq. 2-19 becomes

$$e_o = RC \frac{de_i}{dt} \qquad (2\text{-}20)$$

Equation (2-20) expresses the ideal output voltage of the circuit as the time derivative of the input voltage multiplied by the factor RC.

To illustrate the operation of the differentiating circuit, consider an input voltage in the form of a ramp that increases linearly with time at a rate of A volts per second. If $e_i = 0$ at $t = 0$, the input equation is

$$e_i = At \qquad (2\text{-}21)$$

From Eq. (2-20), the ideal output voltage is

$$e_o = RC \frac{de_i}{dt} = RC \frac{d(At)}{dt} = RCA \qquad (2\text{-}22)$$

By comparison, it can be shown that the actual output voltage of the differentiating circuit with a ramp input is

$$e_o = RCA\,(1 - e^{-t/RC}) \qquad (2\text{-}23)$$

The ideal and actual outputs are compared in Fig. 2-10. From Fig. 2-10 we note that there is an initial error in the actual output. Obviously, this error can be reduced by decreasing the circuit time constant, that is by making the resistor and/or capacitor smaller. However, the output voltage will also be decreased so that increased accuracy is again realized only at the price of greater attenuation of the input signal.

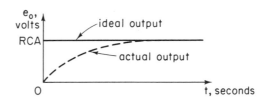

FIGURE 2–10   Ideal and actual outputs of differentiating circuit with ramp input.

From a theoretical standpoint, differentiation can be performed equally as well as integration. However, in practice, RC differentiation is not advised for the reasons discussed below, and it is seldom used in actual analog computation.

Any electrical signal contains extraneous components, commonly referred to as *noise* or *hum*. These are caused by factors such as power supply ripple, pickup on leads or components, and noise generated within components themselves. Almost invariably, the frequencies constituting the noise are well above the frequencies constituting the signal itself. Generally, these noise variations are negligible and do not affect our computation. However, let us consider the effect of differentiating a signal containing high-frequency noise. Since the derivative of a sine wave is proportional to its frequency, the noise components will have a proportionately greater output than the lower-frequency signal components. Thus, differentiation accentuates or magnifies any noise present in a signal and, although the noise in the signal may have been negligible to begin with, the resultant noise in the derivative of the signal will frequently be objectionable. Recalling the differentiating circuit of Fig. 2-9, higher frequencies will obviously undergo less attenuation than low frequencies.

The inverse condition with respect to noise is true with the integrating circuit of Fig. 2-6. In this circuit, noise frequencies will be more attenuated than signal frequencies, which is obviously to our advantage.

A second limitation involves the differentitaion of a discontinuous function such as the voltage step shown in Fig. 2-11. The derivative at the discontinuity is theoretically a pulse of infinite amplitude and zero width. An

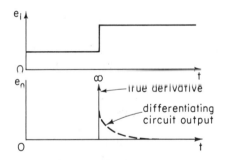

FIGURE 2–11   Differentiation of step function.

actual differentiating circuit cannot produce an output such as this; rather it can only provide a poor approximation of the derivative.

Fortunately, the difficulties of differentiation do not seriously limit the application of analog computing methods. In using the computer to solve differential equations, the need to obtain the derivative of a function arises very infrequently. Almost invariably, we begin by knowing the derivatives of a function. The computer then solves the differential equation containing these derivatives by performing appropriate integrations.

So far, we have only considered resistors and capacitors in passive computing circuits and have made no mention of the use of inductors. Since the

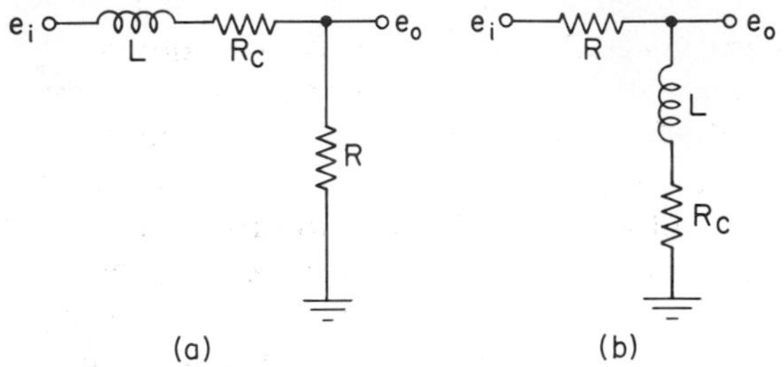

FIGURE 2–12 *RL* circuits for (a) integration and (b) differentiation.

voltage–current relationship of an inductor is the inverse of that of a capacitor, an inductor could, in theory, be used in lieu of a capacitor. Figure 2-12 shows possible integrating and differentiating circuits using an inductive element.

However, inductors are not used as computing elements, primarily because a pure inductor cannot be realized in practice. Any inductance must also contain distributed resistance (R_c in Fig. 2-12) which alters the voltage–current relationship from that given by Eq. 2-2. In addition, an inductor must incorporate a magnetic core to obtain reasonable values of inductance. The core introduces non-linearities and hysteresis into the characteristics of the inductor. Inductors are also relatively bulky components and it is difficult to shield them from pickup due to stray magnetic fields.

2-4 OPERATIONAL AMPLIFIERS

We have seen that the fundamental linear operations of algebra and calculus may be performed by simple electrical circuits composed only of passive components. However, several limitations were shown to be inherent in applying these circuits. Large signal losses are associated with reasonable computing accuracy and the network output is affected by the load placed on the circuit. The addition of a simple followup amplifier to increase the output voltage to a useable level is not a practical solution because the gain characteristics of the amplifier are overly critical.

Fortunately, an electronic amplifier may be used with passive circuit elements in such a way that circuit operation is essentially independent of amplifier characteristics and loading of the amplifier. This arrangement employs the principle of negative feedback in which a portion of the amplifier output signal is connected back to the input in an out-of-phase relationship. In analog computer use, the amplifier is identified as an *operational amplifier* since it is capable of accurately performing various mathematical operations.

The operational amplifier is the basic functional unit in an electronic analog computer.

To function adequately as an operational amplifier, an electronic amplifier must have certain characteristics. The amplifier is direct coupled with a very high gain (usually 10^5 or higher) and must be carefully designed for stability and freedom from drift. Direct coupling is required since the amplifier must handle dc voltages which are constant or vary slowly with respect to time. The amplifier must have an extremely small input current and, for negative feedback purposes, a phase inversion from input to output. The characteristics and design of operational amplifiers will be discussed in detail in the next chapter.

From a functional standpoint, the operational amplifier may be considered a three-terminal device in which the input and output terminals are referenced to a common or ground terminal. Figure 2-13 shows the schematic symbol for an operational amplifier (a pie-shaped wedge with the apex pointing in the direction of the output). The amplifier input voltage* is identified as e_b and the output voltage as e_o. The amplifier voltage gain is shown as $-A$ since a phase inversion, or polarity change, is required from input to output. For simplicity, the ground line is not included on computer circuit diagrams. The equation for the amplifier output voltage is

$$e_o = -Ae_b \qquad (2\text{-}24)$$

where the voltage gain A is commonly taken as the dc gain of the amplifier.

The schematic arrangement of an operational amplifier incorporating negative feedback is shown in Fig. 2-14. The voltage e_i is applied to the ampli-

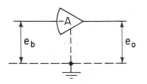

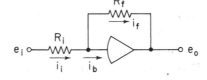

FIGURE 2–13   Symbolic
representation of operational amplifier.

FIGURE 2–14   Operational
amplifier with feedback.

fier by the input resistor R_i and the output voltage is coupled back to the amplifier input by the feedback resistor R_f.

The currents at the amplifier input, which is referred to as the *summing junction* or *summing point*, may be summed using Kirchhoff's current law.

---

*Since almost all operational amplifiers now use transistors, the amplifier input voltage is commonly applied to a transistor base. Hence the use of the subscript "*b*" for input voltage.

Thus

$$i_i = i_b + i_f \tag{2-25}$$

The base current i_b to the input stage of the amplifier is quite small and is considered negligible for all practical purposes. For $i_b = 0$, the currents through the input and feedback resistors are equal. These currents may be expressed in terms of the voltage drops across their respective resistors so that Eq. (2-25) may be written

$$\frac{e_i - e_b}{R_i} = \frac{e_b - e_o}{R_f} \tag{2-26}$$

Replacing e_b by $-e_o/A$, we obtain

$$\frac{e_i + e_o/A}{R_i} = \frac{-e_o/A - e_o}{R_f} \tag{2-27}$$

The voltage gain with feedback may be obtained by solving Eq. (2-27) for the ratio e_o/e_i. Thus

$$\frac{e_o}{e_i} = \frac{-AR_f}{R_f + R_i + AR_i} \tag{2-28}$$

Multiplying numerator and denominator of Eq. (2-28) by $1/A$ and factoring R_i from the denominator gives the result

$$\frac{e_o}{e_i} = -\frac{R_f}{R_i}\left[\frac{1}{1 + (1 + R_f/R_i)/A}\right] \tag{2-29}$$

The ratio of the output of a device to its input is known as the *transfer function* of the device. The concept of transfer functions is widely used in analyzing physical systems and is commonly applied to operational amplifier circuits. The transfer function given by Eqs. (2-28) and (2-29) is the *closed-loop gain* of the amplifier circuit. If the amplifier gain A is very high and the ratio R_f/R_i is not excessive, then, to a close approximation, Eq. (2-29) becomes

$$\frac{e_o}{e_i} = -\frac{R_f}{R_i} \tag{2-30}$$

Equation (2-30) reveals a very important fact. For a high-gain operational amplifier with negative feedback, the transfer function is essentially *independent* of amplifier characteristics. The ratio of output to input voltages becomes simply the negative ratio of the feedback and input resistors. Thus, the accuracy of the circuit is determined *entirely* by the precision of these two resistors.

Let us define the ratio or fraction of the output voltage that is fed back to the input as a *feedback factor* β. If the input resistor in Fig. 2-14 is returned to ground through a very low resistance, then R_f and R_i act as a simple voltage divider for e_o. Hence

$$\beta = \frac{e_b}{e_o} = \frac{R_i}{R_i + R_f} = \frac{1}{1 + R_f/R_i} \tag{2-31}$$

From Eq. (2-31), $1/\beta = 1 + R_f/R_i$. Substituting this result in Eq. (2-29), we have

$$\frac{e_o}{e_i} = -\frac{R_f}{R_i}\left(\frac{1}{1 + 1/A\beta}\right) = -\frac{R_f}{R_i}\left(\frac{A\beta}{A\beta + 1}\right) \tag{2-32}$$

The product $A\beta$ is known as the *loop gain* of the circuit. Where $A\beta \gg 1$, Eq. (2-32) may be written in an equivalent form that is more convenient for computing e_o/e_i. Thus

$$\frac{e_o}{e_i} = -\frac{R_f}{R_i}\left(\frac{A\beta - 1}{A\beta}\right) = -\frac{R_f}{R_i}\left(1 - \frac{1}{A\beta}\right) \tag{2-33}$$

EXAMPLE 2-3

In the circuit in Figure 2-15 the amplifier gain is 10,000. Determine (a) the exact output voltage and (b) the percentage error if we assume the amplifier gain to be infinitely large.

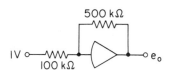

500 kΩ

$1V$ ——/\/\/——▷——o e_o
100 kΩ

FIGURE 2–15   Circuit   for Example 2-3.

SOLUTION:

(a) Using Eq. (2-31), the feedback factor is

$$\beta = \frac{1}{1 + 500\,k\Omega/100\,k\Omega} = 0.167$$

The loop gain is then

$$A\beta = (10,000)(0.167) = 1670$$

Using Eq. (2-33), the exact output voltage is

$$e_o = -\frac{500 \text{ k}\Omega}{100 \text{ k}\Omega} \left(1 - \frac{1}{1670}\right) (1) = -4.997 \text{ volts}$$

(b) For A assumed infinitely large,

$$e_o = -\frac{R_f}{R_i} e_i = -5.0 \text{ volts}$$

The error is then

$$\epsilon = \frac{5.0 - 4.997}{5.0} \times 100 = 0.06\%$$

2-5 SCALE CHANGING

In the preceding section, it was shown that an operational amplifier can provide a simple transfer function that is determined solely by the ratio of the feedback to the input resistances. By using appropriate combinations of input and feedback elements, it is possible for the amplifier to perform the linear operations which are basic to algebra and calculus.

Before discussing other operational amplifier circuits, let us again consider the basic feedback arrangement shown in Fig. 2-14. Using Eq. (2-30), the amplifier output voltage is

$$e_o = -\frac{R_f}{R_i} e_i \tag{2-34}$$

Two conclusions are apparent from Eq. (2-34). First, the operational amplifier changes the sign or polarity of the input and, secondly, it multiplies the input by a constant equal to the ratio R_f/R_i. By selecting appropriate values for R_f and R_i, the input voltage e_i may be multiplied by a desired constant, or coefficient. This operation of multiplication by a constant is called *scale changing.*

When the value of the input resistor is the same as the feedback resistor, the amplifier output voltage has the same amplitude as the input, but is opposite in polarity. In this case $e_o = -e_i$ and the operation of inversion is performed. The amplifier in this connection is called an *inverter* or *sign changer.*

In Fig. 2-14 the operational amplifier circuit is shown with the input and feedback resistors in schematic form. In programming an analog computer, a simplified form of this diagram proves convenient. Assume that the closed-loop gain of an operational amplifier is five ($R_f = 5R_i$). For programming purposes the entire circuit is represented by a triangle as shown in Fig.

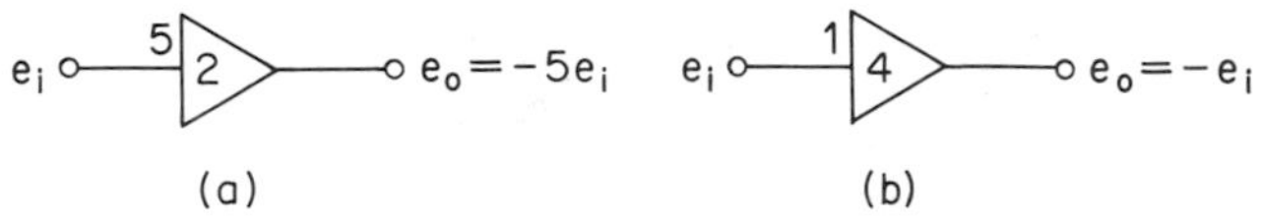

$$e_i \multimap \boxed{5 \triangleright 2} \multimap e_o = -5e_i \qquad e_i \multimap \boxed{1 \triangleright 4} \multimap e_o = -e_i$$

(a)   (b)

FIGURE 2–16 Operational amplifier programming symbols for (a) scale changing, (b) inversion.

2-16(a). The number at the amplifier input indicates the closed-loop gain or coefficient associated with that input (5 in this case). The number within the triangle identifies that particular amplifier. The symbol for an inverter is shown in Fig. 2-16(b).

EXAMPLE 2-4

(a) Determine the output of the operational amplifier shown in Fig. 2-17(a).

(b) Draw the circuit using programming symbology.

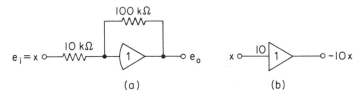

(a)   (b)

FIGURE 2–17 Circuits for Example 2 4.

SOLUTION:

(a) $$e_o = -\frac{R_f}{R_i} e_i = -\frac{100 \text{ k}\Omega}{10 \text{ k}\Omega} x = -10x$$

(b) The symbolic diagram is shown in Fig. 2-17(b). In this example, the input voltage is multiplied by -10 causing a scale change of the variable by a factor of 10.

2-6 COEFFICIENT POTENTIOMETERS

Multiplying a variable by a coefficient according to Eq. (2-34) requires two precision resistors of appropriate values. When the coefficients are not convenient whole numbers, this scheme becomes impractical since we would need an infinite number of resistors to satisfy any possible scaling requirement. To overcome this difficulty and permit continuous variation of the scale factor, variable resistance elements known as *coefficient potentiometers*

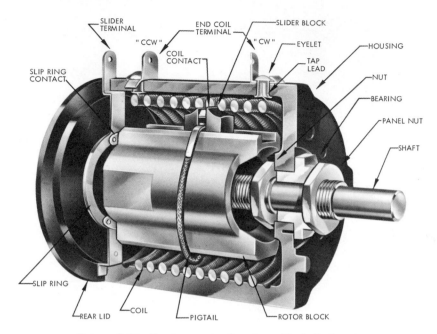

FIGURE 2–18   Ten-turn potentiometer with helical resistance element. (Helipot Division of Beckman Instruments, Inc.)

are used in conjunction with a limited number of fixed resistors. For example, a general-purpose analog computer may provide fixed resistors in 10,000 and 100,000 ohm values only.

A potentiometer is a resistor which has a sliding tap or wiper. Potentiometers find uses in many kinds of electronic circuits where an adjustable level of operation is required. A familiar example of potentiometer use is the volume control of a radio receiver. The coefficient potentiometer used in an analog computer differs from commonly used potentiometers in that it is a high-precision, more expensive device. It generally has a wire wound resistance element, although elements of carbon or metal film deposited on ceramic are also employed. For greater accuracy, the resistance is in the form of a ten-turn helix so that the shaft turns through 3600° in moving the wiper or slider from one end of the winding to the other. Figure 2-18 shows the internal construction of a ten-turn potentiometer with a helical resistance element. The resistance of coefficient potentiometers varies between 1000 and 100,000 ohms depending upon the particular application. Their linearity is typically 0.1 per cent or better.

A dial mechanism is sometimes used with a potentiometer to show accurately the mechanical position of the wiper as a decimal percentage of

FIGURE 2–19 Multiturn potentiometer and turn-counting
dial. (Helipot Division of Beckman Instruments, Inc.)

the total allowable rotation. Figure 2-19 shows a ten-turn dial and potentiometer of the type used in analog computers. Ten-turn dials commonly provide 1000 divisions over the full 3600° range so that setting accuracies of 1 part in 1000 are possible. This arrangement permits the wiper to be positioned such that the resistance from the wiper to one end of the potentiometer (generally referred to as the low end) is accurately that percentage of the total resistance shown by the dial.

The resetting precision of a potentiometer cannot be better than its *resolution*. The resolution of wirewound potentiometers is limited by the small stepwise changes that occur as the wiper moves from one turn of the resistance element to the next. Ten-turn potentiometers can provide resolutions of better than 0.01 per cent; that is, the wiper can detect a resistance change to better than 1 part in 10,000. On the other hand, deposited film potentiometers have practically infinite resolution.

A coefficient potentiometer multiplies a voltage by a positive constant less than unity; hence it is frequently referred to as an *attenuator*. When used as an attenuator, the end of the potentiometer designated Low (L) is connected to ground, the High (H) end to the input voltage, and the wiper is the output terminal. Figure 2-20 shows these potentiometer connections.

If the potentiometer is unloaded, that is, if no current flows through the potentiometer wiper, the current i through the potentiometer is

$$i = \frac{e_i}{R_p} \tag{2-35}$$

where R_p is the total resistance of the winding. If we denote the dial setting

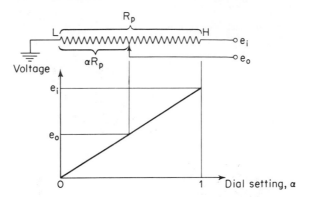

FIGURE 2–20   Grounded potentiometer, unloaded.

ratio as α, then the fraction of R_p from the wiper to ground is αR_p. The output voltage e_o is then

$$e_o = \alpha R_p i = \frac{\alpha R_p e_i}{R_p} = \alpha e_i \qquad (2\text{-}36)$$

The ratio α determines the position of the wiper and can assume any value between zero and one. As shown in Fig. 2-20, the output voltage is linearly related to wiper position. If we define a voltage attenuation ratio as $k = e_o/e_i$, then for an unloaded potentiometer, the ratios α and k are equal. For example, to obtain an output of 6.89 volts with $e_i = 10$ volts, the dial is set at 0.689 as long as no current is drawn from the wiper.

The programming symbol used for a grounded potentiometer is shown in Fig. 2-21. The potentiometer attenuation ratio k is commonly written outside the circle and a number identifying the potentiometer is written inside.

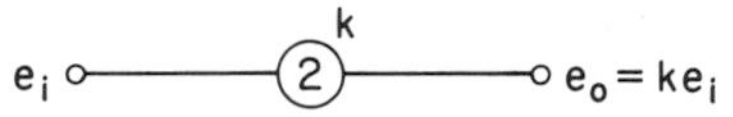

$$e_i \;\circ\!\!-\!\!-\!\!-\!\!-\!\!\overset{k}{\underset{}{\fbox{2}}}\!\!-\!\!-\!\!-\!\!-\!\!\circ\; e_o = k e_i$$

FIGURE 2–21   Grounded potentiometer programming symbol.

In some special applications, an ungrounded potentiometer is used. Voltages are applied to both the High (H) and Low (L) ends as shown in Fig. 2-22(a). The wiper voltage in this case is

$$e_o = \alpha R_p i + e_2 = \alpha R_p \left(\frac{e_1 - e_2}{R_p}\right) + e_2$$

$$= \alpha(e_1 - e_2) + e_2$$

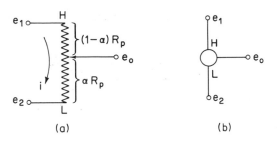

FIGURE 2–22 Ungrounded potentiometer (a) and programming symbol (b).

The programming symbol for an ungrounded potentiometer is shown in Fig. 2-22(b).

So far, we have assumed that no current is drawn from the potentiometer wiper. In practice however, the potentiometer output voltage is invariably used as an input to an operational amplifier or other computing circuit. When the potentiometer is operated with a load, there is a *loading effect* due to the fact that an output current flows. This is shown in Fig. 2-23. The

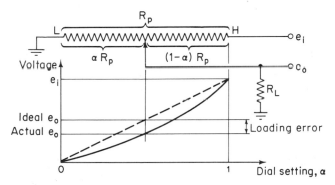

FIGURE 2–23 Grounded potentiometer with load.

load current causes the output voltage to be reduced so that the non-linear characteristic shown in Fig. 2-23 is obtained. As we shall see, the error due to loading depends on both the wiper position and the magnitude of the load.

With the wiper set at a ratio α, the effective resistance of the potentiometer is

$$R_{\text{eff}} = (1 - \alpha)R_p + \frac{\alpha R_p R_L}{R_L + \alpha R_p} \qquad (2\text{-}37)$$

Since the input current i to the potentiometer is e_i/R_{eff}, we may express the output voltage as

$$e_o = i\left(\frac{\alpha R_p R_L}{R_L + \alpha R_p}\right) = \frac{e_i}{R_{eff}}\left(\frac{\alpha R_p R_L}{R_L + \alpha R_p}\right) \tag{2-38}$$

Substituting Eq. (2-37) in Eq. (2-38), we obtain an expression for the voltage attenuation as

$$k = \frac{e_o}{e_i} = \frac{\alpha}{1 + \alpha(1 - \alpha)R_p/R_L} \tag{2-39}$$

EXAMPLE 2-5

A 10kΩ potentiometer is driving a 50kΩ load resistor. For an input of 5 volts and a shaft setting of 0.6, determine the actual output voltage.

SOLUTION:

From Eq. (2-39), the output is

$$e_o = \frac{(0.6)(5)}{1 + (0.6)(0.4)(10,000)/50,000} = 2.86 \text{ volts}$$

If the loaded potentiometer is set to a ratio α, the error due to loading will be the difference between the ideal and actual attenuations as given by Eqs. (2-36) and (2-39) respectively. This error is

$$\epsilon = \alpha - \frac{\alpha}{1 + \alpha(1 - \alpha)R_p/R_L} = \frac{\alpha^2(1 - \alpha)}{R_L/R_p + \alpha(1 - \alpha)} \tag{2-40}$$

From Eq. (2-40), we see that the error depends on both the setting α and the the ratio R_L/R_p. If (as is generally the case) $R_L > 5R_p$, the error may be approximated as

$$\epsilon \cong \alpha^2(1 - \alpha)R_p/R_L \tag{2-41}$$

Figure 2-23 is an error curve based on Eq. (2-41). Maximum error occurs at a setting two-thirds of the potentiometer travel. To determine attenuation error using Fig. 2-24, the value of $\alpha^2(1 - \alpha)$ corresponding to the setting α is read from the curve and then multiplied by the ratio R_p/R_L.

For light loads where $R_L > 5R_p$, approximate compensation for the loading can be obtained by increasing the ideal dial setting ratio by an amount equal to the attenuation error. The corrected setting will place the wiper at a slightly higher position so that e_o is now very nearly ke_i, where k is the desired attenuation.

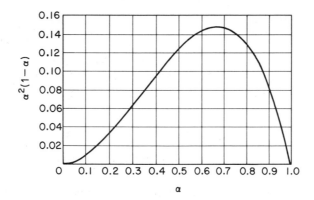

FIGURE 2–24   Approximate potentiometer-loading correction curve.

EXAMPLE 2-6

For the potentiometer given in Ex. 2-5, determine the corrected dial setting to provide $k = 0.6$.

SOLUTION:

Using Fig. 2-24, the loading error for $k = 0.6$ is

$$\epsilon - \frac{(0.144)(10,000)}{50,000} - 0.0288$$

Adding this error to the ideal setting, we have a corrected setting α_c of

$$\alpha_c = 0.6 + 0.0288 = 0.629$$

Using Eq. (2-39) with $\alpha = 0.629$, the output voltage is 3.00 volts which is the desired value.

The above correction process would become rather tedious if many potentiometers are being set. Consequently, a more direct setting method is preferable in a general-purpose computer. This involves setting coefficients by measurement of the potentiometer output with the load connected to the wiper and a reference voltage as the input. The dial calibration is needed only for rough setting and possibly for resetting coefficients used previously.

A common scheme of direct potentiometer setting is to balance or null the potentiometer output with a standard or reference potentiometer. A simplified nulling circuit is shown in Fig. 2-25. In setting a potentiometer, the High end is switched from the input signal to a reference voltage and a null-meter is connected to the wiper.

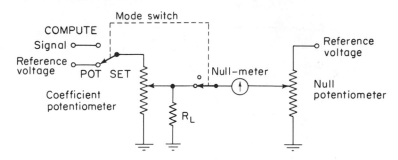

FIGURE 2–25   Potentiometer-nulling arrangement.

The null-meter is generally an extremely sensitive current meter (or galvanometer) and the precision of the null potentiometer is quite high. The wiper of the null potentiometer is positioned to the desired coefficient by means of a calibrated dial. The loaded coefficient potentiometer is then adjusted so that a null or zero reading is obtained on the meter. Since no current flows through the meter at null, there is no load on the null potentiometer. By means of this method, attenuation ratios may be quickly and easily set to within better than 0.1 per cent.

Although more expensive than the null potentiometer, the most convenient read-out device for direct potentiometer setting is a digital voltmeter (DVM). A DVM permits the potentiometer wiper voltage to be measured directly to an accuracy of three or four significant figures without placing any additional load on the potentiometer itself.

In addition to simplifying the setting of potentiometers under load conditions, a direct setting circuit makes it possible to use uncalibrated coefficient potentiometers in a computer. Since the cost of a potentiometer increases substantially with its accuracy of calibration, the reduced cost of using uncalibrated potentiometers more than offsets the cost of a nulling circuit or, possibly, a DVM.

2-7 SUMMATION

An operational amplifier may be used for the addition or summation of voltages. In this application the amplifier arrangement is referred to as a *summing amplifier*.

The output of a summing amplifier can be determined by extending our previous analysis of the feedback amplifier with a single input. Figure 2-26 shows an operational amplifier having n inputs connected in parallel to the amplifier input. The currents in this circuit may be combined at the summing point according to Kirchhoff's current law. If the amplifier input current is

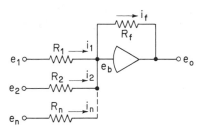

FIGURE 2–26   Schematic diagram of summing amplifier.

assumed to be zero, we may write the equation

$$i_1 + i_2 + \cdots + i_n = i_f \tag{2-42}$$

Expressing the currents in terms of voltage drops, we have

$$\frac{e_1 - e_b}{R_1} + \frac{e_2 - e_b}{R_2} + \cdots + \frac{e_n - e_b}{R_n} = \frac{e_b - e_o}{R_f} \tag{2-43}$$

Substituting $-e_o/A$ for e_b in Eq. (2-43), we may derive an equation for e_o as

$$e_o = -\left(\frac{R_f}{R_1} e_1 + \frac{R_f}{R_2} e_2 + \cdots + \frac{R_f}{R_n} e_n\right)$$

$$\times \left[\frac{1}{1 + \dfrac{1}{A(1 + R_f/R_1 + R_f/R_2 + \cdots + R_f/R_n)}}\right] \tag{2-44}$$

If the amplifier gain A is extremely high, Eq. (2-44) becomes simply

$$e_o = -\left(\frac{R_f}{R_1} e_1 + \frac{R_f}{R_2} e_2 + \cdots + \frac{R_f}{R_n} e_n\right) \tag{2-45}$$

Equation (2-45) is the basic equation for the operation of a summing amplifier.
The amplifier output is the negative sum of the inputs where each input is weighted according to the ratio of the feedback resistor and the input resistor associated with that input.

Because of the high amplifier gain, the input voltage e_b is generally of the order of tens of microvolts and may be assumed negligible. The current into each input resistor is then determined only by the corresponding input voltage and there is no interaction or coupling between the inputs as a consequence of their connection to the amplifier. Since the summing point is very near zero (ground) potential, it is referred to as a *virtual ground,* even though the actual resistance between the summing point and ground may be quite high.

We may again define the feedback factor as the ratio of the voltage fed back to the input to the total output voltage. For a summing amplifier, the feedback factor may be expressed as

$$\beta = \frac{e_b}{e_o} = \frac{R_{eq}}{R_f + R_{eq}} \tag{2-46}$$

where R_{eq} is the parallel combination of the n input resistors. Writing Eq. (2-46) in terms of the resistors, we have

$$\beta = \frac{\dfrac{1}{1/R_1 + 1/R_2 + \cdots + 1/R_n}}{R_f + \dfrac{1}{1/R_1 + 1/R_2 + \cdots + 1/R_n}} = \frac{1}{1 + R_f/R_1 + R_f/R_2 + \cdots + R_f/R_n} \tag{2-47}$$

If this result is substituted in Eq. (2-44), we obtain an alternate form:

$$e_o = -\left(\frac{R_f}{R_1} e_1 + \frac{R_f}{R_2} e_2 + \cdots + \frac{R_f}{R_n} e_n\right)\left(\frac{1}{1 + 1/A\beta}\right) \tag{2-48}$$

The product $A\beta$ is again the loop gain.

Subtraction of one or more of the inputs may be accomplished by introducing these inputs to the summing amplifier with the opposite or negative polarity.

The programming symbol for the summing amplifier is shown in Fig. 2-27. The gain associated with each input is indicated by the corresponding numeral. In Fig. 2-27, inputs 1, 2, and 3 have gains of 2, 5, and 10 respectively.

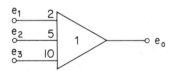

FIGURE 2–27   Programming symbol for summing amplifier.

EXAMPLE 2-7

(a) Determine the output of the summing amplifier shown in Fig. 2-28(a).

(b) Draw the circuit using programming symbology.

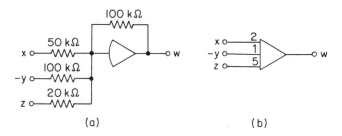

FIGURE 2–28   Circuits for Example 2-7.

SOLUTION:

(a) Using Eq. (2-45)

$$e_o = w = -\left[\left(\frac{100\text{k}\Omega}{50\text{k}\Omega}\right)(x) + \left(\frac{100\text{k}\Omega}{100\text{k}\Omega}\right)(-y) + \left(\frac{100\text{k}\Omega}{20\text{k}\Omega}\right)(z)\right]$$

$$w = -2x + y - 5z$$

(b) The symbolic diagram is shown in Fig. 2-28(b).

In the preceding section, it was pointed out that coefficient potentiometers are invariably used to obtain a wide range of scaling constants. The potentiometer output is connected to the amplifier input resistor and adjusted so that its attenuation ratio multiplied by the amplifier gain yields the desired constant. The schematic diagram of this arrangement is shown in Fig. 2-29 together with the corresponding programming diagram. The output voltage

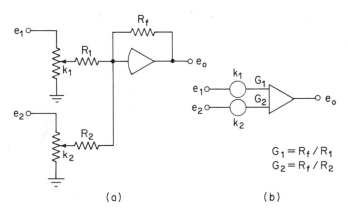

FIGURE 2–29   Summing amplifier schematic diagram (a) and programming diagram (b).

of this circuit is given by the equation

$$e_o = -\left(\frac{k_1 R_f}{R_1} e_1 + \frac{k_2 R_f}{R_2} e_2\right)$$ (2-49)

EXAMPLE 2-8

Determine the output of the summing amplifier shown in Fig. 2-30.

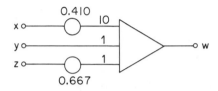

FIGURE 2–30   Circuit for Example 2-8.

SOLUTION:

Using Eq. (2-49), the output is

$$e_o = w = -[(0.410)(10)(x) + (1)(y) + (0.667)(1)(z)]$$
$$w = -4.1x - y - 0.667z$$

In some cases, an operational amplifier and its input network are used without feedback or with some special feedback arrangement. A circuit without feedback is shown in Fig. 2-31(a). Its output voltage is given by the equation

$$e_o = \left(\frac{R_2 e_1}{R_1 + R_2} + \frac{R_1 e_2}{R_1 + R_2}\right)(-A)$$

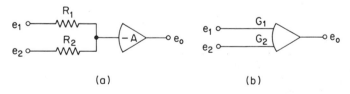

(a)   (b)

FIGURE 2–31   Amplifier without feedback.

where $-A$ is the voltage gain of the amplifier. The absolute gains from the inputs through the amplifier cannot be determined since $-A$ is extremely high and not exactly known. However the ratio of the gains depends only on the relative values of R_1 and R_2 and may be expressed as

$$\frac{G_1}{G_2} = \frac{R_2/(R_1 + R_2)}{R_1/(R_1 + R_2)} = \frac{R_2}{R_1} \tag{2-50}$$

where G_1 and G_2 are relative gain magnitudes. Thus, we may represent the open-loop amplifier circuit by the symbol shown in Fig. 2-31(b), where G_1 and G_2 are determined using Eq. 2-50.

EXAMPLE 2-9

Determine the values of G_1 and G_2 in Fig. 2-31 if $R_1 = 20\mathrm{k}\Omega$ and $R_2 = 10\mathrm{k}\Omega$.

SOLUTION:

The gain ratio G_2/G_1 is $20\mathrm{k}\Omega/10\mathrm{k}\Omega = 2$. Therefore, we may simply choose $G_2 = 2$ and $G_1 = 1$ in the programming symbol.

One of the input resistors (R_2, for example) in Fig. 2-31(a) may be connected as a feedback element. Referring to Eq. 2-30, we may write

$$e_o = -\frac{R_2}{R_1} e_i$$

Substituting Eq. 2-50, the output may also be expressed as

$$e_o = -\frac{G_1}{G_2} e_i$$

We have seen that a potentiometer connected to an input resistor reduces the gain normally available through that input. Let us now consider the effect of coupling the amplifier output to the feedback resistor by a potentiometer, as shown in Fig. 2-32(a). If the potentiometer ratio k is set under load conditions, the voltage applied to the feedback resistor is ke_o. Referring to Eq. (2-34), we have

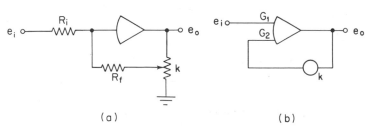

(a)   (b)

FIGURE 2–32 Amplifier with potentiometer feedback schematic diagram (a) and programming diagram (b).

$$ke_o = -\frac{R_f}{R_i} e_i$$

from which

$$e_o = -\frac{R_f}{kR_i} e_i \tag{2-51}$$

The effect of a potentiometer in the feedback circuit is to increase the closed-loop amplifier gain by the factor $1/k$. The programming symbol for the potentiometer feedback circuit is shown in Fig. 2-32(b), where G_1 and G_2 are the relative open-loop gains associated with R_i and R_f, respectively. Since gain is inversely proportional to resistance value, the output given by Eq. (2-51) may be expressed as

$$e_o = -\frac{1/G_2}{k/G_1} e_i = -\frac{G_1}{kG_2} e_i \tag{2-52}$$

EXAMPLE 2-10

(a) Determine the output voltage of the summing amplifier shown in Fig. 2-33(a).

(b) Draw the circuit using programming symbols.

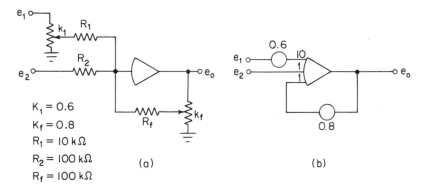

$K_1 = 0.6$
$K_f = 0.8$
$R_1 = 10\ k\Omega$
$R_2 = 100\ k\Omega$
$R_f = 100\ k\Omega$

(a)   (b)

FIGURE 2–33   Circuit for Example 2-10.

SOLUTION:

(a) The equation for e_o is

$$e_o = -\left(\frac{k_1 R_f}{k_f R_1} e_1 + \frac{R_f}{k_f R_2} e_2\right)$$
$$= -\left[\frac{(0.6)(100k\Omega)e_1}{(0.8)(10k\Omega)} + \frac{(100k\Omega)e_2}{(0.8)(100k\Omega)}\right]$$
$$= -7.5e_1 - 1.25e_2$$

(b) The programming diagram is shown in Fig. 2-33(b).

It should be noted that a change in the setting of the feedback potentiometer will affect the gains of both inputs by the same factor. Consequently, a potentiometer feedback circuit proves convenient when we wish to change the gain of a summing amplifier with respect to all inputs.

2-8 INTEGRATION

An analog computer circuit that performs integration is the basic element in simulating dynamic systems. As was mentioned in Chapter 1, a differential equation expresses the relationships between the derivatives of a function. The purpose of solving the differential equation is to find the function and, from basic calculus, we know that integrating the derivative of a function leads to the function itself. *Hence, integration is a basic operation in solving differential equations.*

We have seen that a simple resistor–capacitor network can function as an integrator if the capacitor voltage is kept small compared to the input voltage. However, as charge builds up on the capacitor, the resultant voltage opposes the charging current so that the integration is far from perfect. To perform exact integration, we must maintain a charging current that is proportional to the input voltage regardless of the voltage developed across the capacitor.

By combining an operational amplifier with the resistor–capacitor network, we can achieve near-perfect integration. The basic circuit for performing integration uses a resistor as the input element and a capacitor for the feedback component as shown in Fig. 2-34. To analyze this circuit, let us assume that current i_i flows in the input element and current i_f flows in the feedback element. If the amplifier input current is considered negligible, then

$$i_i = \frac{e_i - e_b}{R} = i_f \tag{2-53}$$

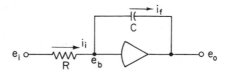

FIGURE 2–34   Basic integrator circuit.

To obtain an expression for i_f, we may differentiate Eq. (2-5) with respect to time, which gives

$$i_f = C\frac{de_c}{dt} = C\frac{d(e_b - \epsilon_o)}{dt} \tag{2-54}$$

From Eq. (2-54) we see that the feedback current is proportional to the rate of change of voltage across the capacitor. Substituting Eq. (2-54) into Eq. (2-53), we have

$$\frac{e_i - e_b}{R} = C\frac{d(e_b - e_o)}{dt} \qquad (2\text{-}55)$$

If the amplifier gain is so large that the input voltage e_b is negligible compared to the output e_o, then Eq. (2-55) may be written as

$$\frac{e_i}{RC} = -\frac{de_o}{dt} \qquad (2\text{-}56)$$

Integrating both sides of Eq. (2-56) with respect to time, we obtain the definite integral

$$e_o = -\frac{1}{RC}\int_0^t e_i \, dt + E_0 \qquad (2\text{-}57)$$

where zero and t are the lower and upper limits of the time interval.

Equation (2-57) states that the output of the integrator circuit is proportional to the input voltage integrated with respect to time. Zero time ($t = 0$) is the time at which we start the simulation of the system under study. The time t corresponds to any later time at which we observe the results of the simulation. In other words, the output of the circuit at any time is the integral of the input over the interval from the time the computer was started to that time. As in previous amplifier circuits, the polarity of the output voltage is the opposite of the input voltage.

In Eq. (2-57), E_0 is the value of e_o at the start of operation. It is known as the *initial-condition voltage* and is analogous to the constant of integration which occurs in indefinite integrals.

The constant $1/RC$ which multiplies the integral represents a gain factor for the integrating circuit. From basic circuit theory, the quantity RC is defined as a *time constant* and has the dimensions of seconds when R is expressed in ohms and C in farads. The dimension of the gain factor $1/RC$ is then seconds^{-1}. Therefore, if the variable of integration is time measured in seconds, the output of the circuit is a voltage of the same units as the input voltage.

In a manner similar to the summing amplifier, more than one input may be applied to the integrating circuit. For multiple inputs, the output is given by

$$e_o = -\int_0^t \left(\frac{e_1}{R_1C} + \frac{e_2}{R_2C} + \cdots + \frac{e_n}{R_nC}\right) dt + E_0 \qquad (2\text{-}58)$$

In Eq. (2-58), the output voltage is the integral of the weighted sum of the input voltages. The input elements can be the same resistors used by the amplifier as a summer; however, the feedback element is a capacitor rather than a resistor. In general, integrators use a fixed capacitor value and the desired gain is established by selecting an appropriate value of the input resistor, or by a combination of a resistor and coefficient potentiometer. The schematic diagram of an integrating circuit having two inputs is shown in Fig. 2-35 together with the corresponding programming symbol. The symbol (Fig. 2-35b) is similar to that of a summing amplifier except for a rectangle adjacent to the triangle.

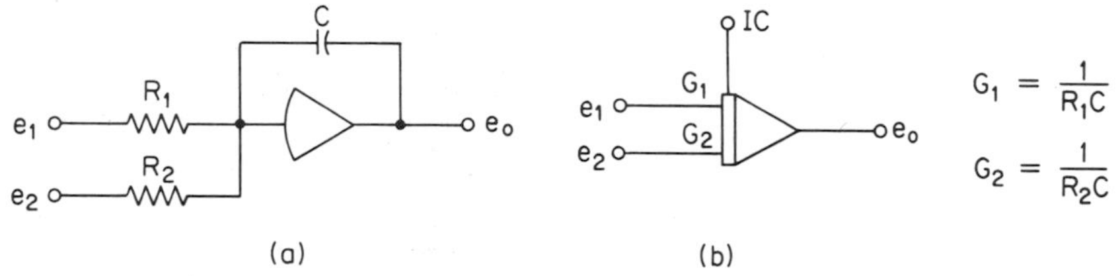

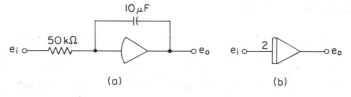

FIGURE 2–35   Integrator schematic diagram (a) and programming symbol (b).

Note that an additional input labeled *IC* is shown on the integrator symbol. This is the initial-condition input terminal which introduces the initial-condition voltage E_0 onto the feedback capacitor. On some computers the voltage applied to the *IC* input appears at the output in inverted form; on others it is not inverted. For the sake of discussion, we will hereafter assume the first type of operation; that is, if a positive E_0 is desired, a negative voltage of magnitude E_0 is applied to the *IC* input. The method by which the *IC* voltage is actually applied to the capacitor will be described in Chapter 6 as part of the sections on control of the computer.

EXAMPLE 2-11

(a) Determine the output of the integrating circuit shown in Fig. 2-36(a).
(b) Draw the circuit using programming symbology.

SOLUTION:

(a) Using Eq. (2-57) the output is

$$e_o = \frac{-1}{5 \times 10^4 \times 10^{-5}} \int_0^t e_i \, dt = -2 \int_0^t e_i \, dt$$

(b) The symbolic diagram is shown in Fig. 2-36(b).

FIGURE 2–36   Circuit for Example 2-11.

EXAMPLE 2-12

(a) Write an equation for the output of the circuit shown in Fig. 2-37(a).
(b) Sketch a graph of this output.

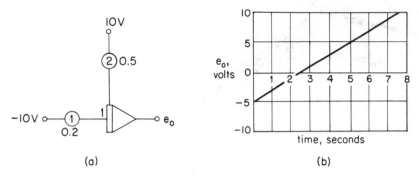

(a)   (b)

FIGURE 2-37   Circuit and graph for Example 2-12.

SOLUTION:

(a) The initial condition input from potentiometer 2 is 5 volts so that
$E_0 = -5$ volts. The equation of the output is

$$e_o = -0.2 \int_0^t (-10)dt - 5 = 2t - 5 \text{ volts}$$

(b) The output is graphed in Fig. 2-37(b).

The output voltage in Example 2-12 increases linearly with time. Such a
circuit is referred to as a *ramp generator*. Note that the integration time was
limited by the voltage range of the amplifier (assumed in this case to be ± 10
volts). As with all operational amplifier circuits, we must be sure that the output voltage is held within the specified operating range. If this range is
exceeded, the input and output voltages are no longer linearly related and the
amplifier is in an *overloaded* or *saturated* state. A means of warning the operator of an overload condition in the computer is generally provided; this
feature is discussed in Chapter 6.

2-9   DIFFERENTIATION

In discussing the use of a passive network to perform differentiation, several
limitations were pointed out. These include the amplification of noise and
power supply ripple which are present on the input signal and the inability
to differentiate a step input. These same drawbacks apply to a differentiation
circuit incorporating an operational amplifier. An additional complication

is the possibility of amplifier instability or oscillation when connected as a differentiator. Consequently, the operation of differentiation is seldom used in analog computation. However, since we may on occasion need to use a differentiator, a brief description of the circuit will be provided.

Figure 2-38 shows the differentiator connection of an operational amplifier. As was the case with a passive network, the resistor and capacitor are simply interchanged from the integrator circuit.

Expressing the input and feedback currents in terms of voltage drops and equating, we have

$$C\frac{d(e_i - e_b)}{dt} = \frac{e_b - e_o}{R} \qquad (2\text{-}59)$$

Assuming e_b is negligible, we may solve for e_o, giving the result

$$e_o = -RC\frac{de_i}{dt} \qquad (2\text{-}60)$$

Thus, the output voltage is the negative time derivative of the input voltage multiplied by the time constant (RC) of the circuit.

When differentiation cannot be avoided, the approximate circuit shown in Fig. 2-39 is sometimes used. For effective operation, the resistor R_1 should be such that the time constant R_1C is five to ten times smaller than the smallest time constant in the input.

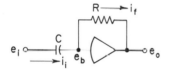

Figure 2–38   Basic differentiator circuit.

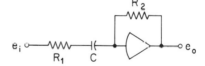

Figure 2–39   Practical differentiator circuit.

2-10   TRANSFER FUNCTIONS

In Section 2-3, the concept of a transfer function as a mathematical relationship between input and output was introduced. The representation of linear systems by means of transfer functions is commonplace in engineering analysis, particularly in the design of control systems. Consequently, in analog computation, the need frequently exists to simulate transfer functions of physical devices. In addition, it may be necessary to incorporate some particular transfer function into the system itself to obtain the desired performance. Operational amplifier circuits provide a convenient means of obtaining a linear transfer function. Therefore, we will conclude this chapter by briefly discussing transfer function generation.

The quantities related by a transfer function are a function of some independent variable such as time. If the input and output are sinusoidal signals, then frequency may be taken as the independent variable. In this case, the generalized transfer function is

$$\frac{e_o(j\omega)}{e_i(j\omega)} = G(j\omega) \tag{2-61}$$

where the transfer function $G(j\omega)$ is a complex quantity whose magnitude and phase angle are a function of the frequency, ω.

There are a wide variety of transfer functions which may be obtained using an operational amplifier. Although we will only consider two simple functions, the method of analysis may be extended to more complex cases.

Figure 2-40 shows a generalized operational amplifier circuit in which the input and feedback elements are complex impedances. Following our usual method of analysis, including the assumption that e_b is negligibly small, the circuit output is

$$e_o = -\frac{Z_f}{Z_i} e_i \tag{2-62}$$

where e_o and e_i are ac voltages. Thus, the transfer function of the circuit is the negative ratio of the feedback and input impedances. If Z_i and/or Z_f contain reactive elements, the transfer function is a complex quantity which is frequency dependent.

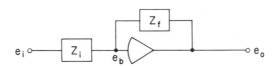

FIGURE 2-40   Generalized amplifier circuit.

Let us reexamine the integrator circuit in Fig. 2-34 assuming e_i is an ac voltage. In this circuit, $Z_i = R$ and $Z_f = 1/j\omega C$. Substituting these values in Eq. 2-62, we obtain

$$e_o = -\frac{1/j\omega C}{R} e_i = -\frac{1}{j\omega CR} e_i = -\frac{1}{j\omega\tau} e_i \tag{2-63}$$

where $\tau = RC$.

A convenient means of representing a transfer function is to plot the magnitude of e_o/e_i as a function of frequency. In making such a graph, it is convenient to use logarithmic scales for both the magnitude ratio and frequency axes.

The integrator circuit transfer function given by Eq. (2-63) is plotted in Fig. 2-41. In this case, the output is inversely proportional to frequency.

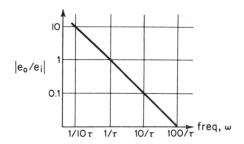

FIGURE 2-41 Transfer characteristic of integrator circuit.

EXAMPLE 2-13

Derive the transfer function of the operational amplifier circuit shown in Fig. 2-42(a).

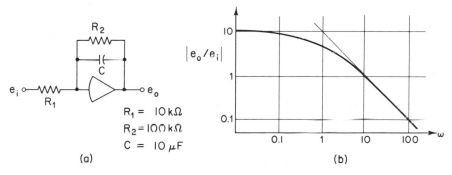

$R_1 = 10\,k\Omega$
$R_2 = 100\,k\Omega$
$C = 10\,\mu F$

(a)   (b)

FIGURE 2-42 Operational amplifier circuit and characteristic for Example 2-13.

SOLUTION:

In this circuit, Z_f is the parallel combination of R_2 and C. The transfer function is

$$\frac{e_o}{e_i} = -\frac{Z_f}{Z_i} = -\frac{\dfrac{R_2/j\omega C}{R_2 + 1/j\omega C}}{R_1} = -\frac{R_2}{R_1}\left(\frac{1}{1 + j\omega C R_2}\right) = -\frac{R_2}{R_1}\left(\frac{1}{1 + j\omega\tau}\right)$$

where $\tau = CR_2$.
Substituting component values, we obtain the result

$$\frac{e_o}{e_i} = \frac{-10}{1 + j\omega}$$

Evaluating the transfer function at various frequencies gives the following table.

ω (rad/s)	e_o/e_i	
	Magnitude	Phase angle
0.1	9.99	$-5.7°$
0.4	9.28	$-21.8°$
1.0	7.07	$-45.0°$
4.0	2.42	$-76.0°$
10.0	1.00	$-84.3°$

These data are plotted in Fig. 2-42(b). Note that the asymptotes of the straight-line portions of the characteristic intersect at the frequency $\omega = 1/\tau$. This provides a useful way of graphing the approximate characteristics of this particular transfer function. The frequency $\omega = 1/\tau$ is designated the *half-power point* and always exhibits a 45° phase angle.

A number of the more common transfer impedances using resistors and capacitors are tabulated in Appendix C. A desired transfer function can be obtained by selecting appropriate networks from the table in order to satisfy the relationship of Eq. (2-62).

PROBLEMS FOR CHAPTER 2

1. Determine the output voltage of the summing network shown below. What change in voltage occurs if a 50kΩ load resistor is connected to the output?

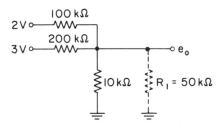

2. Show that the output of the following circuit is given by the equation

$$e_o = \int \left(\frac{e_1}{R_1 C} + \frac{e_2}{R_2 C} \right) dt$$

for $e_o \ll e_1, e_2$.

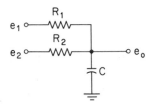

3. What are the advantages of a computing circuit containing active elements as compared to one composed of passive components only?

4. What scale change is introduced by an operational amplifier with a 1MΩ feedback resistor and having a 2-volt input applied to a resistance of 250kΩ?

5. In the circuit below, at left, determine the feedback factor, loop gain, and exact output voltage. What percentage error is introduced by assuming infinite amplifier gain?

6. What is the difference between the two amplifier symbols below, at right?

7. A scaling amplifier has a 100kΩ feedback resistor. What value of input resistor is required for a gain of -1? For a gain of -10?

8. In the circuit below, at left, determine the feedback factor, loop gain, and exact output voltage. What percentage error is introduced by assuming infinite amplifier gain?

9. Write the equation for the output of the summing amplifier shown below, at right.

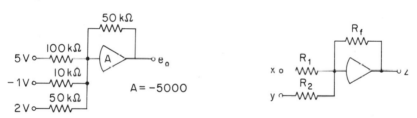

10. Draw a programming diagram for an operational amplifier to implement the equation

$$z = -(10x + 2y)$$

where x and y are input variables. Draw a schematic diagram for the same amplifier using 10kΩ and 100kΩ resistance values.

11. Draw a Thévenin equivalent circuit for the potentiometer with load resistor shown in Fig. 2-23. Using the Thévenin circuit, derive an equation for e_o/e_i. Compare with Eq. (2-39).

12. What is the attenuation of the potentiometer below if the dial setting ratio is 0.7?

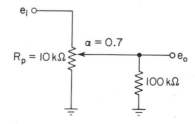

13. In the circuit of Problem 12, what dial setting is required to obtain an actual attenuation of 0.7?

14. A 100kΩ coefficient potentiometer, which is set by means of a dial having 1000 divisions, is loaded by a 1MΩ resistor. What dial setting is required to obtain an attenuation of $k = 0.488$?

15. A 2kΩ coefficient potentiometer, which is set by means of a dial having 1000 divisions, is loaded by a 5kΩ resistor. Plot a curve showing the dial correction required to obtain a desired attenuation k for $0 \leq k \leq 1$.

16. Write the equation for the output of each of the following circuits.

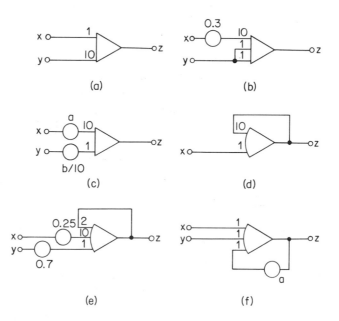

(a)   (b)

(c)   (d)

(e)   (f)

17. Using the amplifier below, at left, draw schematic diagrams for the circuits in Problem 16. Assume potentiometers are available as required.

18. Derive the equation for the output of the circuit below, at right.

19. An operational amplifier has an output capability of $\pm 10V$ at 20mA maximum. What range of load resistance can be connected to the amplifier?

20. Write the equation for the output of each of the following circuits. The capacitor values are given in microfarads.

(a)

(b)

(c)

(d)

(e)

21. Draw an operational amplifier circuit in schematic diagram form to implement the following equations. Assume a $10\mu F$ capacitor is available.

(a) $$y = -0.1 \int_0^t v_y \, dt$$

(b) $$q = -\int_0^t 2i \, dt$$

Repeat using programming symbols.

22. Sketch a graph of the output voltage of circuit below as a function of time. Assume that the amplifier limits at ± 100 volts.

23. Sketch a graph of the output voltage of integrator 2 as a function of time. Assume that the voltage range of the amplifier is ± 10 volts.

24. Using programming symbols, design a computer circuit to implement the

equation

$$e_o = 2e_1 + \int_0^t (e_2 + 5e_3)\, dt$$

25. Determine the proper value of the missing term in each of the following circuits.

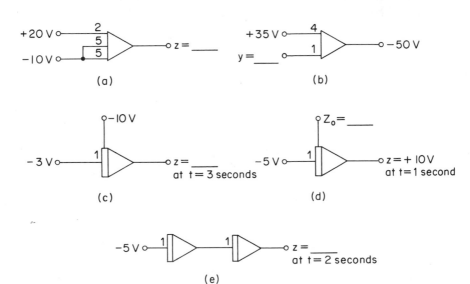

(a)

(b)

(c)

(d)

(e)

26. What problems are associated with using an operational amplifier to perform differentiation?

27. Derive an equation for the output of the circuit below.

28. Derive the transfer function $G(j\omega)$ for each of the following circuits.

29. A sine wave $e_i = 10 \sin 100t$ volts is applied to each of the circuits below. Give the equation for the output voltage e_o and sketch the input and output. waveforms.

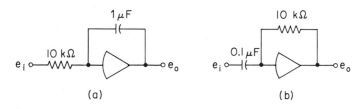

(a)   (b)

3-1 INTRODUCTION

Operational amplifiers are the basic elements of analog computers. Chapter 2 described the way in which amplifier circuits perform the linear operations of scale changing, summation, integration, and differentiation. In addition to analog computation, operational amplifiers are widely applied in signal conditioning, servo and process controls, active filters, and analog instrumentation. Non-linear applications of operational amplifiers are also widespread. Analog-to-digital and digital-to-analog converters, logarithmic amplifiers, and non-linear function generators are typical of the many non-linear devices which incorporate operational amplifiers.

Because of the importance of operational amplifiers in analog computers and elsewhere, this chapter will be devoted to describing their characteristics and design. We shall examine the desired behavior of these devices, departures from the ideal that occur in practice, and the design techniques used to approximate the ideal and achieve satisfactory performance.

Solid-state operational amplifiers have almost entirely superseded amplifiers employing electron tubes. In addition to their inherent advantages in size, power requirements, heat dissipation, and reliability, solid-state amplifiers have surpassed tube amplifiers in performance specifications and, in many ways, permit greater design flexibility.

Solid-state operational ampli-

3

OPERATIONAL
AMPLIFIERS

fiers are available in two basic forms: discrete-component amplifiers and integrated circuit amplifiers. Within each form, a wide variety of circuits and characteristics are provided. At present, most analog computers incorporate discrete-component amplifiers because of their superior performance. In addition, numerous models of discrete-component amplifiers in modular form are used in general-purpose applications. Integrated circuit amplifiers are becoming increasingly popular, however, since they provide extremely small size and low cost at some sacrifice of performance and design flexibility. Continuing improvements in their characteristics indicate that integrated circuits will find increasing use as operational amplifiers in analog computation and for other applications.

3-2 ERRORS IN OPERATIONAL AMPLIFIERS

In Chapter 2, transfer functions of various operational amplifier circuits were derived. However, little mention was made of the imperfections of the amplifiers and the effects of these imperfections on the operations being performed. Rather, an ideal operational amplifier was assumed. An ideal amplifier would exhibit infinite input impedance so that it would not load any source, and zero output impedance so it could drive any load. It would have infinite open-loop gain and bandwidth, and zero input current and noise. Under these conditions, the circuit output would be determined entirely by the input signal and the input and feedback components. Although no amplifier has these ideal qualities, the performance of the better solid-state amplifiers closely approaches this ideal.

The principal sources of errors that distinguish the practical operational amplifier from the ideal are the following:

    1. Finite amplifier gain.
    2. Finite amplifier bandwidth.
    3. Noise.
    4. Amplifier input current.
    5. Non-zero output voltage with zero input voltage.
    6. Change in characteristics with temperature, supply voltages, and time.

There are also other considerations such as common-mode voltage characteristics and finite input and output impedances which affect the performance of operational amplifier circuits.

3-3 FINITE GAIN

The generalized equation for the output of a summing amplifier was developed in Chapter 2. This equation is

$$e_o = -\left(\frac{R_f}{R_1}e_1 + \frac{R_f}{R_2}e_2 + \cdots + \frac{R_f}{R_n}e_n\right)\left(\frac{1}{1 + 1/A\beta}\right) \qquad (3\text{-}1)$$

where A is the amplifier gain and β is the feedback factor as defined by Eq. (2-46). If the amplifier gain is infinite, Eq. (3-1) reduces to the ideal case as given by Eq. (2-45). Therefore, we may regard the second factor in Eq. (3-1) as an *error factor* which, when multiplied by the ideal closed-loop gain, gives the actual closed-loop gain. Thus, we may state that

$$\text{error factor} = \frac{1}{1 + 1/A\beta} \cong 1 - \frac{1}{A\beta} \qquad (3\text{-}2)$$

for $A\beta \gg 1$.

The output error ϵ due to finite amplifier gain may be determined as follows.

$$\epsilon = \text{ideal output} - \text{actual output}$$

$$= \text{ideal output} - (\text{ideal output})(\text{error factor})$$

$$= (\text{ideal output})\left[1 - \left(1 - \frac{1}{A\beta}\right)\right]$$

$$= \frac{\text{ideal output}}{A\beta}$$

The percentage error is then

$$\epsilon\,(\%) = \frac{\epsilon}{\text{ideal output}} \times 100 = \frac{100}{A\beta} \qquad (3\text{-}3)$$

From the above analysis, we see that the loop gain is a significant factor in operational amplifier performance. Operational amplifiers themselves provide extremely high dc voltage gain, generally in the order of 10^4 to 10^8. However, with high closed-loop gains or a large number of inputs, β becomes small and the loop gain may be reduced to the point that a significant error is introduced.

EXAMPLE 3-1

Find the output voltage of the amplifier circuit in Fig. 3-1 if the open-loop gain of the amplifier is 1000. What amplifier gain is required in order that the output error will be less than 0.1%?

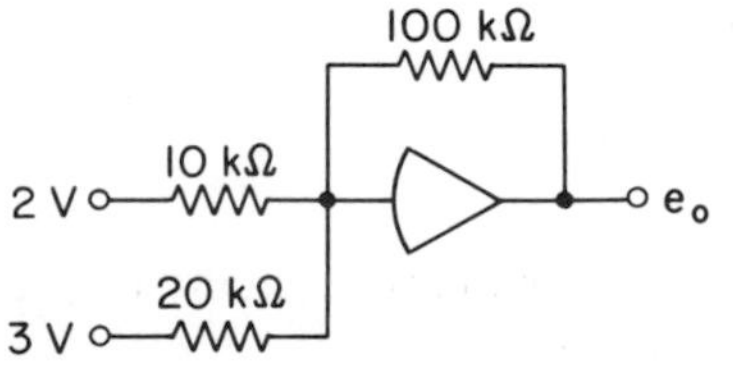

FIGURE 3–1   Circuit for Example 3-1

SOLUTION:

Using Eq. (2-46), the feedback factor is

$$\beta = \frac{(10k\Omega)(20k\Omega)/(10k\Omega + 20k\Omega)}{100k\Omega + (10k\Omega)(20k\Omega)/(10k\Omega + 20k\Omega)} = 0.0625$$

From Eq. (3-1), we obtain the output voltage as

$$e_o = -\left[\left(\frac{100k\Omega}{10k\Omega}\right)2 + \left(\frac{100k\Omega}{20k\Omega}\right)3\right]\left[\frac{1}{1 + 1/(10^3 \times 0.0625)}\right]$$

$$= -(20 + 15)(0.984) = -34.4 \text{ volts}$$

Using Eq. (3-3) with $\epsilon(\%) = 0.1$, the required amplifier gain is

$$A = \frac{100}{0.1 \times 0.0625} = 16,000 \text{ (minimum value)}$$

3-4   OFFSETS, DRIFT, AND NOISE

An ideal operational amplifier should have exactly zero output for zero input. This is never entirely true in practice since an amplifier will exhibit some output for a zero input signal. This output will contain random and spurious ac signals which are generally called *noise* and a dc signal which is known as *offset*. It is customary in specifying these signals to refer them to the input of the amplifier so that they are independent of amplifier gain. *Input offset* is then defined as the input required to zero the dc offset component of the output with zero input signal.

Offset in operational amplifiers appears in two forms: voltage offset and current offset. *Input offset voltage* is the input voltage required to zero the dc component of the output under conditions of zero input signal and zero source impedance (input terminal grounded). Solid-state amplifiers typically have input voltage offsets between 10 microvolts and 10 millivolts. This offset can be adjusted to zero by applying a small voltage, derived from the amplifier's power supplies, to the input.

Input offset current is the input current required to zero the dc output with zero signal and infinite source impedance (input terminal open). Input current offsets as low as 10 picoamperes are specified for some amplifiers while values as high as 0.1 milliampere are found in others. This offset can be zeroed by applying a compensating current to the input.

A fixed input offset (whether voltage or current) is usually not a problem since simple biasing circuits can be used to cancel the offset. However, the components of an electronic amplifier have characteristics that change with time and temperature. In addition, the voltages in the amplifier circuit are dependent upon the magnitude of the supply voltages which may, themselves, change. Thus, for several reasons, the voltages throughout the circuit tend to change with time. In an amplifier employing direct coupling, the voltage and current changes are transmitted from stage to stage and, unfortunately, are amplified in the process. We can interpret a change in the output as being due to a change in input offset. An offset change is customarily referred to as *drift*. Drift in a dc amplifier is a serious problem since offset changes cannot be distinguished from changes in an input signal. Although drift cannot be entirely eliminated, it can be minimized by proper design so that its effect is negligible.

The primary causes of drift in solid-state amplifiers are variations in temperature and supply voltages and aging of components. Drift is usually specified as the *coefficient of input offset change*. For example, voltage drift versus temperature is stated in microvolts per degree centigrade ($\mu V/°C$), drift versus supply voltage in microvolts per volt ($\mu V/V$), etc.

To evaluate the effects of offset and drift on the closed-loop operation of an amplifier, we will make use of the equivalent circuit shown in Fig. 3-2. The voltage offset is represented by a voltage source e_{os} connected in series

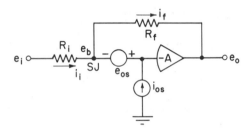

FIGURE 3-2   Operational amplifier including drift equivalent circuit.

with the summing junction and the current offset by a current source i_{os} in parallel with the summing junction. The amplifier following the equivalent input circuit is considered ideal to the extent that it has zero offsets. Since the magnitudes of the voltage and current offsets are functions of temperature, supply voltage, and time, they may be expressed by the following equations:

$$e_{os} = E_{os} + \frac{\Delta e_{os}}{\Delta T} \Delta T + \frac{\Delta e_{os}}{\Delta V_s} \Delta V_s + \frac{\Delta e_{os}}{\Delta t} \Delta t \qquad (3\text{-}4)$$

where

E_{os} is the initial offset voltage, usually measured at 25°C ambient temperature with nominal power supply voltages,

$\dfrac{\Delta e_{os}}{\Delta T}$ is the temperature drift coefficient,

$\dfrac{\Delta e_{os}}{\Delta V_s}$ is the supply voltage drift coefficient,

$\dfrac{\Delta e_{os}}{\Delta t}$ is the drift coefficient with time, and

$$i_{os} = I_{os} + \dfrac{\Delta i_{os}}{\Delta T}\,\Delta T + \dfrac{\Delta i_{os}}{\Delta V_s}\,\Delta V_s + \dfrac{\Delta i_{os}}{\Delta t}\,\Delta t \qquad (3\text{-}5)$$

where the current offset coefficients are defined in a similar manner to the voltage coefficients.

Applying Kirchhoff's current law at the summing junction of the circuit of Fig. 3-2, we have

$$i_i + i_{os} = i_f \qquad (3\text{-}6)$$

In terms of voltage drops, Eq. (3-6) may be written as

$$\dfrac{e_i - e_b}{R_i} + i_{os} = \dfrac{e_b - e_o}{R_f} \qquad (3\text{-}7)$$

The amplifier output voltage is related to the summing junction voltage by the equation

$$e_o = -(e_b + e_{os})A \qquad (3\text{-}8)$$

Equation (3-8) may be solved for e_b and the result substituted into Eq. (3-7). Equation (3-7) is then solved for the output voltage, giving the result

$$e_o = -\left(\dfrac{R_f}{R_i}e_i + \dfrac{e_{os}}{\beta} + R_f i_{os}\right)\left(\dfrac{1}{1 + 1/A\beta}\right) \qquad (3\text{-}9)$$

From Eq. (3-9), we see that the output voltage is the sum of three terms: the amplified input signal and error terms due to the voltage and current offsets. It should be emphasized that the presence of negative feedback around a computing amplifier does not eliminate drift but rather considerably reduces its effects.

EXAMPLE 3-2

An operational amplifier with the indicated offset and drift characteristics is used in the circuit shown in Fig. 3-3. Determine the maximum offset error for

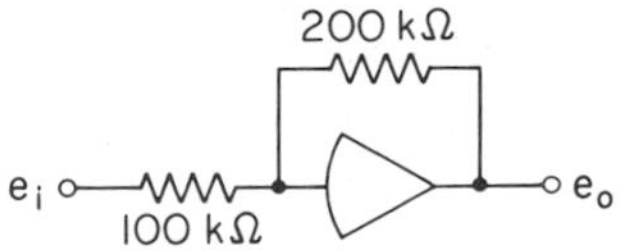

$\dfrac{\Delta e_{os}}{\Delta T} = 15\,\mu V/°C$	$I_{os} = 20\,nA$
$\dfrac{\Delta e_{os}}{\Delta V_s} = 10\,\mu V/\%$	$\dfrac{\Delta i_{os}}{\Delta T} = 1\,nA/°C$
$\dfrac{\Delta e_{os}}{\Delta t} = 50\,\mu V/day$	$\dfrac{\Delta i_{os}}{\Delta V_s} = 2\,nA/\%$

FIGURE 3-3   Circuit and data for Example 3-2.

a temperature range of $\pm 25°C$ and a supply voltage regulation of $\pm 1\%$ over a period of one day. The initial offset voltage is balanced to zero by an internal amplifier adjustment. Assume that the gain error factor is negligible.

SOLUTION:

Using Eqs. (3-4) and (3-5), the maximum voltage and current offsets are found to be

$$e_{os} = (15\mu V/°C)(25°C) + (10\mu V/\%)(1\%) + (50\mu V/day)(1\ day) = 435\mu V$$

$$i_{os} = 20nA + (1nA/°C)(25°C) + (2nA/\%)(1\%) = 47nA$$

From Eq. (3-9), the output error is determined as

$$e_o = \frac{e_{os}}{\beta} + R_f i_{os} = \frac{(435\mu V)(300k\Omega)}{100k\Omega} + (47nA)(200k\Omega) = 10.71\ mV$$

Several conclusions can be drawn from the results of Example 3-2. Amplifier output voltages should be as large as possible so that the percentage error due to offsets will be small (10mV is 0.1% of 10 volts while it is 1% of 1 volt). The effect of current offset is proportional to the value of the feedback resistance; for example, if R_i and R_f were made 10kΩ and 20kΩ respectively, the output error would be reduced to 2.25mV.

We have seen that offsets cause a steady-state error in the output of a summing amplifier. In practice, this error is quite small and can generally be neglected. However, the situation in an integrator differs in that offsets cause the output to drift as a function of time. This behavior may be analyzed by means of the circuit shown in Fig. 3-4. After summing currents and substituting Eq. (3-8), we obtain the equation

$$\frac{e_i}{R} + \frac{e_{os}}{R} + i_{os} = C\left(\frac{de_{os}}{dt} - \frac{de_o}{dt}\right) \tag{3-10}$$

Assuming $e_i = 0$ and $de_{os}/dt = 0$, Eq. (3-10) is solved for the output drift

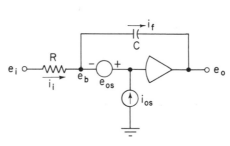

FIGURE 3–4 Integrator circuit including offsets.

rate, giving

$$-\frac{de_o}{dt} = \frac{e_{os}}{RC} + \frac{i_{os}}{C} \tag{3-11}$$

The output error is obtained by integrating Eq. (3-11) yielding the result

$$e_o = -\int_0^t \left(\frac{e_{os}}{RC} + \frac{i_{os}}{C}\right) dt = -\left(\frac{e_{os}t}{RC} + \frac{i_{os}t}{C}\right) \tag{3-12}$$

Since the error builds up with time, it will eventually exceed an acceptable value. Amplifier offsets are thus a significant source of error in integrators and impose a practical limit on the time of integration. Output drift may be minimized by using the smallest value for R and the largest value for C. This follows since the drift due to offset voltage is fixed by the gain of the circuit $(1/RC)$ whereas the drift caused by offset current is reduced by using a large C. However, our choice of values for R and C is limited by several practical considerations. The source impedance sets a minimum value on the input resistance and physical size, price, and quality limit capacitor values to about 10 microfarads.

EXAMPLE 3-3

The amplifier in Example 3-2 is used as an integrator with $R = 10\text{k}\Omega$ and $C - 10\mu\text{F}$. (a) Determine the maximum output drift rate. (b) What is the maximum time of integration in order that the drift error does not exceed 1% of the full-scale output of 10 volts?

SOLUTION:

(a) From Example 3-2, the maximum voltage and current offsets are $435\mu\text{V}$ and 47nA respectively. Using Eq. (3-11), the drift rate is

$$\frac{de_o}{dt} = \frac{435 \times 10^{-6}}{10^4 \times 10^{-5}} + \frac{47 \times 10^{-9}}{10^{-5}} = 9.05 \text{ mV/second}$$

(b) To reach an output voltage of 1% of 10 volts (0.1 volt), the integration time is

$$t = \frac{e_o}{\frac{de_o}{dt}} = \frac{0.1}{0.00905} = 11 \text{ seconds}$$

Strictly speaking, noise can be considered as any spurious output which is not contained in the input signal. Hence, drift is a special case of noise which occurs at very low frequencies. The analysis of drift and the equations to predict drift effects are equally applicable to high frequency signals. In general, noise, like drift, can be represented by a voltage source in series with the summing junction and a current source in parallel with the summing junction as shown in Fig. 3-2.

Noise may be caused by *pickup* from external sources or generated internally within the amplifier. In the first case, it may appear at a discrete frequency such as 60Hz (due to coupling from power lines) or it may arise from an RF source such as arcing contacts. Noise pick-up can be minimized by adequate shielding, the use of low-pass filters on incoming power leads to the amplifier, and by careful attention to grounding.

Random noise is generated internally in semiconductors and other components. It is usually broadband although its energy content is a function of frequency.

Internal amplifier noise is commonly specified as an equivalent input noise voltage. Since noise is related to the bandwidth over which the measurement is made, no noise specification is meaningful unless a frequency band is specified. *Wideband noise* includes frequencies up to the range of 1 kHz to 1MHz and is usually specified in rms volts. Solid-state amplifiers typically have wideband noise figures of 1–10μV rms. Some low-frequency or dc amplifiers also specify peak-to-peak noise in the range of dc to 1kHz; this is usually from 5–10μV p-p.

3-5 INPUT AND OUTPUT IMPEDANCES

Our discussion so far has assumed infinite input impedance and zero output impedance of the amplifier. In reality, solid-state amplifiers have input impedances that range from 10kΩ to as high as 10^6MΩ and output impedances from a few ohms to a few thousand ohms. Figure 3-5 shows an amplifier circuit including finite input and output impedances. For simplicity, pure resistances rather than complex impedances are shown.

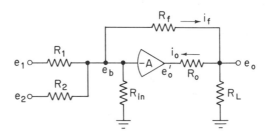

Figure 3–5 Amplifier with input and output resistances.

The effect of the finite input resistance R_{in} is to reduce the loop gain which, in turn, results in larger gain and offset errors in the output. The calculation of β from Eq. (2-46) must be modified to account for the fact that R_{in} appears in parallel with the input resistors in the feedback voltage divider. Thus, for the circuit of Fig. 3-5, we have

$$\beta = \frac{R_p}{R_f + R_p} \tag{3-13}$$

where R_p is the parallel combination of R_1, R_2, and R_{in}.

The closed-loop input resistance is the resistance seen by a signal source applied to the amplifier. In Fig. 3-5, the current through the feedback resistor is

$$i_f = \frac{e_b - e_o}{R_f} \tag{3-14}$$

Since $e_o = -Ae_b$, Eq. (3-14) may be written as

$$i_f = e_b \left(\frac{1 + A}{R_f} \right) \tag{3-15}$$

Solving Eq. (3-15) for the effective resistance R_{eff} at the summing point, we obtain

$$R_{\text{eff}} = \frac{e_b}{i_f} = \frac{R_f}{1 + A} \tag{3-16}$$

If the amplifier gain is reasonably large, then R_{eff} is sufficiently small to be negligible compared to the summing resistors. Thus, the closed-loop input resistance is almost exactly that of the respective input resistor.

The output resistance of an amplifier is defined as the internal resistance seen at the output terminals. For the circuit of Fig. 3-5, output resistance can be determined in the following manner. If we assume an ideal amplifier with output e_o', the actual output resistance can be represented by series resistor R_o. We may write the equation

$$i_o = \frac{e_o - e_o'}{R_o} \tag{3-17}$$

Substituting the relationships $e_o' = -Ae_b$ and $e_b = \beta e_o$ into Eq. (3-17), we obtain

$$i_o = \frac{e_o + A\beta e_o}{R_o} \tag{3-18}$$

The closed-loop output resistance R_{oc} can be determined by taking the ratio of e_o to i_o. Thus, from Eq. 3-18,

$$\frac{e_o}{i_o} = R_{oc} = \frac{R_o}{A\beta + 1} \tag{3-19}$$

We again see that negative feedback reduces the open-loop output resistance by a factor approximately equal to the loop gain.

EXAMPLE 3-4

The amplifier shown in Fig. 3-5 has the following specifications: $R_{in} = 100\text{k}\Omega$, $R_o = 1\text{k}\Omega$, $A = 10^4$. If $R_1 = 50\text{k}\Omega$, $R_2 = 100\text{k}\Omega$, and $R_f = 200\text{k}\Omega$, determine: (a) the effective summing point resistance, and (b) output resistance.

SOLUTION:

(a) From Eq. (3-13), the feedback factor is

$$\beta = \frac{25\text{k}\Omega}{25\text{k}\Omega + 200\text{k}\Omega} = 0.111$$

The loop gain $A\beta$ is then 1110. From Eq. (3-16),

$$R_{\text{eff}} = \frac{200\text{k}\Omega}{10^4} = 20 \text{ ohms}$$

(b) Using Eq. (3-19), we find

$$R_{oc} = \frac{1000}{1111} = 0.90 \text{ ohms}$$

We note from Example 3-4 that R_{eff} is much less than the input resistors R_1 or R_2. Also R_{oc} is sufficiently small so that the output voltage is almost completely independent of amplifier load.

3-6 FREQUENCY RESPONSE AND STABILITY

Thus far, we have considered amplifier gain to be independent of frequency. Unfortunately, this is not the case and the assumed constant high open-loop gain is available only at dc and very low frequencies. At higher frequencies the amplifier gain attenuates markedly, due largely to the effects of stray capacitances and the fall-off of transistor current gain. Associated with the gain attenuation is an increasing lag in the phase of the output voltage with respect to the input voltage.

The attenuation of amplifier gain with frequency has two adverse effects. It creates the possibility of self-oscillation or frequency instability and, as loop gain becomes less, the output error increases.

The problem of frequency instability is inherent in any negative feedback circuit. Let us begin by examining the equation for the output of an operational amplifier. For example, a simple scaling amplifier has an output according to the equation

$$e_o = -\frac{R_f}{R_i}\left(\frac{1}{1 + 1/A\beta}\right)e_i \tag{3-20}$$

Now consider the situation if $A\beta = -1$, which corresponds to 180° of phase shift with unity gain through the amplifier and feedback network. This is an unstable condition since, according to Eq. (3-20), the output is equal to $-\infty$ (in practice, of course, the output will limit at its saturation value). This instability is a consequence of the fact that the overall phase shift is now 360° (recall that 180° of phase shift is designed into an operational amplifier). This means that the feedback signal is in phase with the input signal (positive feedback) causing oscillations to develop.

If the open-loop characteristics of an amplifier satisfy certain criteria, stable closed-loop operation is assured. A common method of analyzing frequency stability is from a graph which shows voltage gain as a function of frequency. There are several ways in which the gain may be expressed in a frequency response plot. The easiest is simply the ratio of output voltage to input voltage, and this method is sometimes used. However, the conventional way of expressing gain is in logarithmic units known as *decibels* (dB). The voltage gain in decibels is defined as

$$\text{gain in dB} = 20\log\frac{e_o}{e_i} \tag{3-21}$$

where e_o and e_i are the output and input voltages respectively. Thus, a voltage gain of 10 corresponds to 20 dB, a gain of 100 is 40 dB, etc.

Using a dB gain scale, the frequency response (on a logarithmic scale) of a typical operational amplifier might be as shown in Fig. 3-6. As frequency increases, the various stray capacitances and other high frequency effects in the amplifier cause the rate of gain attenuation, or "roll-off," to become progressively greater. Tangent lines corresponding to multiples of -20dB per decade* are identified on the response plot.

According to feedback theory, closed-loop operation will be stable if the added phase shift around the loop is less than 180° at the frequency where the open-loop gain is unity. Phase shift and rate of change of gain are explic-

---

*This is simply a way of stating that the gain is down by a factor of ten if the frequency is increased by a factor of ten.

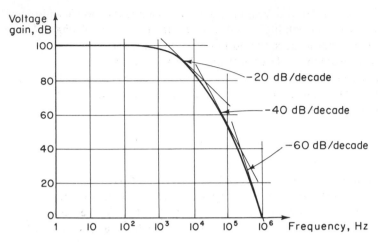

FIGURE 3-6　Open-loop frequency response of uncompensated operational amplifier.

itly related; it can be shown that 90° of phase lag corresponds to a roll-off of −20 dB/decade, 180° to −40 dB/decade, etc. Hence, as a stability criterion, we can state that the attenuation rate must be *less* than 40 dB/decade in the region of *crossover* of unity loop gain (0 dB). Note that in Fig. 3-6 the attenuation rate is higher than −40dB/decade when the loop gain is 0 dB, showing the instability of this operational amplifier.

Considerable care is exercised in designing the frequency response of an operational amplifier to prevent it from breaking into oscillation. Circuits known as *compensating networks* are used to shape the frequency response characteristic so that the above stability criterion is satisfied. Operational amplifiers are usually designed to have a smooth constant attenuation of −20 dB/decade so that stable operation is assured under widely varying feedback and load conditions. Figure 3-7 shows the open-loop gain characteristic of a 20 dB/decade compensated amplifier where A_o is the dc gain, f_c is the cutoff frequency, and f_1 is the unity gain (0 dB) crossover frequency.

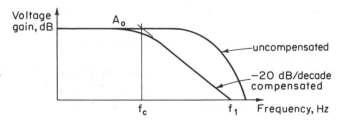

FIGURE 3-7　Open-loop frequency response of compensated operational amplifier.

If we compare the frequency response shown in Fig. 3-7 with the transfer characteristic derived in Example 2-13, we note that the two are similar in form. Therefore, the gain of this amplifier as a function of frequency can be expressed mathematically by the equation

$$A(\omega) = \frac{A_o}{1 + j\omega/\omega_c} \tag{3-22}$$

where ω_c is the cut-off frequency in rad/sec. For frequencies much greater than ω_c, the gain becomes

$$A(\omega) \cong \frac{A_o \omega_c}{j\omega} \tag{3-23}$$

At the crossover frequency ω_1, $A(\omega) = -j$. Substituting this identity in Eq. (3-23), we have

$$\omega_1 = A_o \omega_c$$

from which

$$A_o = \frac{\omega_1}{\omega_c} \tag{3-24}$$

Substituting Eq. (3-24) in Eq. (3-23) and replacing A by $A(\omega)$ in Eq. (3-20), the closed-loop gain as a function of frequency is

$$\frac{e_o}{e_i} = -\frac{R_f}{R_i}\left(\frac{1}{1 + j\omega/\beta\omega_1}\right) = -\frac{R_f}{R_i}\left(\frac{1}{1 + jf/\beta f_1}\right) \tag{3-25}$$

Thus, we see that the closed-loop frequency response has a cut-off frequency of βf_1. As closed-loop gain is increased (smaller β), the bandwidth is decreased.

Let us now examine a graphical representation of the closed-loop response. The frequency at which the loop gain is unity depends upon both the amplifier gain and the feedback factor. Loop gain can be expressed in decibels as

$$\text{loop gain} = 20 \log A\beta = 20 \log \frac{A}{1/\beta} = 20(\log A - \log 1/\beta) \tag{3-26}$$

Thus, the difference between A and $1/\beta$ on a logarithmic frequency response plot represents the *loop gain* (graphical subtraction of dB is equivalent to arithmetic division). Figure 3-8 illustrates the closed-loop frequency response for the case where β is a real quantity (input and feedback elements are resistive). Note that the closed-loop response is flat until it approaches the frequency at which the loop gain becomes unity (zero dB *difference* between

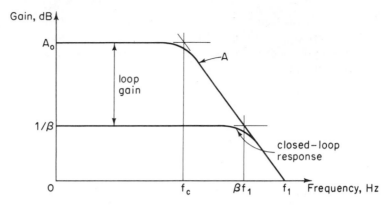

FIGURE 3–8   Closed-loop frequency response.

A and 1/β), whereupon it merges with the open-loop response. Since the effect of the negative feedback disappears as the loop gain drops below unity, the closed-loop response becomes the response of the amplifier itself.

EXAMPLE 3-5

An amplifier whose open-loop characteristic is shown in Fig. 3-9 is used with $R_i = 10\text{k}\Omega$ and $R_f = 100\text{k}\Omega$. (a) Sketch the closed-loop response and (b) determine the exact closed-loop gain at a signal frequency of 1kHz.

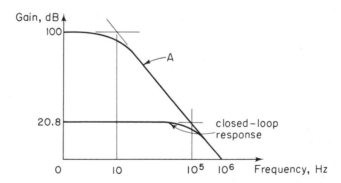

FIGURE 3–9   Frequency response curves for Example 3-5.

SOLUTION:

(a) The feedback factor β is $R_i/(R_i + R_f) = 0.091$ and 1/β is then 11 or 20.8 dB. Combining the 1/β curve with the amplifier gain curve in Fig. 3-9 gives a closed-loop response whose cut-off frequency is approximately 100kHz.

(b) The gain at 1 kHz is found with the aid of Eq. (3-25). Substituting values, we obtain

$$\frac{e_o}{e_1} = -\frac{100\text{k}\Omega}{10\text{k}\Omega}\left[\frac{1}{1+j10^3/(0.091\times10^6)}\right] = \frac{-10}{1+j0.011}$$

$$= \frac{-10}{1.0001\ \angle\ 0.63°} = -9.999\ \angle\ -0.63°$$

Example 3-5 shows that the gain magnitude is much closer to the ideal value than would be the case if A were real. Thus, the 20 dB/decade gain roll-off at 1 kHz actually results in improved amplitude accuracy, although a slight phase shift is introduced as a consequence.

3-7 DESIGN OF OPERATIONAL AMPLIFIERS

The first part of this chapter described the characteristics of operational amplifiers and analyzed the computing errors caused by amplifier imperfections. In the remaining sections, we will consider the techniques which are commonly used for dc amplification including differential amplifiers, chopper-stabilized amplifiers, and integrated circuit amplifiers.

An extensive treatment of these techniques is beyond the scope of this book, as there are numerous variations of each. Therefore we will discuss the basic features of each technique; typical designs will be illustrated. As previously mentioned, our discussion will be limited to solid-state circuits. The reader interested in this subject will find descriptions of amplifier circuits and design methods in references listed in the bibliography.

Operational amplifiers may be classified in several ways. In addition to grouping them according to basic design techniques, amplifiers are classified according to general application requirements. These categories include:

1. General-purpose, moderate performance
2. Wideband, fast response
3. High input impedance, low input current
4. Low voltage drift
5. High output voltage and power

In general, an operational amplifier must satisfy the following design specifications.

1. Extremely high dc voltage gain, generally in the range from 10^4 to 10^9.
2. Wide bandwidth starting at dc and rolling-off to unity gain at from 1 to 10 MHz with a slope of 20–30 dB per decade.
3. Plus or minus output voltage over a large

dynamic range, typically either ± 10 or ± 100 volts.

4. Very low input offset and drift with time and temperature.
5. High input impedance.

The design of a dc amplifier normally proceeds from the output stage back to the input stage. A choice of the output stage is made on the basis of required output, available power supplies, and environment.

The type and number of intermediate amplification stages are determined on the basis of overall gain requirements. The design of these stages is similar to that of an ac amplifier except for the provision of conductive coupling between the stages.

The design of the input (or first) stage is most critical because the amplifier drift and noise characteristics are largely determined at this point. A careful choice of input stage components and operating points is necessary to achieve high quality performance.

A necessary step in the design procedure is the evaluation of amplifier frequency response and the incorporation of stabilizing networks to assure stable operation.

3-8 DIFFERENTIAL AMPLIFIER STAGE

The major limitation on the ultimate sensitivity of a dc amplifier is the drift caused by variations of transistor operating point with temperature. This is especially true in the input stage since drift developed at this point is greatly amplified in succeeding stages. If the drift can be balanced by an equal drift, the amplifier sensitivity can be extended many orders of magnitude. This is the principle of the *differential amplifier*, so called because its output voltage is proportional to the *difference* of the voltages applied to two separate inputs.

In addition to the reduction in drift, a differential amplifier provides other advantages including the mixing of two input voltages (or an input and feedback signal), an output of either polarity or push-pull, ease of choosing dc operating levels, and rejection of what is known as a common-mode signal.

Two transistors are necessary to perform the differential operation as can be seen in the basic circuit shown in Fig. 3-10. The emitters of Q_1 and Q_2 are each coupled by small resistors R_E whose value is typically several hundred ohms. These resistances are generally provided by a potentiometer which can be adjusted to balance small inequalities between the two halves of the circuit. The series resistance R_{EE} is relatively large, usually 10kΩ or greater. If R_{EE} is connected to ground, the two inputs would necessarily be off ground. By returning R_{EE} to a negative supply voltage, the circuit can be designed so

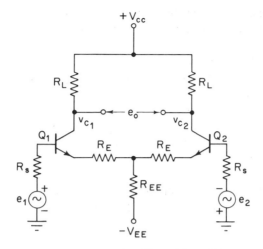

FIGURE 3-10   Basic differential amplifier.

that the terminals for inputs e_1 and e_2 are normally at zero voltage. The resistors R_S represent the internal resistance associated with the signal sources.

Two out-of-phase inputs are shown applied to the differential amplifier circuit. These signals cause one base to go positive while the other goes negative with respect to the emitters. Current will then rise in one transistor and fall in the other. This will result in an amplified voltage difference between the collectors, which voltages may be fed to another differential stage for further amplification. Since the oppositely phased emitter voltages cancel each other, the circuit amplifies as if the resistor R_{EE} were shorted.

The circuit will also amplify if only one signal is applied and the other input is grounded. For example, assume e_1 goes positive causing v_{c_1} to drop. The emitter voltage of Q_1 will tend to follow its base voltage so that a positive signal is applied to the emitter of Q_2. This will cause a decrease in current through Q_2 producing a rise in v_{c_2}.

A detailed analysis of the operation of a differential stage is beyond our scope. However, with certain simplifications, the differential output voltage is given by the equation

$$e_o = v_{c_1} - v_{c_2} = \left(\frac{\beta R_L}{\beta R_E + R_S}\right)[e_1 - e_2 + V_{BE_1} - V_{BE_2} + R_S(I_{CBO_1} - I_{CBO_2})]$$

$$(3\text{-}27)$$

where β is the common-emitter short-circuit current gain of the transistor,* V_{BE} is the base-emitter voltage drop, and I_{CBO} is the collector leakage current.

---

*Recall that β is also used to designate feedback factor; this should not be confused with its use here for transistor current gain.

Equation (3-27) assumes that the transistor current gains are equal and that the internal transistor resistances r_e, r_b, and r_c are negligible compared to the external circuit resistors.

The first factor in Eq. (3-27) specifies the differential gain A_D of the stage. The second factor contains the differential input signal $e_1 - e_2$ as well as input offsets due to the V_{BE} and I_{CBO}. If $V_{BE_1} = V_{BE_2}$ and $I_{CBO_1} = I_{CBO_2}$, the internal effects cancel and do not appear in the output. As was noted before, this is one of the primary advantages of a differential stage.

If desired, the stage output may be taken single-ended between a collector and ground. In this case the output voltage will be one-half the value given by Eq. (3-27).

The crucial test of a dc amplifier is its drift performance. Good circuit design must minimize drift effects, especially in the amplifier input stage. Drift originates almost exclusively in the transistors, primarily from the effects of aging and temperature changes in the saturation current, the base-emitter voltage, and the current gain.

The use of silicon transistors having room temperature saturation currents of the order of 1nA largely eliminates this source of drift with signal sources of nominal impedance.

Temperature variation of V_{BE} is a more serious source of drift. This quantity exhibits marked temperature dependence, decreasing by about 2mV for every degree centigrade rise in temperature. Even though the base-emitter voltage drops in a differential stage are in series opposition, close matching is necessary to obtain low drift. For example, if the changes in V_{BE} with temperature are matched to one part in 100, there will be a differential change of $20\mu V/°C$ change in ambient temperature. Even if the base-emitter voltage drops are exactly matched, an equivalent input drift of $20\mu V$ will result for every $0.01°C$ temperature difference between the transistors. Thus, in low-drift input stages, it is imperative to employ a good common heat sink or, preferably, a dual transistor unit.

The remaining source of drift is the variation of current gains of Q_1 and Q_2. Since the collector current of each transisor is stabilized by the large resistor in the emitter circuit, the base current is a function of current gain. Inasmuch as the base current flows through the signal source, any variation gives rise to a spurious input signal. By matching the two current gains to within about 10 per cent over a specified temperature and collector current range, this drift effect can be reduced to secondary importance.

EXAMPLE 3-6

The 2N2060 is a dual NPN transistor designed for use in high-performance differential amplifier circuits. The base voltage differential change is $10\mu V/°C$ maximum and the maximum collector cutoff current is 2nA at 25°C. If the circuit is balanced at 25°C, determine the input offset voltage at 45°C. Assume $R_S = 10\text{k}\Omega$.

SOLUTION:

The input offset voltage due to V_{BE} is

$$\left(\frac{\Delta V_{BE}}{\Delta T}\right)\Delta T = 200\mu V.$$

To determine the offset due to I_{CBO}, we will assume that the leakage current of one transistor is much less than the specified maximum. Thus, $I_{CBO_1} - I_{CBO_2} \cong I_{CBO_1}$. If we take I_{CBO} as doubling for each 10°C rise in temperature, then $\Delta I_{CBO} = 6\text{nA}$. The related offset voltage is $6 \times 10^{-9} \times 10^4 = 60\mu V$.
The total offset referred to the input is then $260\mu V$.

Differential amplifiers are particularly useful because signals common to both inputs are eliminated or reduced. Theoretically, if a differential amplifier is perfectly balanced and ideal transistors are assumed, a common-mode signal would produce no output voltage, as can be seen by letting $e_1 = e_2$ in Eq. (3-27). This is especially important in instrumentation applications where a small differential signal exists between two points and the points also have a large in-phase signal. For example, a transducer such as a thermocouple or strain gage will likely have power line pickup or other common-mode voltage appearing on its pair of signal wires. In this case a differential amplifier will amplify the desired data signal while rejecting the common-mode interference.

Because the two sides of an amplifier are not exactly alike, a common-mode signal produces a small differential output. The ability of an amplifier to prevent conversion of a common-mode signal into an output is expressed by its *common-mode rejection* (*CMR*). *CMR* is defined as the ratio of the gain of the amplifier for a differential signal to the gain of the amplifier for a common-mode signal.

Many applications require a single-ended output from a differential stage. Since a common-mode signal drives both inputs in-phase with equal magnitude voltages, the circuit behaves as though the transistors were in parallel. In this case, the large emitter resistor R_{EE} introduces emitter feedback, which substantially decreases the common-mode gain. Using the simplifying assumptions made in Eq. (3-27), the gain for a common-mode input voltage is

$$A_{CM} = \frac{v_c}{e_1} = \frac{\beta R_L}{\beta(R_E + 2R_{EE}) + R_S} \cong \frac{R_L}{2R_{EE}} \qquad (3\text{-}28)$$

High common-mode rejection requires large values of R_{EE} which, in turn, necessitates an unrealistically large emitter supply voltage. Fortunately, large values of R_{EE} can be simulated by means of a third transistor used as a constant-current source as shown in Fig. 3-11. With a low dc voltage drop, this circuit maintains a constant current through the transisors, providing even better common-mode rejection than a high-value resistor.

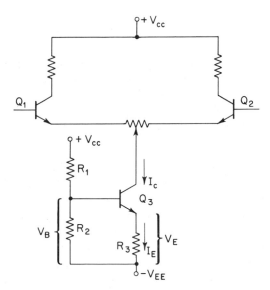

FIGURE 3–11   Differential amplifier with constant-current source.

Resistors R_1 and R_2 form a voltage divider which sets the base and, in turn, the emitter voltage of Q_3. With the emitter voltage fixed, R_3 determines the value of current in the circuit. If we assume that the base current of Q_3 is small compared to the current through the voltage divider, the following equations can be used to define the operation of the circuit.

$$V_B = \frac{(V_{CC} + V_{EE})R_2}{R_1 + R_2} \simeq V_E \tag{3-29}$$

$$I_E = \frac{V_E}{R_3} \simeq I_C$$

The resistance which Q_3 introduces into the differential stage is the collector-to-base resistance of a common-emitter stage in which large emitter degeneration is present. This may be determined from the equation for the output resistance of a common-emitter stage which is approximately

$$R_o \simeq \frac{R_E r_c}{R_E + R_B} \tag{3-30}$$

where r_c is the collector resistance of Q_3 and R_B is the parallel combination of R_1 and R_2.

EXAMPLE 3-7

The differential amplifier shown in Fig. 3-12 is operated with a single-ended input and output. Determine: (a) dc operating points under balanced circuit condition; (b) differential gain; (c) common-mode rejection. Assume $\beta = 100$ and $r_c = 5\text{M}\Omega$.

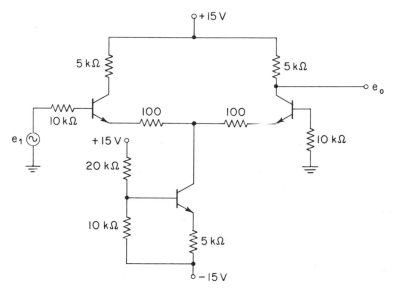

FIGURE 3–12   Circuit for Example 3-7.

SOLUTION:

(a) Using Eq. (3-29), the current to the differential pair may be calculated as follows:

$$V_B \cong V_E = \frac{(15 + 15)10\text{k}\Omega}{10\text{k}\Omega + 20\text{k}\Omega} = 10\text{V}$$

$$I_E \cong I_C = \frac{10}{5\text{k}\Omega} = 2\text{mA}$$

The currents through Q_1 and Q_2 are each 1mA. Their dc collector voltage is then

$$V_C = 15 - (10^{-3})(5\text{k}\Omega) = 5\text{V}$$

(b) The differential gain is determined from Eq. (3-27). Thus

$$A_D = \frac{1}{2}\left(\frac{\beta R_L}{\beta R_E + R_S}\right) = \frac{100 \times 5\text{k}\Omega}{2(100 \times 100 + 10\text{k}\Omega)} = 12.5$$

(c) To compute the common-mode rejection, it is necessary to first determine the resistance of the constant-current source. From Eq. (3-30), the equivalent resistance is

$$R_o = 5\text{M}\Omega\left(\frac{5\text{k}\Omega}{11.7\text{k}\Omega}\right) = 2.13\text{M}\Omega$$

The common-mode gain is then

$$A_{CM} = \frac{5\text{k}\Omega}{2 \times 2.13\text{M}\Omega} = 1.17 \times 10^{-3}$$

The common-mode rejection is

$$CMR = \frac{A_{CM}}{A_D} = \frac{1.17 \times 10^{-3}}{12.5} = 9.4 \times 10^{-5} = -81\text{ dB}$$

3-9 DIFFERENTIAL OPERATIONAL AMPLIFIER

A differential operational amplifier consists of a low-drift differential input stage, one or more additional differential stages for voltage amplification, and an output stage to supply the desired load power. The differential stages may be directly coupled without gain-reducing interstage networks by complementary symmetry in the form of alternate NPN and PNP stages. The output stage in most operational amplifiers employs a transformerless push-pull amplifier with single-ended input and output. Since the quiescent output voltage must be zero, some form of level shifting is generally necessary in driving the output stage. In addition, compensating networks must be provided to shape the frequency response for stable operation.

Figure 3-13 shows a typical differential amplifier for analog computer use by which some points of amplifier design can be illustrated. This circuit was chosen because it is simple, straightforward, and easily understood. The amplifier consists of the input stage Q_1-Q_2, a second differential stage Q_3-Q_4, a buffer stage Q_5, and the output stage Q_6-Q_7.

The input stage is designed for low drift. Transistors Q_1 and Q_2 are matched for V_{BE} change with temperature and are mounted in a common heat sink. The cross-coupling resistors R_3 and R_4 are selected so that no current flows through R_1 and R_2 when the inputs are grounded. Since the signal voltages in a computer do not contain common-mode signals, a resistor R_{10} is used in the emitter circuit rather than a constant-current transistor. Diodes D_1 and D_2 are included to prevent damage from excessive voltages at the base of Q_1.

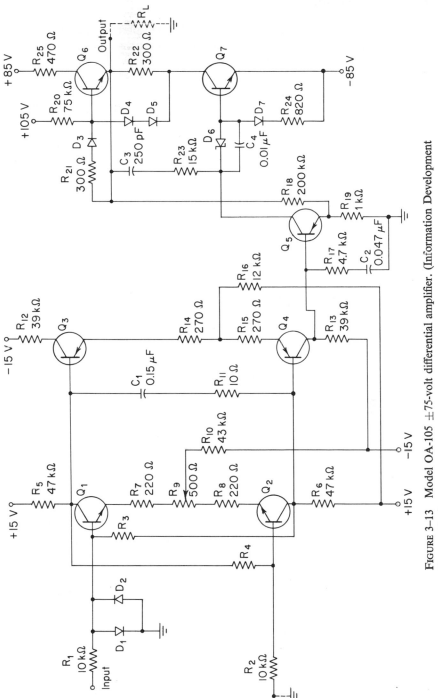

FIGURE 3–13   Model OA-105 ±75-volt differential amplifier. (Information Development Corporation)

The second differential stage is conventional in design. The dc operating points of the differential stages are selected so that the NPN collectors are directly connected to the PNP bases. The collector voltage of Q_4 is coupled to the output stage by a common-emitter amplifier Q_5.

The output stage is known as a *totem-pole stage* because of the particular arrangement of the transistors. Its operation may be described by means of the simplified circuit shown in Fig. 3-14. Series transistors Q_6 and Q_7 are slightly forward biased for Class AB operation which provides high efficiency and low crossover distortion. With a quiescent current of several mA, the output voltage is nominally zero. With a positive input voltage, Q_7 conducts more heavily causing a drop in its collector voltage. The increased voltage drop across R_{22} is coupled to the base of Q_6 through diodes D_4 and D_5 causing Q_6 to cut-off. Thus, the load is effectively in the collector circuit of Q_7. A negative input signal causes the collector voltage of Q_7 to rise. This tends to back bias D_4 and D_5 so that more base current flows into Q_6 through R_{20}. As Q_6 becomes more conductive, it supplies the current to the load as an emitter follower.

The collector of Q_5 must be operated with a positive bias while the base of Q_7 is approximately 85 volts negative. A shift in dc voltage between these stages is therefore necessary. This is provided by Zener diode D_6 which introduces a dc drop of 80 volts without attenuating the signal.

Compensating networks $C_1 R_{11}$, $C_2 R_{17}$, and $C_3 R_{23}$ provide an open-loop high frequency roll-off of about -20 dB/decade.

One of the criteria for an operational amplifier is that the output should

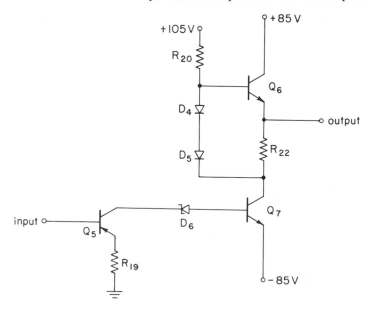

FIGURE 3–14   Totem-pole output stage.

be zero when the input voltage is zero. To obtain zero correspondence between input and output voltages, some means of manual adjustment is usually provided. The process of adjusting zero output voltage with zero input is called *amplifier balancing*. In Fig. 3-13, balancing is done by means of potentiometer R_9 in the input stage. Depending upon the application and drift behavior of an amplifier, if may need to be balanced as frequently as several times daily, or as infrequently as several times a year.

The amplifier shown in Fig. 3-13 has an output capability of ± 75 volts dc at 20mA. The open-loop gain exceeds 100,000 (100 dB) from dc to 50 Hz. The unity-gain crossover frequency is in the vicinity of 500 kHz. Input drift with temperature is less than $25\mu V/°C$ and $1nA/°C$.

3-10 FET INPUT STAGES

A limitation of transistor differential amplifiers is that the input impedance is too low and the offset current and drift are too high for many applications. The use of *field-effect transistors** in the input state of a differential amplifier has provided a new class of amplifiers for these applications.

The FET input stage is similar to the differential amplifier described in Section 3-8 except for the use of FET's rather than transistors. FET input stages are characterized by input impedances as high as 10^{10} to 10^{12} ohms. Newer types of amplifiers using (MOS) FET's achieve input offset currents as low as 1pA and the drift of offset current with temperature tends to be an order of magnitude lower than for transistor type amplifiers. A low offset current is essential in applications where the amplifier is to be used with input currents below 100 pA. Such applications include very low drift integrators and the amplification of signals from high impedance sources such as electrochemical cells, piezoelectric transducers, and photomultiplier tubes.

Figure 3-15 shows the arrangement of an FET differential amplifier. As in the case of the transistor differential stage, some degree of matching is required between certain characteristics of the FET devices. The forward

---

*A field-effect transistor (FET) uses a high-intensity electric field, directed transversely across a bar of semiconductor material, to control the conductance between the ends of the bar (the semiconductor bar is called the *channel* and its ends are identified as the *source* and the *drain*). Two types of field-effect devices are widely used. In the *junction FET*, two P–N junctions are formed on opposite sides of the bar. The input signal is applied as a reverse bias to the junctions which are known as the *gate*. As the reverse voltage is increased, the conductance of the channel decreases because of a widening of the space-charge regions. A second type of construction has a thin metal oxide separating the gate and the channel. This type is termed the metal-oxide-semiconductor [(*MOS*) *FET*]. Since the gate is not in direct contact with the channel, conductance modulation is through the small capacity between the gate and the channel. The voltage–current curves of the FET are shaped like those of a pentode and the device is used both as a voltage amplifier and switch. FET's are characterized by input impedances ranging upward of 10^9 ohms and by extremely low offset currents. Typically, values are 1nA for junction devices and 1pA for the (MOS) FET.

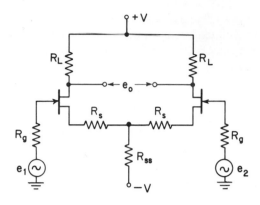

FIGURE 3–15   FET differential amplifier.

transfer admittance y_{fs} and the gate-source voltage V_{GS} should be matched. In addition, if the impedance of the driving source is greater than a megohm or so, the gate-source leakage current I_{GSS} should also be matched.

One very important difference between the transistor and the FET is the nature of the voltage offset at the input. In the case of the FET, the input offset is determined by V_{GS} which, in turn, is a function of the drain current and the temperature. The general approach to obtain low voltage drift is to choose the optimum operating point from a drift standpoint and then incorporate some form of drift compensation into the circuit. Using such techniques, drifts of a few microvolts per degree centigrade can be achieved over a wide temperature range.

The differential voltage gain A_D is the same as that for a single common source stage. If the sides are well matched, the gain is

$$A_D = \frac{y_{fs}R_L}{1 + y_{os}R_L} \qquad (3\text{-}31)$$

where y_{fs} is the forward transfer admittance, y_{os} is the output admittance, and R_L is the load resistance.

The common-mode voltage gain is given approximately by the equation

$$A_{CM} \cong \frac{R_L}{2R_{SS}} \qquad (3\text{-}32)$$

where R_{SS} is the value of the resistor in the common source circuit of the two FET's.

3-11   DRIFT STABILIZATION

We have seen that the drift in differential amplifiers may be kept low through careful design and selection of components. Although the resulting amplifiers can be quite good from a drift standpoint, the operator must still balance them occasionally for best results. A significant improvement in drift performance is possible by providing automatic means of maintaining amplifier balance. This is known as *drift stabilization* of the amplifier, sometimes referred to as *chopper stabilization*. This technique makes use of an auxiliary amplifier that increases the loop gain at dc and low frequencies and therefore acts to reduce the effect of offset voltages.

To understand how drift stabilization functions, let us consider the generalized operational amplifier circuit shown in Fig. 3-16(a). Referring to Eq. (3-9), the output voltage can be expressed as

$$e_o = -\frac{Z_f}{Z_i}\left(\frac{A\beta}{1+A\beta}\right)e_i - \left(\frac{A}{1+A\beta}\right)e_{os} \tag{3-33}$$

where e_{os} is the input offset voltage of the dc amplifier. If $A\beta \gg 1$, then the output due to the offset voltage is e_{os}/β.

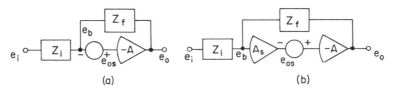

(a)   (b)

FIGURE 3–16   Generalized operational amplifier (a) and inclusion of stabilizing amplifier (b).

Now let an auxiliary drift-free amplifier of gain A_s be inserted ahead of A as shown in Fig. 3-16(b). This amplifier is known as the *stabilizing amplifier*. The circuit may be analyzed following our usual method. Thus

$$\frac{e_i - e_b}{Z_i} = \frac{e_b - e_o}{Z_f} \tag{3-34}$$

and

$$e_o = -AA_s e_b - Ae_{os} \tag{3-35}$$

Combining these equations, we obtain the equation for the output voltage as

$$e_o = -\frac{Z_f}{Z_i}\left(\frac{AA_s\beta}{1+AA_s\beta}\right)e_i - \left(\frac{A}{1+AA_s\beta}\right)e_{os} \tag{3-36}$$

For $AA_s \gg 1$, the offset at the output is $e_{os}/A_s\beta$. Comparing Eqs. (3-36) and (3-33), we see that the inclusion of A_s has reduced the drift to $1/A_s$ times its former value. In addition, the signal term in Eq. (3-36) is more nearly equal to the ideal because of the increased loop gain.

The crux of drift stabilization lies in the provision of amplifier A_s which is free from drift effects. Drift-free amplification is possible in a capacitively coupled amplifier since the stages are dc isolated. However, for this same reason, it cannot respond to dc signals but can only amplify ac voltages. On the other hand, if a dc voltage modulates an ac carrier and the carrier is amplified and then demodulated, then dc amplification is effectively obtained using an ac amplifier.

Figure 3-17 shows the arrangement of a drift-stabilized amplifier composed of dc and ac amplifiers and a modulator-demodulator. We will examine the operation of the stabilizing circuit with the aid of the waveforms shown

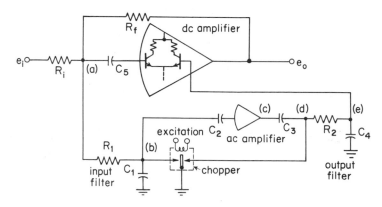

FIGURE 3–17   Block diagram of drift-stabilized amplifier.

in Fig. 3-18. Assume that the summing junction voltage is varying slowly as shown by waveform (a). This voltage is applied to the modulator through a low-pass filter $R_1 C_1$ that removes noise and other high-frequency components which are present in the signal. The modulator is known as a *chopper*, a name descriptive of the action of the device. Choppers are discussed more fully in the next section; at this time we will merely identify this chopper as a switch which alternately grounds the two contacts at a frequency determined by an exciting voltage. Waveform (b) shows the chopped input voltage which is applied to the ac stabilizing amplifier through capacitor C_2. The amplified voltage at the output is shown in waveform (c). Note that the dc level of the input is lost in the amplifier (also note the change in scale between input and output voltages). The amplifier output is coupled by C_3 to the other chopper contact where it is grounded during the half cycles when the input is not grounded. The demodulated signal is then filtered by the action of $R_2 C_4$. This filter must have a very long time constant, generally 10–100 seconds, to reduce the ripple to a very small value.

Since the two inputs to a differential stage cause opposite effects upon the output, the signal from the stabilizer must be of opposite polarity to that at the summing junction. If the ac amplifier introduces no phase reversal, a positive voltage at the summing junction will produce a negative voltage from

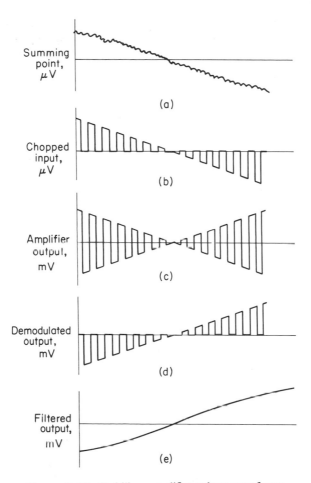

FIGURE 3–18   Stabilizer amplifier voltage waveforms.

the stabilizer, and vice versa, as can be seen by comparing waveforms (a) and (e). The stabilizer gain A_s is actually the gain through the modulator, amplifier, and demodulator. In typical stabilized amplifiers, A_s is of the order of 1000.

If we compare the diagram of Fig. 3-17 with the generalized circuit shown in Fig. 3-16(b), we note that the summing junction voltage is applied to the dc amplifier as well as to the stabilizer amplifier. This is necessary since the bandwidth through the stabilizer channel is quite low because of the long time constant output filter. The connection through C_s permits high-frequency signals to be amplified just as though the stabilizing amplifier were not present. The blocking capacitor C_s is a high-quality unit having extremely low leakage. This reduces the current offset at the summing junction to less than 0.1 nA.

The relative frequency responses of the amplifiers are shown in Fig. 3-19. The gain of the stabilizing amplifier starts to fall off at a much lower frequency than does that of the dc amplifier due to the low cut-off frequency of the output filter. On a logarithmic plot the combined response of the amplifiers may be obtained by adding their individual gains (this is equivalent to

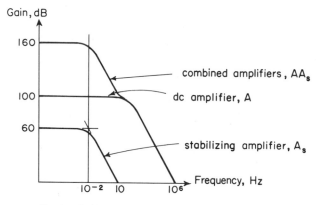

FIGURE 3-19   Frequency responses of A and A_s.

arithmetic multiplication). The combined curve shows a very high dc and low-frequency gain. This is of particular benefit in integration, where the leveling of the gain at low frequencies is a primary source of error. By carefully proportioning the gains of the two circuits, the combined response can have smooth roll-off over its full bandwidth. The gains and cut-off frequencies shown in Fig. 3-19 are typical of stabilized computing amplifiers.

A disadvantage of the chopper-stabilized amplifier is its slow recovery from an overload conditon. An overload causes a signal much larger than normal to be applied to the filter capacitor C_4 and the blocking capacitor C_5. After removal of the overload, sufficient time must be allowed to restore these capacitors to their normal condition. Since time constants of the order of 10 to 25 seconds are common, as much as a minute is sometimes necessary before the amplifier completely recovers. Hence, a temporary overload will have a much more detrimental effect on computer operation when using stabilized amplifiers than when unstabilized amplifiers are used. For this reason, analog computers generally include provisions for automatically indicating to the operator the fact that an overload exists. The method of accomplishing this is described in Section 6-5.

3-12   CHOPPERS

As we have seen, a chopper is a device which "chops" a dc signal into a square wave of some fixed frequency. The performance of a stabilized amplifier is closely tied to the chopper; hence, this section will be devoted to describing various types of choppers and their characteristics.

Modern choppers assume many forms. Electromechanical, transistor, and photoelectric choppers are by far the most common and we will consider these types.

The *electromechanical chopper* was the first type to find wide acceptance. It is still popular because of its excellent performance at microvolt signal levels. Figure 3-20 shows the construction of a mechanical chopper that is used for amplifier stabilization. The chopper consists of a contact-carrying

FIGURE 3-20 Construction of electromechanical chopper. (Airpax Electronics, Inc.)

metal reed positioned between fixed contacts and actuated by an ac voltage applied to the drive coil. The excitation causes the reed to vibrate, so that the contacts open and close on each half cycle of the excitation. The magnetic circuit is designed so that switching occurs close to the zero point of the exciting waveform. The 60Hz ac power line is generally used for excitation because of its convenience. However, some choppers are designed to perform at higher frequencies in the range of 400 to 1000 Hz.

The voltage drift in a stabilized amplifier using a mechanical chopper is largely due to minute offset voltages generated by electrochemical, thermoelectrical, and piezoelectrical effects in the contact assembly, as well as to pickup from the excitation circuit. Offsets as low as several microvolts are

possible in high-quality choppers. Operating life is an important consideration in applying electromechanical choppers; with proper use, an operating
life of from 5,000 to 10,000 hours can generally be expected.

Despite the continued improvement of electromechanical choppers,
the trend is toward the use of electronic choppers for amplifier stabilization.
Solid-state choppers overcome many of the limitations of electromechanical
choppers such as limited life, low chopping frequency, and sensitivity to shock
and vibration. Although the low-level performance of mechanical choppers
is unequaled, the characteristics of some solid-state choppers now approach
those of the best mechanical units.

The *transistor chopper* is shown in its basic form in Fig. 3-21. The transistor is alternately biased on to saturation and off to cut-off by the excitation
voltage. This causes the current flow to the load to be interrupted at the frequency of the excitation, and the dc signal is thereby converted to an ac
voltage across the load.

Unfortunately, this simple arrangement has several undesirable characteristics. When the transistor is switched on, a small potential in the range of
10 to 500mV appears between the collector and the emitter. Since this produces an ac output voltage, even with zero signal, a voltage offset is intro-

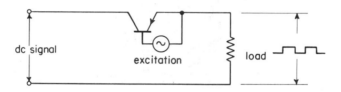

FIGURE 3–21   Basic transistor chopper circuit.

duced. Another troublesome characteristic is due to the collector cutoff
current of the transistor, which ranges between 1nA and 1μA. This also causes
an offset to appear if the load impedance is high.

With most transistors a lower saturation voltage and leakage current are
obtained by using the collector of the transistor for the emitter and the emitter for the collector. This is known as the *inverted connection*; it gives as much
as a ten-fold improvement in offset characteristics. Special transistors for
chopper applications (e.g., 2N2944) have an offset voltage of 0.5mV and a
leakage current of 0.1nA when operated in the inverted connection.

Most transistor chopper circuits use two transistors in such a way that the
offset voltages and/or leakage currents appearing at their outputs either
oppose each other or add to produce a constant dc voltage. Figure 3-22 shows
two simple circuits which illustrate this principle. The success of this approach
depends on the degree to which the saturation voltages and offset currents can
be matched over the operating temperature range. In the series connection, the

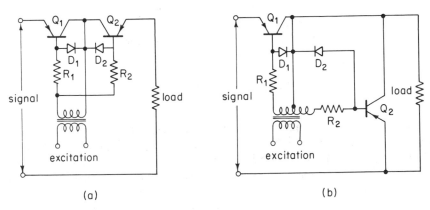

FIGURE 3-22   Transistor chopper circuits: (a) series connection, and (b) series-shunt connection.

transistors are switched together and their offsets tend to cancel. Resistors
R_1 and R_2 are for balancing the base drive currents, and diodes D_1 and D_2
prevent an excessive base voltage during the off half cycle.

In the series-shunt arrangement, the transistors are connected back-to-
back and are driven out of phase so that when one is on, the other is off.
Consequently, the signal is connected to the load during one half cycle, and
during the other half cycle the output is very nearly zero. In this connection,
the saturation voltage drops are alternately coupled to the load during each
half cycle. Although this produces a dc voltage at the output, there is no ac
component to cause an offset. Matched transistors fabricated in a common
collector structure are used for best performance.

For convenience, the chopper excitation voltage may be sinusoidal.
However, a square-wave drive usually produces smaller offsets since the circuit
need only be balanced at one value of base current. Since transistor choppers
generally use a floating-transformer drive circuit to prevent coupling the
drive into the output, square-wave excitation has the disadvantage of requiring a more expensive wideband transformer. In addition, during the instant of
switching a noise spike will apear in the output due to capacitance coupling.
The offset-producing effect of this spike can be minimized by filtering and by
operating the circuit at a lower switching frequency.

Field-effect transistors (FET's) have proved to be especially suitable as
electronic choppers. Two characteristics of the FET make it an excellent
device for low-level switching: it does not have an inherent voltage offset
between the input and output terminals, and the input impedance is extremely
high.

The simple chopper circuit shown in Fig. 3-23 offers most of the advantages of both mechanical and transistor choppers and few of the disadvan-

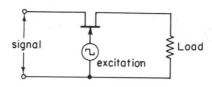

FIGURE 3–23   Series FET chopper.

tages. With no bias applied from gate to source, current flows freely through the channel. When a reverse bias is applied, a very high value of resistance will be seen from drain to source. Since the gate-to-source junction is reverse biased, a very high impedance is seen at the gate and no transformer is needed to isolate the drive.

There are no offset voltages, as there are in the transistor chopper, because when the FET is in the on state, the path from drain to source is a pure resistance. When the FET is turned off, the performance approaches that of a mechanical chopper. The drain–source off resistance is of the order of 10^{12} ohms and the gate leakage current is less than 1pA at room temperature.

The major disadvantage of the FET chopper occurs when chopping a very low level signal at a high frequency. Due to capacitance from gate to source, the drive–signal transition is coupled into the output and causes spikes to appear in the output waveform.

Because of the extremely small off current, the series chopper circuit is commonly used. However, the series-shunt arrangement offers an advantage at high chopping frequencies. Both junction and MOS type FET's are used in chopping applications.

A form of electronic chopper which has microvolt sensitivity at medium switching speeds is the photochopper which employs photoresistive cells and associated light sources. The resistance of a photocell varies inversely with the level of illumination. Thus, if the light source is modulated, the resistance of the photocell will be modulated accordingly.

Figure 3-24 shows the internal schematic of a photochopper which uses neon lamps for the actuating light source. The photocells are usually a material such as cadmium sulfide and have an on resistance of several thousand ohms and an off resistance on the order of 10^9 ohms. The illustrated circuit uses a series-shunt arrangement for the photocells. The neon lamps fire on alternate half cycles of the excitation, so that R_1 is high when R_2 is low (switch open), and R_1 is low when R_2 is high (switch closed).

Photochoppers can yield long-term offsets as low as $2\mu V$, negligible temperature effects, and an operating life measured in years. Unfortunately, the switching time of suitable photocells is of the order of milliseconds so the useful range of exciting frequencies is about 1 kHz maximum. Another handicap in solid-state circuit application is the fact that the neon lamps require a high ac supply voltage.

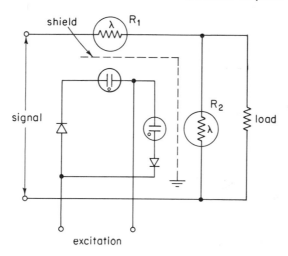

FIGURE 3–24   Schematic diagram of photochopper.

The characteristics of various types of choppers are summarized in the table below. Best overall performance can be obtained from the FET chopper which combines high-speed operation with good low-level sensitivity. For minimum offset at lower switching frequencies, the electromechanical or photochopper is used.

SUMMARY   OF   CHOPPER   CHARACTERISTICS

Type	Excitation		Resistance(ohms)		Offset noise (μV)	Drift (μV/°C)	Life (hours)
	frequency	voltage	on	off			
Electro-mechanical	60–400Hz	6–120 rms	$\cong 0$	$\cong \infty$	1–5	1	5000
Transistor	0–100kHz	5–10 p-p†	50	10^9	50	3	$> 10^4$
FET	0–1MHz	1–5 p-p	100–1kΩ	10^{12}	5–10	1	$> 10^4$
Photo	0–500Hz	120 p-p	1–10kΩ	10^9	3	1	$> 10^4$

†Peak to peak

3-13   STABILIZED AMPLIFIER DESIGN

The basic principle of the stabilized amplifier was discussed in Section 3-11. In this section we will examine the details of a typical stabilized amplifier for analog computer application.

Figure 3-25 is a schematic diagram of the amplifier, which consists of a dc amplifier, an electromechanical chopper, and a stabilizer amplifier. The summing junction is connected to the input terminal of the amplifier. The ac

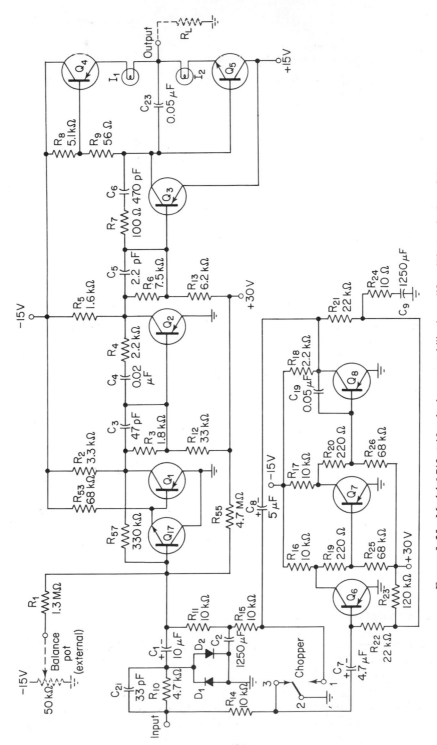

FIGURE 3-25 Model 6.712 ±10-volt chopper-stabilized amplifier. (Electronic Associates, Inc.)

96

components of the input signal are applied to the base of transisor Q_{17} through R_{10}, C_{21}, and C_1. The input signal is also coupled through R_{14} to the input to the stabilizer section. Two reverse-connected diodes (D_1 and D_2) are connected from the input to ground so that capacitor C_1 cannot be charged to a high voltage during overload conditions. This feature allows the amplifier to recover more quickly should an overload occur. The normal signal at this point is below the diode conduction point.

Transistors Q_{17} and Q_1 comprise the amplifier input stage. Transistor Q_1 is connected in a common-emitter configuration with R_{53}, providing self-bias. Transistor Q_{17} is used in a common-collector configuration and uses the voltage drop (0.3 volt) across the base-emitter diode of Q_1 as its operating voltage. The base-emitter resistance of Q_1 serves as the load for Q_{17}. This configuration gives the amplifier a relatively high input impedance. The base circuit of Q_{17} is competed through R_{55}, R_1, and the balance potentiometer. These components form a voltage divider between -15 volts and $+30$ volts; adjusting the balance potentiometer sets the optimum operating point for Q_{17}. In practice, the balance potentiometer is adjusted for zero output from the stabilizer.

The output at the collector of Q_1 is directly coupled to the base of Q_2, which is also connected in the common-emitter configuration. Bias is supplied from voltage divider R_3 and R_{12}, connected between the collector of Q_1 and the $+30$ volt supply. The high-frequency roll-off of the Q_2 stage is controlled by the series combination of R_4 and C_4, which provides an increasing amount of negative feedback at higher frequencies. Capacitors C_3, C_5, and C_{23} provide additional high-frequency compensation to assure frequency stability.

Transistor Q_3 is the driver for the output stage. This stage is similar to Q_2, except that the emitter is returned to $+15$ volts instead of ground in order to establish the correct operating point for Q_3, Q_4, and Q_5. The output stage of the dc amplifier consists of Q_4 and Q_5, each connected in a common-collector (emitter-follower) arrangement. Transistor Q_4 is a PNP type transistor and Q_5 is an NPN type with similar characteristics. The circuit employs complementary symmetry to provide push-pull operation with single-ended input. A phase inverter is not required to drive a stage of this type. The NPN transistor (Q_5) conducts when the output of Q_3 goes positive and the PNP transistor (Q_4) conducts when the output of Q_3 goes negative.

With no signal, the forward bias across resistor R_9 causes a small current flow from the negative supply through Q_4, I_1, I_2, and Q_5 to the positive supply. Because the transistors are similar, the voltage drop is the same across each, and the circuit is similar to a balanced bridge: there is no current flow through the load. An input to the amplifier causes one of the output transistors to conduct more heavily than the other (unbalancing the bridge) and current flows through the external load on the amplifier. The output voltage appears between the common-emitter point and ground. Incandescent lamps

(I_1 and I_2) are connected in series with each emitter. Since the resistance of these lamps increases with increasing current (higher temperature), the lamps serve to stabilize and protect the output stage by limiting the maximum current flow through each transistor.

The stabilizer amplifier consists of a three-stage amplifier (Q_6, Q_7, and Q_8) and a 60Hz chopper. The stabilizer amplifies the dc and low-frequency components of the input signal and the resulting signal is summed with the ac components at the input of the dc amplifier section. Any dc or low-frequency voltage appearing at the summing junction is modulated by contacts 2 and 3 of the chopper. The resulting 60Hz square wave is applied to the base of Q_6 and is amplified by Q_6, Q_7, and Q_8. The ac signal from the amplifier at the collector of Q_8 is coupled through C_8 to contact 1 to the chopper. Contacts 1 and 2 function as a phase-sensitive demodulator and produce a pulsating dc signal which is applied to a filter (R_{15}, C_2). The filter removes the carrier frequency generated by the chopper action; its output is a smooth dc which is applied to the base of Q_{17}. Since a differential input stage is not used in the dc amplifier, the stabilizer channel does not have a phase reversal.

The amplifier has an output voltage range of ± 10 volts at 20mA load current. The dc amplifier section has a typical low-frequency gain of 3×10^4 and the stabilizer gain is approximately 10^3, giving an overall dc gain of 3×10^7. Noise referred to the input is typically $40\mu V$ peak from dc to 200Hz. The input voltage offset after balancing is typically $\pm 10\mu V$ and the temperature drift coefficient is about $\pm 1\mu V/°C$.

3-14 INTEGRATED CIRCUIT AMPLIFIERS

An *integrated circuit* (IC) is a complete circuit assembly which is fabricated from a basic chip of semiconductor or other material. Several processing techniques are used in the manufacture of IC devices. The most common type is the *monolithic* IC in which all circuit elements, both active and passive, are diffused into a single-crystal block of silicon. The individual elements are then simultaneously interconnected by depositing metallic conduction paths onto the surface of the monolithic block.

A distinct advantage of the IC is that a large number of individual circuits can be processed in one large wafer of silicon. This makes possible large volume production at reduced cost as compared to assembling the same circuit from discrete components. Other inherent advantages of IC devices are small size and weight, good uniformity, and high reliability.

The integrated circuit approach is especially well suited to operational amplifiers. Although amplifiers using discrete components offer better performance in some specialized applications, IC amplifiers are appropriate to a variety of uses including servo and process control, signal conditioning and filtering, and analog computation.

The differential amplifier configuration is the basic circuit employed in IC operational amplifiers. This circuit is highly compatible with monolithic fabrication because of its balanced nature. A close matching of transistor characteristics, especially with respect to temperature changes, is obtained. Gain in a differential amplifier is dependent on resistance ratios (rather than absolute values of resistors) and such ratios are readily controlled in the IC manufacturing process.

IC operational amplifiers differ in one respect from their discrete component counterpart. Because of the difficulty in fabricating large capacitance values in integrated circuits, amplifiers usually omit the compensating networks necessary for frequency stability. To obtain stable closed-loop operation, the user must add external networks.

IC amplifiers generally follow the differential amplifier design described in the previous sections of this chapter. The schematic diagram of a representative IC operational amplifier (type MC-1530) is shown in Figure 3-26. This amplifier has a typical open-loop voltage gain of 5000, output voltage swing of $\pm 5V$ with supply voltages of $\pm 6V$, input and output impedances of 20kΩ and 25 ohms respectively, and common-mode rejection of 75 dB.

The excellent matching of electrical characteristics within IC amplifiers is evidenced by their offset and drift specifications. Typical input offsets of the MC-1530 are 1mV and 0.2μA and the voltage drift with temperature is about 4μV/°C.

The operation of the amplifier in Figure 3-26 may be briefly described as follows. Transistors Q_1 and Q_2 differentially amplify the input signal applied between terminals 1 and 2. Transistor Q_3 serves as a constant-current source to provide high common-mode rejection. The second differential stage (Q_4 and Q_5) is directly coupled to the first stage and provides additional voltage gain. Since this stage will not have an appreciable input common-mode swing, a resistor R_6 is used as a current source. The signal is taken single-ended from the collector of Q_5 and is coupled to the output stage through emitter follower Q_6.

A positive dc voltage is present at the point where the single-ended connection is made. Some level translation is therefore necessary since the dc output voltage should nominally be zero. Transistor Q_7 provides the level shift between Q_6 and the output stage driver Q_8.

The output transistors Q_9 and Q_{10} are connected in a totem-pole circuit so that the load can be driven in both positive and negative directions. Resistor R_{10} provides negative feedback around the output stage to reduce the crossover distortion and lower the output impedance.

The collectors of the first stage are brought to case pins to provide connection points for open-loop frequency compensating networks. Additional compensation may be provided by connecting a small capacitor in parallel with R_9. The values for the compensating networks can be optimized so that

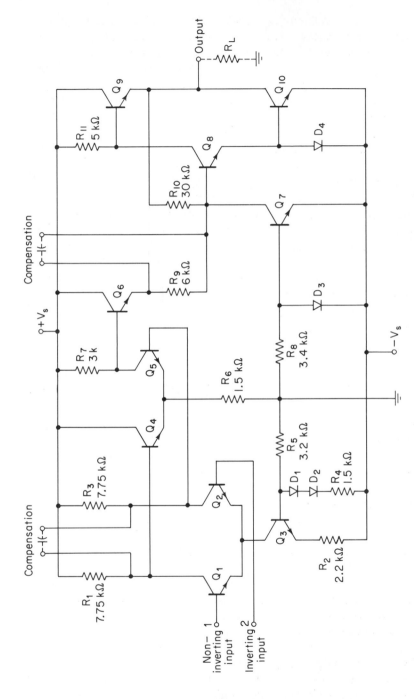

FIGURE 3–26 Model MC-1530 integrated circuit amplifier. (Motorola Semiconductor Products, Inc.)

both overall gain and bandwidth can be maximized for a particular case. IC manufacturers usually provide optimum value curves that are based on various gain-bandwidth characteristics of the amplifier.

3-15 SUMMARY OF OPERATIONAL AMPLIFIER CHARACTERISTICS

We have seen that operational amplifiers are available in various basic designs. Within each category, a wide range of characteristics is possible depending upon circuit complexity and, ultimately, amplifier cost. A choice of amplifier type should be related to the application for which it is intended. Insofar as analog computation is concerned, chopper-stabilized amplifiers are used wherever the best possible results are desired. Smaller, lower-cost computers incorporate differential amplifiers at some reduction in computer performance. In many special-purpose computing applications such as control and instrumentation, IC amplifiers are finding wide acceptance.

The following table summarizes typical characteristics of currently available solid-state amplifiers. This table is intended to only indicate the general range of characteristics; obviously, because of the overlaps, no one type is necessarily unique to a particular application.

TYPICAL CHARACTERISTICS OF OPERATIONAL AMPLIFIERS

Characteristic	Unit	General-purpose differential	FET input	Chopper-stabilized	Integrated circuit
dc voltage gain		10^4–10^5	10^4–10^5	10^6–10^8	10^3–10^5
Unity gain crossover frequency	MHz	0.5–10	1–30	0.2–10	1–10
Input offset voltage	mV	0.3–10	1–10	0.01–0.1	1–10
current	nA	2–200	0.001–0.1	0.01–0.1	100–500
Input drift with temperature voltage	μV/°C	2–20	5–50	0.2–2	2–20
current	nA/°C	0.2–5	0.02–0.1	5×10^{-4}–0.02	0.1–5
Input impedance	megohms	0.1–0.5	10^5–10^6	0.5–1	0.01–0.5
Common-mode rejection	dB	50–100	60–80	single-ended	60–100
Output voltage	± volts	10–100	10–100	10–150	3–12
Output current	mA	1–20	1–20	2–100	1–10

3-16 COMPUTING RESISTORS AND CAPACITORS

So far we have not examined in detail the resistors and capacitors which form the input and feedback elements of an operational amplifier. As we have seen, the accuracy of analog computer results is largely dependent upon the characteristics of these components.

Computing resistors are invariably of either wirewound, deposited carbon, or deposited metal-film construction. Although relatively high in cost, wirewound resistors are the most stable and reliable of the three types. Wirewound resistors are fabricated of special alloy resistance wire noninductively wound on ceramic or plastic rods. Resistance values can be established with a tolerance as close as ±0.01 per cent and a long-time stability of 50 to 500 parts per million* (ppm) at constant temperature. Suitable resistance-wire alloys provide temperature coefficients as low as 20 ppm/°C. When highest precision is desired, the computing resistors may be mounted in an oven whose temperature is maintained constant. Wirewound resistors are generally limited to values less than one megohm and are physically larger than other types.

Deposited film resistors have gained wide acceptance in analog computers because of their low cost. These resistors are made by depositing a thin film of carbon or metallic resistive on an insulating substrate. The desired resistance value is then obtained by cutting a helical groove in the film. Although the tolerances of deposited film resistors are typically one per cent, resistors may be readily matched to within 0.1 per cent for computer applications. Carbon-film resistors have stabilities of about 500 ppm at constant temperature and temperature coefficients of several hundred ppm/°C. Metal-film resistors most nearly approximate the performance of wirewound resistors, having temperature coefficients of 50 ppm/°C.

The feedback capacitors used in integrators must also have precise values and stability. The value of capacitance should generally be as high as possible but, as mentioned previously, physical size, price, and quality must be considered. Precision capacitors are available with capacitance tolerances of ±0.5 per cent. For greater precision, small trimmer capacitors are connected in parallel. The long-term stability of these capacitors is about 0.1 per cent per year.

Various precision capacitors differ primarily in their dielectric material. The accompanying table gives the characteristics of capacitors using three common materials: mylar, polystyrene, and teflon.

---

*This is a common way of specifying variations in the values of precision components such as resistors and capacitors. For example, 100 ppm would indicate a variation of 100 ohms for each one megohm of resistance. In the case of a 100 kilohm resistor, this would be 10 ohms.

TYPICAL CHARACTERISTICS OF COMPUTING CAPACITORS

Dielectric material	Insulation resistance, $M\Omega/\mu F$	Temperature coefficient, ppm/°C	Dielectric absorption, % at 25°C
Mylar	2×10^5 at 25°C		
	10^3 at 100°C	+250	0.1
Polystyrene	10^6 at 25°C		
	10^5 at 100°C	−100	0.01
Teflon	10^6 at 25°C		
	10^5 at 100°C	−250	0.1

Insulation resistance is an important characteristic for relatively long computing times or where it is desired to accurately retain or hold the output voltage of an integrator.

When a capacitor is discharged, it will gradually recover a fraction of its earlier charge. In some cases, the delay may be relatively long and there may be an appreciable residual voltage creating errors in the circuit operation. This effect is known as *dielectric absorption* and, in the table, is expressed as a percentage of the applied voltage measured approximately one second after the capacitor is discharged.

PROBLEMS FOR CHAPTER 3

1. Determine the exact output voltage of the circuit below for $A = -5000$. What percentage error is caused by the finite amplifier gain?

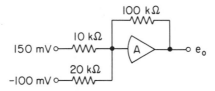

2. An operational amplifier sums five input signals. Each input has a closed-loop gain of 10 associated with it. What amplifier gain is necessary in order that the output error be less than 0.5%?

3. An amplifier has a nominal open-loop gain of −10,000 subject to ±25% variation. What percentage variation in closed-loop gain is possible if the value of β is 0.1?

4. An operational amplifier has the following drift characteristics:

$$\frac{\Delta e_{os}}{\Delta T} = 10\mu V/°C \qquad \frac{\Delta i_{os}}{\Delta T} = 500pA/°C$$

$$\frac{\Delta e_{os}}{\Delta t} = 100\mu V/day \qquad \frac{\Delta i_{os}}{\Delta t} = 1nA/day$$

What maximum input offsets can be expected if the amplifier operates for one day over a temperature range of 0 to 50°C? Assume that the amplifier is initially balanced at 25°C.

5. An amplifier has an input voltage offset of 100μV and offset current of 1nA. What will be the voltage offset at the output of each of the following circuits?

(a)   (b)   (c)

6. An amplifier having a voltage gain of 2000 and an output resistance of 500 ohms is operated with a feedback factor of 0.1. What percentage change in output voltage occurs when a load resistance of 1000 ohms is connected to the amplifier?

7. Plot the open-loop gain in dB versus frequency for an amplifier with dc gain of 10,000, cut-off frequency of 500Hz, and attenuation of -20 dB/decade. What is the unity-gain crossover frequency?

8. If the amplifier of Problem 7 has an attenuation of -30 dB/decade, determine the cut-off frequency if the other characteristics are unchanged.

9. What is the closed-loop cutoff frequency if the amplifier of Problem 7 is operated with a 10kΩ input and feedback resistor? What is the exact closed-loop gain at a signal frequency of 100kHz?

10. The amplifier of Problem 7 is used as an integrator with $R = 100$kΩ and $C = 10\mu$F. Sketch the loop gain as a function of frequency. [*Hint:* Take $\beta = R/(R - jX_c)$.]

11. In the circuit below, determine the value of R_1 so that $I_c = 2$mA in each transistor. Assume $\beta = 50$ and $V_{BE} = 0.5$V for both transistors.

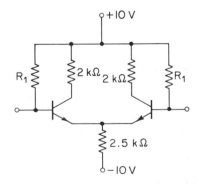

12. It is desired that the 2.5kΩ emitter resistor in Problem 11 be replaced with a constant-current source. Design a suitable circuit for this purpose.

13. Considering one transistor returned to ground through R_s, show that the input resistance of the differential amplifier in Fig. 3-10 is approximately $R_s + 2\beta R_E$. (Note that the second transistor appears as a common-base stage in the emitter circuit of the first.)

14. A differential amplifier has non-equal gains A_1 and A_2 from its two inputs. For $A_1 \cong A_2$, show that the common-mode rejection can be expressed as $A_1/(A_1 - A_2)$.

15. If the dc portion of a stabilized amplifier has a gain of 20,000 and the associated stabilizer amplifier has a gain of 500, what is the total gain of the amplifier expressed in dB?

16. The dc amplifier in Problem 15 has an input offset of 1mV and the stabilizer chopper has an offset of 5μV. What offset appears at the output of the amplifier when $\beta = 0.1$?

17. A non-inverting amplifier having high input impedance is obtained by operating a differential amplifier in the following circuit. If the amplifier gain A is very high, show that

$$\frac{e_o}{e_1} = \frac{R_1 + R_2}{R_1}$$

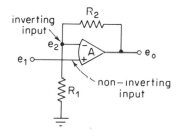

In Chapter 2 we considered the mathematical operations associated with linear equations and linear computing circuits for performing these operations. By combining various of these linear circuits, we may simulate a system that can be represented by a linear differential equation or by a system (or set) of linear differential equations.

Although linear methods of analysis are applied to a large number and variety of problems, in reality we rarely, if ever, encounter a truly linear system. Almost without exception non-linear effects are present which will require the multiplication of variables or the generation of non-linear mathematical functions. Equations which describe a non-linear system always contain terms higher than first degree and are known as *non-linear equations*.

Non-linear equations of a differential nature are extremely difficult to solve by exact analytic means and their treatment is generally beyond the capability of other than skilled mathematicians. Consequently, one common approach in the solution of non-linear problems is simply to approximate the behavior by linear equations. In cases where the non-linear effects are of secondary importance, they can be entirely ignored with little consequence. In other situations non-linearities may be studied in the vicinity of an operating point and the non-linear behavior approximated by linear equations. This tech-

4

COMPUTING SERVO- MECHANISMS

nique is known as *linearization* of the equations. It is recognized of course that the true response will not be exactly that which is predicted. However, the difference should be small if the excursions of the variables around the operating point are small.

To illustrate the linearization process, consider the algebraic equation $y = ax^2$ where x and y are variables and a is a constant. We may approximate this non-linear equation in the vicinity of an operating point x_o, y_o by the equation

$$y_o + \Delta y = a(x_o + \Delta x)^2 = a(x_o^2 + 2x_o\Delta x + \Delta x^2) \qquad (4\text{-}1)$$

where Δx and Δy are excursions of the variables x and y around the operating point. Since $y_o = ax_o^2$ is a constant and Δx^2 will be very small when Δx is small, we may write a linear equation

$$\Delta y \cong 2ax_o\Delta x \qquad (4\text{-}2)$$

The quantity $2ax_o$ is a constant which multiplies the variable Δx to give an approximate expression for the variable Δy.

Linear differential equations can be solved using exactly specified mathematical procedures. However, for large problems these procedures can become arduous and time-consuming. Consequently, we find an analog computer to be a convenient means for studying linear systems. On the other hand, there is no general analytic method for treating all non-linearities. However, analog computer methods for solving non-linear equations are essentially the same as for linear equations. The main difference is the use of non-linear computing devices in addition to linear elements. By means of these auxiliary devices, non-linear characteristics can be introduced directly into the simulation and we can solve problems which would be extremely difficult or even impossible to handle using analytic means.

The non-linear operation most frequently found in the mathematical description of a physical system is the multiplication of variable quantities. If the behavior of such a system is to be investigated using a computer, it becomes necessary to multiply together two or more voltages representing the factors in a product. A variety of multiplying devices and circuits have been developed for analog use. Essentially such equipment operates on variable input voltages such as e_1 and e_2 to produce an output Ke_1e_2 where K is a proportionality constant.

There exist a variety of problems in which we use non-linear mathematical functions such as trigonometric, exponential, and logarithmic functions. In certain other cases we require some function of a variable which is not known as a mathematical expression but is rather based on experimental data. Consequently, a second general category of non-linear equipment is used to generate non-linear functions of an arbitrary nature.

The two main types of non-linear analog equipment are electromechanical and electronic devices. A servomechanism used as either a multiplier or function generator is the most common electromechanical device. Although servomechanisms are simple, accurate, and low in cost, they have a limited frequency response because of their mechanical nature. On the other hand, electronic multipliers and function generators exhibit high accuracy, wide frequency response, and high reliability.

In this chapter, we shall examine the design and application of servomultipliers, servo function-generators, and servo resolvers. The electronic counterparts for performing these operations will be described in the next chapter.

4-2 SERVOMECHANISMS

An early and still widely used method of multiplying variables and generating non-linear functions in analog computers is by a *servomechanism* or *servo*, as it is commonly known. Before considering the various computing applications of a servomechanism, it is desirable that we have some understanding of its basic principles.

Let us begin by examining the concept of closed-loop control. In a closed-loop control system, a sensing device measures the system output and provides a feedback signal. This is compared with the input command to the system, and a difference or error signal is generated which then drives the output to the desired value. Although we may not be conscious of it, man himself functions as a closed-loop system. For example, consider our actions in driving an automobile down a road. The eye senses the position of the car with respect to a desired course. The mind then directs the hands to position the wheel to reduce the error between the actual and desired positions. In addition to responding to immediate errors, we also observe the road some distance ahead so that corrections are anticipated before they are actually needed.

A servomechanism is a closed-loop control device whose basic function is to control in accordance with an input signal a load that is coupled to its output. The load must quickly and precisely respond to any change in the input command. Thus, we may think of a servomechanism as a following device, and it is from this that the name is derived from the words "servant" (or slave) and "mechanism."

The functional arrangement of a servomechanism is shown in the block diagram of Fig. 4-1. The servo input is a *command* or *reference* signal which defines the desired output and is generally in the form of a shaft position or electrical signal. The output is the condition of the load being controlled by the servomechanism. The sensing device measures the output and provides

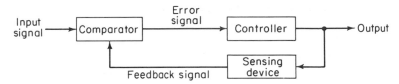

FIGURE 4–1   Functional block diagram of a servomechanism.

a feedback signal which may be either a shaft position or an electrical signal.
The comparator compares the input and feedback and generates an error
signal proportional to the difference between the two. The controller com-
prises the necessary electrical and mechanical means for controlling the output. This is generally an amplifier which amplifies the error signal, and a
motor which supplies the power to vary the load.

Since we are concerned with the use of servomechanisms in electronic
analog computers, we shall consider only electromechanical types. Although
servomechanisms using hydraulic or pneumatic components are also common, they are not appropriate to use in electronic computers. There are
two basic forms of electromechanical servomechanisms used with dc and
low-frequency ac signals. One type, the *dc servomechanism*, operates entirely
with dc voltages. The other uses an ac carrier of higher frequency (commonly 60Hz or 400Hz) which is modulated by the signal frequencies. This
type is known as an *ac servomechanism*.

A dc servomechanism is shown schematically in Fig. 4-2. It consists of
a resistor summing network, a dc amplifier, and a dc motor which is coupled
through a gear train to a potentiometer. The position of the potentiometer
shaft represents the servo output and the wiper voltage provides a measure
of the position. The input e_i is a dc voltage applied to the input resistor R_i.
A dc generator is also shown; its function will be discussed later.

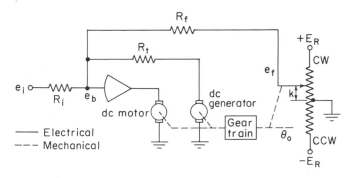

FIGURE 4–2   Schematic diagram of a dc servomechanism.

The servo amplifier is similar to an operational amplifier except that its power output is capable of driving the servo motor. This typically requires from 10 to 20 watts.

The dc motor is generally of the permanent magnet type and has a power rating of the order of 1/100 horsepower. The maximum speed is usually 5,000–10,000 rpm and the armature voltage is typically from 10–20 volts when a transistor servo amplifier is used.

The potentiometer is especially designed for servo use and is characterized by low torque and inertia, as well as long useful life. The resistance element may be either a wirewound or film type. The potentiometer may be a single-turn unit having continuous rotation or a multi-turn unit (generally 3 or 10 rotations) with end stops. A center tap is usually provided to precisely establish the zero-output point. In applying servo potentiometers, it is recommended that the tap and slider connections be fused to prevent burnouts due to faulty connections.

High-performance computer servomechanisms usually have gear trains between the motor and potentiometer shafts. The gear train provides increased torque at the output shaft and, at the same time, reduces the output speed. The gear train ratio is generally selected to obtain optimum static and dynamic performance from the servo. Accurate servo operation requires precision gears with low friction and backlash.

In the circuit shown in Fig. 4-2, the amplifier input voltage e_b is amplified and applied to the motor armature to cause rotation, the direction of which depends upon the polarity of e_b. For correct operation, the potentiometer wiper will rotate in a direction such that e_b is driven toward zero. When e_b becomes zero, the motor then stops. If $R_i = R_f$, the wiper position for $e_b = 0$ is such that $e_f = -e_i$. The rotation of the shaft from the center tap may be expressed by a voltage attenuation ratio

$$k = \frac{e_f}{E_R} = \frac{e_i}{E_R} \tag{4-3}$$

where E_R is a reference voltage applied to the potentiometer.

For illustration, consider that reference voltages of ± 10 volts are applied to the ends of the potentiometer and a positive value of e_b causes counter-clockwise rotation of the wiper. If the wiper is assumed to be initially at the center-tap ($e_f = 0$) and $+5$ volts is applied to the servo input, then e_b is positive. The wiper will rotate counter-clockwise until $e_f = -5$ volts. Since e_b is now zero, the output will come to rest at this point. Since the amplifier input behaves in the same manner as the summing point of an operational amplifier, additional inputs could be provided in which case e_f would be the negative sum of the input voltages weighted according to the values of their respective resistors.

The above discussion ignores a difficulty that is inherent in closed-loop systems. This is the tendency of the system to oscillate about its normal resting point. In the case of the servomechanism, the motor is driving the potentiometer at a rapid rate toward the null position. When zero error is reached and the driving force is removed, the inertia of the rotating elements will cause the system to overshoot the stopping point. The error signal suddenly reverses polarity causing the motor to run in the opposite direction. Again the output may go beyond the null position, causing the process to repeat. The result is an instability in the form of a back-and-forth hunting of the output around the desired position.

Servo design methods and the problem of instability are treated extensively in the literature. Although the subject is beyond the scope of this text, we will briefly examine one common method of achieving stability. This involves the use of a dc generator (tachometer) which is coupled to the motor shaft, as shown in Fig. 4-2. The output voltage of a tachometer is proportional to shaft rotational speed or, expressed in other words, to the rate of change of the output position. This voltage is connected to the amplifier summing point so that it opposes the polarity of the servo input signal. Hence, in addition to the position feedback from the potentiometer, a *rate feedback* is obtained from the generator. Note that the rate signal will not affect the at-rest position of the output since the generator voltage is zero at that time. However, as the servo approaches the null point, the rate feedback causes the motor to slow down and thus overcomes the tendency to overshoot the stopping point. For this reason the rate feedback is frequently referred to as *damping* in the system. By adjusting the amount of damping or rate feedback, the response of a servomechanism can be optimized for the particular components being used.

Figure 4-3 shows the typical response of a servomechanism to a position command. When an input voltage is applied, the response is not instantaneous but will lag slightly since time is required to accelerate the moving parts. The damping is generally adjusted to allow a slight overshoot in the output since this minimizes the time for reaching the final position. As shown in Fig. 4-3, a small error will exist in the at-rest output for the follow-

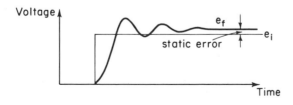

FIGURE 4-3   Servomechanism response.

ing reason. As the output shaft approaches the desired position, the error signal becomes smaller and smaller. When the motor torque drops below the friction level of the moving parts, the shaft stops even though it has not quite reached the desired output. The result is a small static or dc error in the system.

Although simple in concept and implementation, dc servomechanisms have several disadvantages. The amplifier is direct-coupled and must be carefully designed to ensure that no significant drift will appear in its output. The dc motor incorporates a commutator and brushes which increase the friction and require periodic maintenance.

To overcome these drawbacks, an ac servomechanism of the type shown in Fig. 4-4 is frequently used. If we compare this circuit with the dc servo shown in Fig. 4-3, we note that both contain summing resistors, a servo amplifier and motor, and a feedback potentiometer coupled to the motor shaft through a gear train. The principle of operation of the ac servo is the same as that previously described for the dc circuit: the output shaft will assume a position in response to a dc input voltage. The essential difference is that this servomechanism operates with an ac error signal and therefore contains a modulator, ac amplifier, and ac motor. Because of this feature, an ac servomechanism is sometimes referred to as a *modulated-carrier servomechanism*.

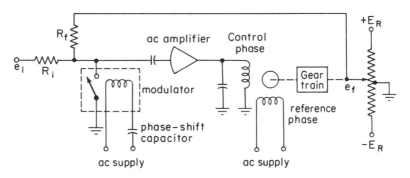

FIGURE 4-4   Schematic diagram of ac servomechanism.

The ac servomotor is a two-phase, induction type, low-inertia motor and requires no electric connections such as brushes or slip-rings between its stator and rotor. Since friction is reduced to a minimum, very smooth operation is possible. The two-phase induction motor contains two windings (or phases) which are spaced 90 electrical degrees apart. These are known as the *reference* and *control* phases respectively. A 60Hz motor is commonly used since the power line provides a convenient ac supply. However 400Hz motors are frequently used since improved dynamic performance of the servo is possible at a higher carrier frequency.

When used in a servomechanism, the reference phase of the motor is connected to a fixed supply voltage. The control winding is energized from the servo amplifier by a variable voltage which is 90° out of phase with the fixed voltage. When the control voltage leads the reference voltage by 90°, motor rotation is in one direction; when it lags the fixed voltage by 90°, the direction of rotation is reversed. The motor speed and torque are approximately proportional to the magnitude of the control voltage.

Since the servo must respond to dc input signals, means must be provided to obtain an ac control voltage for the motor. This is accomplished by modulating the error signal at the summing point, as shown in Fig. 4-4. The resulting high-frequency ac signal is then amplified and applied to the motor winding. The ac servo amplifier has the advantages of being drift free and generally more simple than its dc counterpart. A *resonating capacitor* is usually connected in parallel with the highly inductive motor winding to improve the load power factor.

Modulation may be accomplished quite simply and effectively with an electromechanical chopper of the type described in the preceding chapter. The metal reed vibrating at the carrier frequency acts as a switch contact and grounds the summing point during alternate half-cycles of the excitation. The dc error voltage is converted to an ac signal, as shown by the waveforms in Fig. 4-5. Note that the ac error signal changes phase by 180° as the dc voltage goes from positive to negative. By placing an appropriate capacitor in series with the coil of the chopper, the excitation may be shifted 90° with respect to the supply voltage. As a consequence, the ac control voltage will either lead or lag the reference voltage by 90°, depending on the polarity of the dc error voltage.

Electronic switching circuits are well-suited to modulating a low-level error voltage. Those discussed in the chapter on operational amplifier

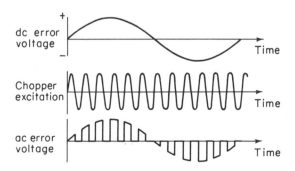

FIGURE 4–5   Modulation waveforms.

design may also be applied as choppers in a modulated-carrier servomechanism.

Although not shown in Fig. 4-4, a tachometer generator may be used as described before to provide damping and prevent hunting of the servo output.

4-3 SERVOMULTIPLIERS

A *servomultiplier* is an electromechanical servo which provides products of analog variables. It basically consists of an amplifier, a motor, and a potentiometer connected as described in the previous section. The essential difference is that a number of linear potentiometers are coupled to the output shaft, rather than only a single potentiometer for shaft-position feedback. These potentiometers are almost always an integral or ganged assembly having a common shaft. The individual wipers are aligned mechanically but are not connected electrically. Since each wiper rotates inside a cylindrical resistance element, the individual potentiometers are frequently referred to as cups. The potentiometer used for feedback is the "follow-up" cup while the remaining sections are multiplying cups. The potentiometers used in servomultipliers are high-precision units having linearities on the order of 0.01 to 0.1 per cent. The potentiometers may be either single turn or multi-turn and generally have a tap at the physical center of the resistance element.

Figure 4-6 shows the functional arrangement of a servomultiplier having two multiplying cups. For simplicity, the servo amplifier and motor are shown in the diagram as a single block. The center taps of all cups are connected to ground so that the zero output point is precisely established.

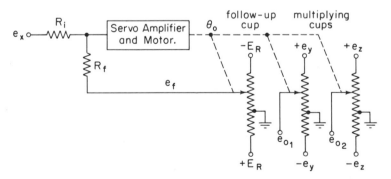

Figure 4–6 Functional diagram of a servomultiplier.

As previously described, the follow-up cup has the computer reference voltages applied to its ends and its wiper voltage is fed back to the amplifier input. With a voltage e_x applied to the servo input, the wiper of the follow-up cup positions itself according to Eq. (4-3). Since the wipers of all cups are at the same mechanical position, the ratios of the voltages applied to the multiplying cups and the voltages at the respective wiper arms are also equal to k.* Thus

$$k = \frac{e_x}{E_R} = \frac{e_{o_1}}{e_y} = \frac{e_{o_2}}{e_z} \tag{4-4}$$

Solving for the outputs of the multiplying cups gives

$$e_{o_1} = \frac{e_x e_y}{E_R} \quad \text{and} \quad e_{o_2} = \frac{e_x e_z}{E_R} \tag{4-5}$$

Equation (4-5) states that the voltage at the wiper arm of the first multiplying cup is equal to the product of the voltages representing variables x and y divided by the reference voltage E_R.

Additional products involving x and other variables are readily obtained by adding more multiplying cups to the servo output shaft. For cup n, the output voltage is given by

$$e_{o_n} = \frac{e_x e_n}{E_R} \tag{4-6}$$

where e_n is the voltage applied to the cup.

The multiplier shown in Fig. 4-6 is capable of four-quadrant multiplication; in other words the inputs x and y may be either positive or negative and the product will have the proper sign. This represents the normal operating mode of the multiplier but does require that the variables connected to the multiplying cups be available as both positive and negative voltages.

In some situations, the variable connected to the servo input may be either always positive or always negative. In this case the accuracy of the multiplier may be improved by grounding one end of the cups rather than the center-tap. The multiplication now obtained is two quadrant, since the voltages applied to the multiplying cups may still be of either polarity.

The output of a multiplying cup is generally connected to an operational amplifier input. This causes a loading of the potentiometer which must be considered in determining multiplier accuracy. Fortunately, a simple method allows us to correct for loading errors. As we have seen in the case of an attenuating potentiometer, loading error may be eliminated by setting the loaded potentiometer to the desired voltage ratio. If the cups of a servomultiplier have the same resistance and are loaded identically, the voltage ratio

---

*This assumes equal loading on the potentiometers as discussed later.

will be the same at all wipers. As the wiper of the follow-up cup positions itself to a slightly higher point to compensate for loading, the multiplying cups will undergo the same compensation and the correct value of k is obtained at all outputs. Because of the loading effect, multiplying-cup wipers should be connected only to fixed resistors, and the cups should always be driven from very low impedance sources such as operational amplifier outputs.

In applying a servomultiplier, consideration should be given to the rate of change of the variables. Because the frequency response of a servomechanism is limited to 10Hz or less, only slowly varying quantities should be used to drive the servo. There is no frequency limitation on the voltages applied to the potentiometers; they can change quite rapidly without an error being introduced.

The programming symbol for a servomultiplier is shown in Fig. 4-7. The information inside the box includes an identifying number for the multiplier, the polarity of the reference voltage applied to the follow-up cup (N indicates the normal mode with $\pm$ voltages) and the value of the load resistor being used. The symbols for the individual multiplying cups need not be adjacent on a programming diagram but may be located where convenient.

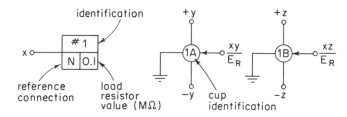

FIGURE 4-7   Programming symbol for servomultiplier.

A servomultiplier may be used for *squaring* a variable. If the same voltage is applied to both the servo input and a multiplying cup, the output of the cup is e_x^2/E_R. Higher integer powers of a variable may be obtained by using additional multiplying cups. If the output of the squaring cup drives a second multiplying cup, then e_x^3/E_R^2 is obtained from that cup. To avoid potentiometer loading, two operational amplifiers must be used to excite the resistance element of the second cup from the wiper of the first cup.

EXAMPLE 4-1

Determine the outputs of the servomultiplier shown in Fig. 4-8. Assume that the reference voltage applied to the feedback potentiometer is ± 10-volts.

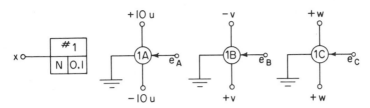

FIGURE 4–8   Servomultiplier for Example 4-1.

SOLUTION:

The output voltages are calculated using Eq. (4-6). For cup A,

$$e_A = \frac{10\,ux}{10} = ux$$

For cup B,

$$e_B = \frac{-vx}{10}$$

For cup C, we note that the output voltage will exhibit the polarity of w for x positive or negative. Hence,

$$e_C = \frac{|x|\,w}{10}$$

4-4   DIVISION

In analog simulation, a need frequently exists to divide one variable by another. A divider unit as such is not necessary since we can accomplish division by employing a multiplier in an inverse relationship. Figure 4-9(a) shows a division circuit in which a multiplier is connected as the feedback element in an operational amplifier circuit. Although any type of multiplier can be used in this circuit, we will consider the use of a servo multiplier as shown in Fig. 4-9(b).

We may analyze the circuit of Fig. 4-9(a) by summing the currents at the amplifier input. If the amplifier input current is assumed to be zero, we have

$$\frac{e_x}{R_1} + \frac{e_o e_y}{E_R R_2} = 0 \tag{4-7}$$

If $R_1 = R_2$, Eq. (4-7) may be solved for e_o giving

$$e_o = -\frac{e_x E_R}{e_y} \tag{4-8}$$

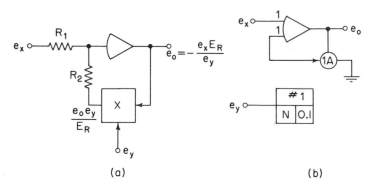

(a)   (b)

FIGURE 4–9   Division circuit.

Several limitations are inherent in the division circuit shown in Fig. 4-9.

1. The divisor (in this case e_y) must not be zero. If e_y were zero, there would be no output from the multiplier and the amplifier would lose its feedback. The amplifier output would now be meaningless—which, of course, is consistent with the fact that division by zero yields an infinite quotient. In actual use, as the divisor nears zero, the circuit becomes too inaccurate to be of practical value.

2. The divisor must always be greater in amplitude than the dividend. If e_x were greater than e_y, the output would exceed E_R. This is not possible since E_R is the maximum value of the computer variable.

3. The divisor must not change sign. Should e_y become negative, the multiplier output will be opposite in sign to the amplifier output. The feedback is then changed from negative to positive causing the circuit to become unstable.

The same technique used in the division circuit can be used to generate the square root of a variable. In the square-root circuit shown in Fig. 4-10, the output of the operational amplifier is connected to both inputs of the multiplier. The nulling equation at the amplifier input is

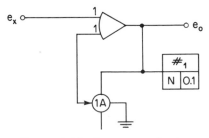

FIGURE 4–10   Square-root circuit.

$$e_x - \frac{e_o^2}{E_R} = 0 \tag{4-9}$$

or

$$e_o = -\sqrt{E_R e_x} \tag{4-10}$$

As with the division circuit, the square-root circuit becomes highly inaccurate for small values of the input voltage. Although negative values of e_x cause this circuit to become unstable, they may be handled by reversing the connections at the ends of the multiplying cup.

4-5 FUNCTION GENERATORS

In some computer problems it is necessary to provide a non-linear function of a particular variable. Certain non-linear functions such as trigonometric and logarithmic functions are well known. In some cases, however, a function is based on experimental data and there may be no simple mathematical expression relating the variables. For example, in studying the behavior of an aircraft we may consider non-linear relationships such as those shown in Fig. 4-11. Most non-linear functions are extremely difficult, if not impossible, to generate in an analog computer which uses linear computing elements. Some simple functions such as the square and square root of a variable may be obtained using the circuits just described. In general, the approach to providing non-linear functions is to use an item of equipment known as a *function generator*.

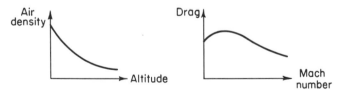

FIGURE 4-11   Examples of non-linear relationships in aircraft simulation.

The non-linear functions which are frequently encountered in simulation are often obtained from fixed function generators. The sine and cosine functions are perhaps the most common of these. Their generation is discussed in detail in the next section.

To generate functions which are peculiar to a given problem and may be largely derived from experimental data, variable function generators are used. These function generators may be quickly and simply changed from one function to another and, since the function is set at the discretion of the user, they are frequently referred to as *arbitrary function generators*. Arbitrary function generators have been devised using various electronic and electro-mechanical principles. In this section we will consider an electromechanical type which is a form of a computing servomechanism.

A common approach to generating a non-linear function of a variable is to approximate the function by a series of straight-line segments. This is illustrated in Fig. 4-12, in which a function of the variable x is approximated by ten segments. Obviously, the more segments used, the more exact will be

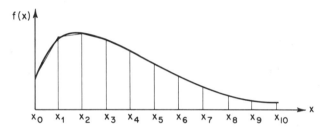

FIGURE 4–12   Straight-line approximation of non-linear function.

the representation of the function. Experience has shown that from ten to twenty segments provide a straight-line approximation sufficiently accurate for most experimental data, provided the functional changes are not too rapid.

Tapped potentiometers provide a convenient means of generating linear segments. In normal use, a multiplying cup is a linear device (if we neglect loading), and its output is proportional to the position of the wiper with respect to the ground terminal. Assume, however, that we provide a number of equally spaced connections, or taps, along the linear potentiometer and apply known voltages to these points. The voltage at the wiper will no longer be proportional only to its position: it will also be dependent on the voltages applied to the taps. This is illustrated in Fig. 4-13, which shows a potentiometer with five taps (four segments). Between taps the output voltage will change linearly from the value at one tap to that at the next (linear inter-polation). As the wiper moves from one end of the pot to the other, its voltage changes along a sequence of straight lines as shown in the figure. If the tapped cup is coupled to the servo output shaft, then its voltage output is a straight-line approximation of a non-linear function of the variable applied to the servo input. The programming symbol for a servo function generator is shown in Fig. 4-14.

To supply the appropriate voltages to the potentiometer taps, a padding unit such as shown in Fig. 4-15 is used. In this circuit a padding potentiom-eter is connected to each tap. A selector switch connects the other end of the padding potentiometer to either the positive or negative reference voltage, to ground, or it may be left open.

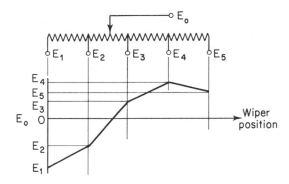

FIGURE 4–13   Function generation with tapped potentiometer.

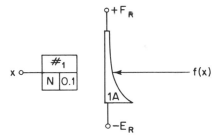

FIGURE 4 14   Programming symbol for servo function generator.

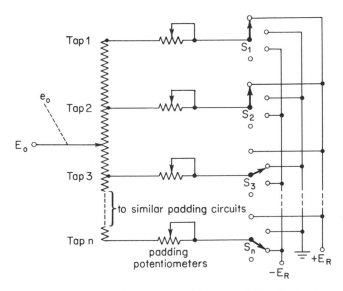

FIGURE 4–15   Tapped-potentiometer padding circuit.

Should we attempt to set the tap voltages sequentially to desired values, we would be severely handicapped by the interaction between voltages applied to the taps. As the voltage on a given tap is adjusted, it will affect the value at every other tap and repeated adjustments would be necessary before an acceptable representation of the function is obtained.

A means of eliminating this interaction and reducing set-up time to a matter of minutes is given in the circuit shown in Fig. 4-16. The tap voltages are again adjusted in sequence starting with the first tap. The difference, however, is in the fact that the next tap in the sequence is maintained at its proper voltage during the adjustment of the preceding tap. For example, in setting Tap 1 in Fig. 4-16, the voltage of Tap 2 is held at its proper value by the inverter amplifier driven by a coefficient potentiometer set to the voltage of Tap 2. Since the output resistance of the amplifier is essentially zero, the

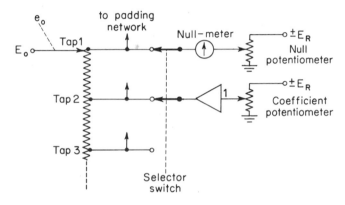

FIGURE 4–16   Circuit for setting tapped potentiometer.

voltage of Tap 2 is maintained regardless of a change in the Tap 1 voltage. The selector switch is then advanced so that Tap 2 may be adjusted while the amplifier holds the proper voltage on Tap 3. Thus, each tap is adjusted with its two adjacent taps at their correct voltages. By positioning the pot wiper to the tap being adjusted, loading effects may be largely eliminated.

One caution must be observed in selecting voltages for the taps. The current-carrying capacity of the resistance element imposes a limitation on the voltage between adjacent taps. Thus, the tapped potentiometer is not well suited to functions having regions of extremely steep slopes.

4-6 RESOLVERS

In the solution of problems that involve angular motions, we invariably make use of trigonometric functions. This is especially true in navigation computers, flight simulators, and trajectory problems. The importance of trigonometric functions has led to the development of computing devices, both servo and electronic, known as *resolvers*. Resolvers are specifically designed to accomplish certain coordinate transformations, usually the transformation of polar to rectangular coordinates or the transformation of rectangular to polar coordinates. The first of these transformations, which is the more easily implemented, is illustrated by the geometry of Fig. 4-17.

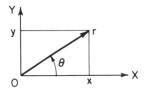

FIGURE 4–17   Geometry of rectangular transformation.

In polar coordinates, a vector is defined by a magnitude r and an angle θ measured with respect to a reference axis. If the polar coordinates are known, we may resolve the vector into rectangular coordinates x and y along the X and Y axes respectively. The rectangular coordinates are expressed as

$$y = r \sin \theta \quad \text{and} \quad x = r \cos \theta \tag{4-11}$$

One application of this transformation is in radar operation, where the slant range and elevation angle of a target (polar coordinates) are converted into altitude and ground distance (rectangular coordinates).

A special potentiometer, known as a sine-cosine potentiometer, is used to accomplish this transformation. This potentiometer, shown schematically by Fig. 4-18, consists of four resistance segments connected together at tap points. As indicated in the diagram, these taps are located at 90° intervals. The taps at 0° and 180° are connected to ground (zero volts) and the 90° and 270° taps are connected to voltages proportional to $+r$ and $-r$ respectively. The voltages at these four points conform to the values of the sine function at the corresponding angles. Between the taps, the resistance element is tapered or shaped so that the wiper voltage varies sinusoidally as shown in the output waveforms of Fig. 4-18.

Two wipers are commonly provided in the potentiometer. The output of one wiper equals $r \sin \theta$. The second wiper is placed on the same shaft, but displaced 90° from the first wiper. This provides an output of $r \sin (\theta + 90)$ which, of course, equals $r \cos \theta$.

Figure 4-19 shows the schematic diagram of a servo resolver connected in the rectangular mode of operation. The linear followup cup provides a

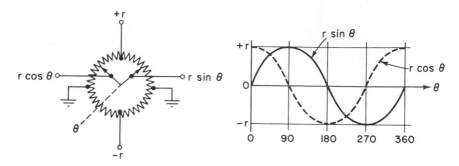

FIGURE 4–18   Sine-cosine potentiometer and output wave-forms.

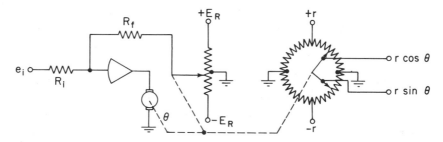

FIGURE 4–19   Servo resolver in rectangular mode.

feedback voltage to null the servo at a shaft angle θ proportional to the input voltage e_i.

The error due to potentiometer loading cannot be compensated by using equal load resistors on the sine-cosine and follow-up potentiometers, since their characteristics are dissimilar. Instead, the sine potentiometer winding is tapered to provide the correct output with a specified load resistance connected between the wiper and ground. For accurate operation, this resistor value must be used and the load on the follow-up cup must be so small as to be negligible. The precision of a sine-cosine potentiometer is commonly stated in terms of conformity to the ideal sine function. This is typically between 0.1 and 0.5 per cent of the peak-to-peak excursion of the function.

The input scale factor of the resolver is established by the number of turns and the applied voltages of the followup cup. For example, if $E_R = \pm 90$ volts and a single-turn potentiometer is used, the scale factor is 0.5 volt per degree and the angle θ may vary between $\pm 180°$. When a ten-turn followup cup is used, the single-turn sine potentiometer can make 10 revolutions or $\pm 1800°$ of travel. The input scale factor is then 50 millivolts per degree.

The second variety of coordinate transformation is required when the rectangular coordinates of a vector are known and we wish to determine its

magnitude and phase angle. If x and y are the rectangular coordinate variables, we may obtain the corresponding polar coordinates by applying the
basic equations

$$\theta = \tan^{-1}(y/x) \qquad r = \sqrt{x^2 + y^2} \qquad (4\text{-}12)$$

To cause a servo resolver to perform the polar transformation, it is
necessary to position the sine-cosine potentiometer shaft at the angle θ.
Since this angle is one of the quantities to be determined, it is not directly
available as an input, as in the case of the previous transformation. However,
let us reexamine the geometry of the problem with the aid of Fig. 4-20.
We see that two additional equations can be developed as follows:

$$x \cos \theta + y \sin \theta = r \qquad (4\text{-}13)$$

and

$$y \cos \theta - x \sin \theta = 0 \qquad (4\text{-}14)$$

Rearranging Eq. (4-14), we obtain

$$y \cos \theta = x \sin \theta$$

$$y/x = \sin \theta/\cos \theta = \tan \theta$$

Thus, we see that equation (4-14) will be valid when $\theta = \tan^{-1}(y/x)$.
This equation suggests a means of nulling the servo since the two terms sum

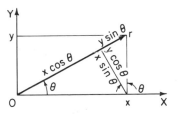

FIGURE 4–20   Geometry of polar
transformation.

to zero only at the desired angle. Figure 4-21 shows the resolver configuration
for performing the polar transformation using these equations. Two sine-
cosine potentiometers are excited by voltages proportional to the rectangular
coordinates, $\pm x$ and $\pm y$. The wiper voltages are $x \sin \theta'$, $x \cos \theta'$, $y \sin \theta'$,
and $y \cos \theta'$, where θ' is any arbitrary angle assumed by the shaft. Summing
voltages $y \cos \theta'$ and $-x \sin \theta'$, we have

$$y \cos \theta' - x \sin \theta' = \epsilon \qquad (4\text{-}15)$$

where ϵ is the error voltage applied to the servo amplifier. Substituting for
x and y in Eq. (4-15) and using the trigonometric identity for the sine of the

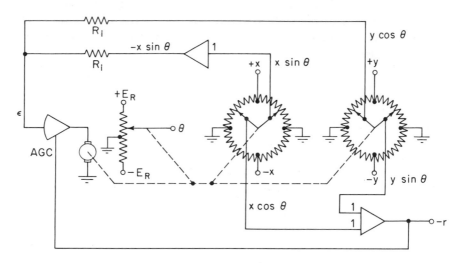

FIGURE 4–21   Servo resolver in polar mode.

difference of two angles, we obtain

$$\epsilon = r \sin \theta \cos \theta' - r \cos \theta \sin \theta'$$

$$\epsilon = r \sin (\theta - \theta') \tag{4-16}$$

If $(\theta - \theta')$ is very small (as will be the case near null), then

$$\epsilon \cong r (\theta - \theta') \tag{4-17}$$

The error voltage ϵ is proportional to the difference between θ' and θ and drives the servo output shaft so that θ' approaches θ. When θ' equals the desired angle θ, $\epsilon = 0$ and the servo is nulled. A voltage proportional to θ may be obtained from the linear followup cup, since it is not used for feedback in this mode. The voltages from the other sine-cosine wipers are summed according to Eq. (4-13) to provide a voltage proportional to r.

An additional factor complicates the operation of a resolver in the polar mode. Referring to Eq. (4-17), we note that the error voltage is proportional to both the angular difference and the magnitude of r. Since the latter may vary over a wide range of values, the gain through the servo loop also varies proportionally. Varying loop gain can result in poor servo operation. For small values of r, the response will be sluggish and inaccurate. Large values of r may cause servo instability. To overcome this undesirable effect, the gain of the servo amplifier may be made to vary approximately as $1/r$ so that the loop gain remains nearly constant. This is accomplished by providing an automatic gain control (AGC) circuit whose function is similar to the automatic volume control circuits in radio receivers. As the voltage representing r increases, the amplifier gain is decreased, and vice versa.

The programming symbols for servo resolvers in the rectangular and polar modes are shown in Fig. 4-22.

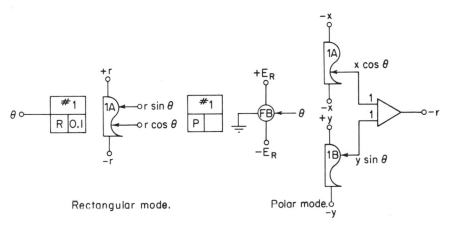

Rectangular mode.   Polar mode.

FIGURE 4–22   Programming symbols for servo resolver.

EXAMPLE 4-2

Develop circuits for generating the following functions:

(a) $\sin^2 \theta$ (b) $\theta \sin \theta$

SOLUTION:

These functions may be obtained using a servo resolver connected as shown in Fig. 4-23 (a) and (b).

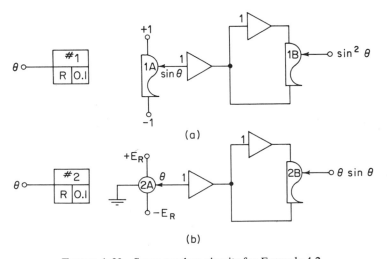

(a)

(b)

FIGURE 4–23   Servo resolver circuits for Example 4-2.

PROBLEMS FOR CHAPTER 4

1. What is the principle of closed-loop control?
2. What is the purpose of a tachometer in a servomechanism?
3. What would be the effect on the response of the servomechanism in Fig. 4-2 if the value of the tachometer feedback resistor R_t was reduced significantly?
4. In the servomechanism in Fig. 4-2, what would be the effect of reversing the voltages applied to the feedback potentiometer?
5. How is potentiometer loading error corrected in a servomultiplier?
6. Write an equation for each output of the servomultipliers shown below.

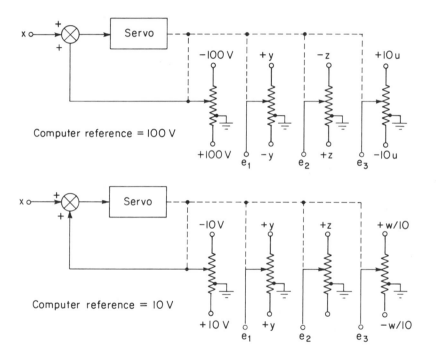

7. Draw a schematic diagram of a servomultiplier circuit for obtaining the product xyz where x, y, and z are variables.
8. Draw a schematic diagram of a servomultiplier circuit which can provide the cube of a variable.
9. What limitations exist in using a servomechanism to perform division?
10. A servo function generator is to provide the function

$$f(x) = x^2 - 10x - 5$$

for $0 \leq x \leq 10$ volts. The function potentiometer has 9 equally spaced taps between its end taps. The computer reference is ± 10 volts.

(a) Plot the function over the specified range of x.

(b) Select a scale factor for $f(x)$. [_____ volts $= 1$ unit $f(x)$].

(c) Prepare a table showing voltages to be applied to taps and ends of potentiometer. (How many straight-line segments are available?)

11. The variables ϕ and x are available at the outputs of operational amplifiers.
Draw a schematic diagram of a circuit to provide $x \sin \phi$. Repeat using programming symbols.

12. Occasionally the need arises to rotate rectangular coordinate axes through
some angle as shown in the figure below. The equations for accomplishing this
coordinate transformation are

$$x_2 = \quad x_1 \cos \theta + y_1 \sin \theta$$

$$y_2 = -x_1 \sin \theta + y_1 \cos \theta$$

where x_1 and y_1 are the coordinates in the original system and x_2 and y_2 are
the coordinates after rotation through the angle θ. Prepare a circuit diagram
for performing this transformation.

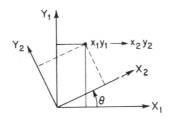

5

ELECTRONIC FUNCTION GENERATORS AND MULTIPLIERS

5-1 INTRODUCTION

We have already examined the need for non-linear operations in analog computation. Methods of implementing various non-linear operations using servomechanisms were described in Chapter 4. In this chapter we shall consider electronic methods of representing non-linear phenomena; in general these methods offer significantly higher frequency response compared to their electromechanical counterparts.

Although circuits employing non-linear resistors, semiconductors, or vacuum tubes can produce continuous non-linear relations, their characteristics are not easily reproduced with precision. Consequently most non-linear circuits involve a simple non-linear component, the diode, in such a way that changes in diode characteristics have only a relatively small effect on the circuit output.

Many physical systems exhibit discontinuous non-linear behavior in which the output changes suddenly at a certain point. Saturation, dead band, and hysteresis are examples of non-linearities of this type. Many of these effects may be simulated in a fairly simple manner by incorporating diodes in operational amplifier circuits.

Continuous non-linear functions are electronically generated by approximating the function in discrete straight-line segments. Diode circuits are then used to generate the various segments.

A number of electronic circuits

have been devised to multiply voltages representing problem variables. The multiplication scheme which has found widest use is based on a diode function generator and is known as the quarter-square multiplier. Two other multiplication circuits which have also proved popular are the time-division multiplier and the Hall effect multiplier.

Before proceeding with descriptions of non-linear circuits based on diode operation, we might examine the characteristics of diodes as they relate to analog computer use. A diode may be regarded as a two-terminal device which acts as a voltage-sensitive on–off switch. With voltage applied such that one terminal (anode) is more positive than the other (cathode), the ideal diode conducts with zero forward resistance as shown in Fig. 5-1. With the reverse polarity of applied voltage, the diode behaves as an open circuit (zero current).

Practical diodes depart from the ideal as shown by the dotted characteristic in Fig. 5-1. They have a finite, low forward resistance and a finite, high back resistance. In addition, the characteristics are not completely linear, especially near the transition or "break" point, which is not as sharply defined as in the ideal case.

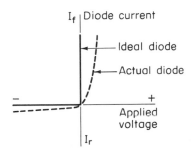

FIGURE 5–1   Diode characteristic.

Various types of diodes, including vacuum tubes and germanium and silicon semiconductor diodes, have been used in analog computer circuits. In evaluating diodes for computer use, the magnitudes of the operating voltages and currents should be considered. The maximum reverse voltage depends upon the computer reference voltage and is generally either 20 or 200 volts. Forward currents of the order of 0.1 to 1.0mA are typical.

The characteristics of silicon junction diodes are well suited to these operating ranges and these diodes are used almost exclusively. The characteristics of a typical silicon diode are shown in Fig. 5-2. In the reverse direction the leakage current is essentially independent of voltage so that the diode acts as a current source. This reverse current, of the order of 10

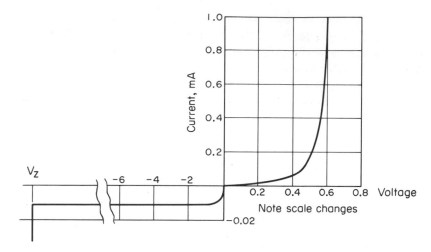

FIGURE 5–2   Characteristic of silicon junction diode.

nanoamperes at 25°C, can be considered negligible for most computer applications.

In the forward direction, the diode makes a fairly sharp transition between non-conduction and conduction at a forward bias of about 0.5 volt. For forward currents above 0.1mA, the dynamic resistance is reasonably small. For analog applications, it is convenient to approximate the diode characteristic by two linear segments as shown in Fig. 5-3(a). The

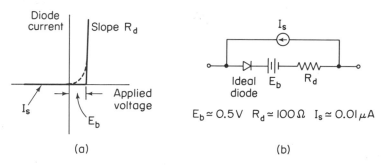

FIGURE 5–3   Linear approximation of diode characteristic (a), and (b) equivalent circuit.

break voltage or breakpoint E_b identifies a bias which must be overcome before the diode forward resistance R_d reduces to a value of the order of several hundred ohms.

A diode equivalent circuit based upon this linear approximation is shown in Fig. 5-3(b) together with typical parameter values at 25°C.

A silicon diode exhibits another characteristic occasionally used in analog applications and shown in Fig. 5-2. If the reverse bias is increased, a potential is reached at which breakdown of the junction occurs. Beyond this so-called *Zener voltage* (V_z), the reverse current increases rapidly with relatively little increase in voltage. The value of V_z can be controlled during manufacture and diodes are available which have Zener voltages in a region between several volts to several hundred volts with tolerances on the order of several per cent if required.

One limitation in the use of silicon diodes is their temperature sensitivity. The forward voltage drop will decrease by approximately 2 to 3 mV per degree centigrade of ambient-temperature increase while the leakage current will double for each 7 to 10 degree rise in temperature. Over the range of temperatures normally found in laboratory and industrial environments, the changes in diode characteristics are small enough to be ignored in most cases. If severe temperature excursions are encountered (as in some military equipment), the changes may be significant and must then be taken into consideration.

5-2 DIODE CIRCUITS

A number of electrical, mechanical, and magnetic devices exhibit a *saturating* or *limiting* effect in their output. Up to a certain input magnitude, the output is more or less proportional to the input. Beyond this, for greater inputs, the output ceases to increase and remains essentially constant. In some devices the transition from linear operation to saturation may be quite abrupt and a "hard limit," as shown in Fig. 5-4(a), is reached. In other cases, as shown in Fig. 5-4(b), the transition is more gradual and is described as a "soft limit."

A number of computer circuits have been devised for simulating saturation. A circuit widely used because of its simplicity and versatility is shown

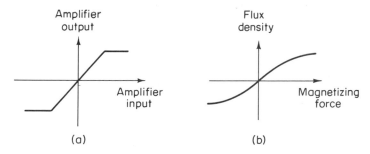

FIGURE 5–4 Examples of saturation in physical devices: (a) hard limit, (b) soft limit.

in Fig. 5-5. This circuit uses an operational amplifier with the usual feedback resistor. However, biased diodes are employed as additional feedback elements.

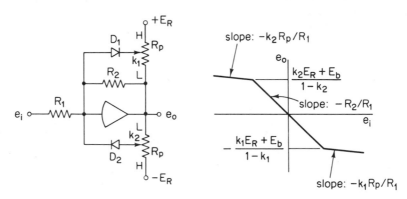

FIGURE 5–5 Diode feedback limiter circuit and input-output characteristic.

For the linear condition when neither diode is conducting, the circuit behaves as an operational amplifier with gain $-R_2/R_1$. As e_i is made increasingly positive, the voltage at the cathode of D_1 (which is a function of the output voltage e_o and the potentiometer setting k_1) will become negative. Diode D_1 then conducts, and a low-impedance feedback path is established. The amplifier gain is significantly reduced so that the output remains essentially constant at a desired limit. As e_i becomes increasingly negative, the anode of D_2 becomes positive and the output limits at a positive level in a manner similar to the negative limit.

The operation of the circuit for a positive limit may be analyzed with the equivalent circuit shown in Fig. 5-6. The cathode of D_2 is connected to

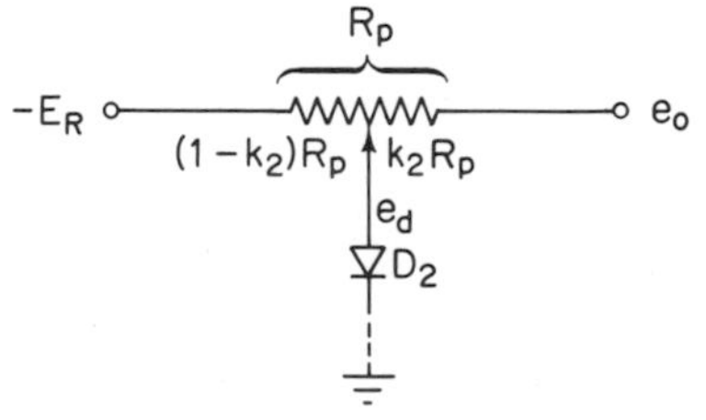

FIGURE 5–6 Equivalent circuit of diode limiter.

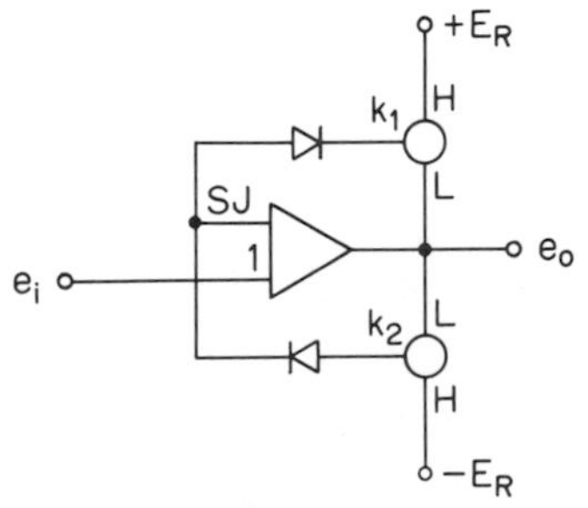

FIGURE 5–7 Programming diagram for diode limiter.

the summing junction and is assumed at ground potential. For D_2 non-conducting, the diode voltage is

$$e_d = e_o - \left(\frac{E_R + e_o}{R_p}\right)k_2 R_p$$

$$= e_o(1 - k_2) - k_2 E_R \qquad (5\text{-}1)$$

When e_d equals the diode offset voltage E_b, D_2 becomes conducting. The value of e_o at which limiting occurs is

$$e_o = \frac{k_2 E_R + E_b}{1 - k_2} \qquad (5\text{-}2)$$

Solving Eq. (5-2) for the potentiometer setting corresponding to a desired limit gives

$$k_2 = \frac{e_o - E_b}{e_o + E_R} \qquad (5\text{-}3)$$

Since the potentiometer introduces some resistance in the diode branch, the output is not constant at the limit. For the usual case where $R_d \ll R_p \ll R_2$, the slope of the output during limiting is

$$e_o/e_i \simeq \frac{-k_2 R_p}{R_1} \qquad (5\text{-}4)$$

Equations (5-2) and (5-3) may also be applied to the negative limit by changing the signs of e_o, E_R, and E_b. In practice, the final settings of the potentiometers are generally made on a trial and error basis so that exact compensation may be made for the diode offset voltage. Note that the potentiometers used in Fig. 5-6 must have both ends available for external connection; therefore ungrounded potentiometers must be used.

When a soft limit is desired, the circuit of Fig. 5-5 may be slightly modified for this purpose. The slope of the characteristic beyond the limit point may be increased by adding an appropriate resistance in series with each diode. To compute e_o/e_i beyond the limit, the value of the series resistance is added to the numerator of Eq. (5-4).

A programming diagram for the diode limiter is shown in Fig. 5-7.

EXAMPLE 5-1

Plot a graph of the output characteristic of the limiter circuit shown in Fig. 5-8(a). Use an input voltage range of ± 10 volts and assume $E_b = 0.5$ volt.

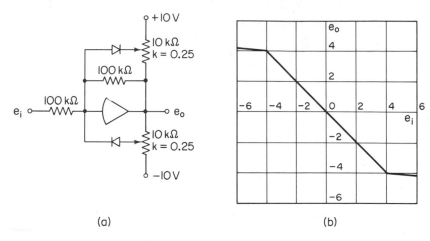

(a)   (b)

FIGURE 5–8   Circuit diagram and output characteristic for Example 5-1.

SOLUTION:

Taking the ratio $-R_f/R_i$, the gain of the amplifier over its linear range is -1. Using Eq. (5-2), the output will limit at

$$e_o = \frac{0.25(10) + 0.5}{0.75} = 4 \text{ volts in positive direction}$$

$$e_o = \frac{0.25(-10) - 0.5}{0.75} = -4 \text{ volts in negative direction}$$

The gain after limiting is

$$e_o/e_i = \frac{-0.25(10\text{k}\Omega)}{100\text{k}\Omega} = -0.025 \text{ in both directions.}$$

The output characteristic is drawn in Fig. 5-8(b).

A diode limiter circuit which makes use of Zener breakdown is shown in Fig. 5-9. Two Zener diodes D_1 and D_2 are connected back to back in parallel with the usual feedback resistor. For outputs less than the Zener voltage, the gain is simply $-R_2/R_1$. When the amplifier output reaches the Zener voltage, breakdown occurs and a low resistance feedback path is established. The output is now clamped at $\pm V_z$.

Leakage current through the diodes can introduce an error in the output. To overcome this limitation, resistor R_3 and diodes D_3 and D_4 are added to the circuit. During normal amplifier operation, R_3 (which is of the order of 1–10kΩ) absorbs the diode leakage current. The small voltage drop across

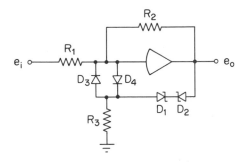

FIGURE 5-9   Zener diode limiter circuit.

R_3 causes only a minute coupling of leakage current into the summing junction.

The circuit of Fig. 5-9 is not as versatile as the biased diode circuit since the limits are not adjustable. The diodes must be replaced if a change in limits is desired.

The Zener diode circuit is sometimes used to prevent an operational amplifier from becoming overloaded by an excessive input voltage. With some types of amplifiers, recovery from an overload may take several seconds after removal of the offending signal. By using a feedback limiter with limits set slightly beyond the rated output voltage of the amplifier, amplifier overload is prevented and recovery time is reduced to milliseconds.

A non-linearity which exists in all physical systems is *Coulomb* (or *dry*) *friction* caused by sliding motion. As shown in Fig. 5-10, the friction force is of constant magnitude and is always in a direction to resist the relative motion. When reversal of motion takes place, a discontinuity occurs.

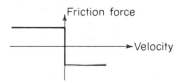

FIGURE 5-10   Coulomb   friction characteristic.

Coulomb friction may be simulated by removing the feedback resistor from the limiter circuit of Fig. 5-5. The limits are set to correspond to the friction force. If the input voltage representing velocity becomes just slightly positive or negative, the output goes to the corresponding limit. The slope between the positive and negative values of e_o is very high since the amplifier is essentially operating open-loop between the limits. The amplifier thus

appears to have two stable conditions: either the positive or negative saturation voltage. Because of this characteristic, the circuit is also known either
as a bistable amplifier or (its more picturesque name) as a "bang-bang"
circuit.

In analog computation, the requirement occasionally exists to compare
the magnitudes of two quantities and develop a signal indicative of the
larger quantity. A circuit which performs this function is known as a *comparator*. The output of a comparator generally drives either a relay or an
electronic switch, making it possible to change a computing circuit as a
function of signal levels. Although relay comparators are well suited to
switching low-level voltages and currents, their dynamic response is limited,
because relays require a number of milliseconds to operate, and because
they suffer from contact bounce. However, in many applications this
imposes no limitation when the switching times are insignificant compared
to computing times in seconds. On the other hand, electronic switches are
extremely fast and provide switching times on the order of microseconds.

A comparator may be formed using a bistable amplifier having two
inputs as shown in Fig. 5-11.

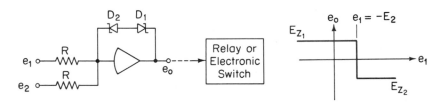

FIGURE 5-11   Electronic comparator and characteristic.

This circuit compares the magnitudes of the input voltages e_1 and e_2
and changes state for some predetermined relationship between these inputs.
The most common relationship between the two voltages being compared
is that the change in state occurs when one voltage goes from less than
to greater than the negative of the other voltage. Thus, for $e_1 + e_2 < 0$,
the output voltage e_o will be positive of magnitude determined by the breakdown voltage E_{Z_1} of the Zener diode D_1. For $e_1 + e_2 > 0$, the output voltage
will be negative as determined by D_2. If one input is a fixed voltage ($e_2 = E_2$
for example), the input-output characteristic of the circuit will be that shown
in Fig. 5-11. In this case, switching will occur as e_1 becomes just greater than
or less than the magnitude of $-E_2$.

Control systems frequently exhibit a non-linearity known as *dead zone*
or *threshold*. A dead zone is that input range for which there is no output.
As an example, a motor displays a dead band when its armature does not
rotate (despite input voltage) until the developed torque exceeds the static
friction of the output shaft.

A dead zone may be simulated by using biased diodes in the input circuit of an operational amplifier, as shown in Fig. 5-12.

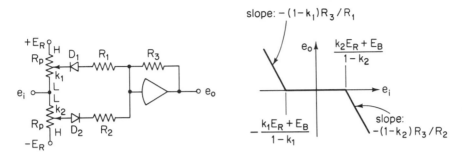

FIGURE 5-12   Dead zone circuit and input-output characteristic.

Note that the diode arrangement in the dead zone circuit is similar to that of the limiter circuit of Fig. 5-5 except that the diodes are associated with the input rather than with the feedback. For small values of e_i, the reverse bias applied to the diodes prevents the signal being applied to the amplifier, and e_o remains zero. As e_i is made increasingly negative, a point is reached at which diode D_1 becomes forward biased. Assuming that R_1 is much larger than both the diode forward resistance and the potentiometer resistance, the amplifier output is now $-[(1 - k_1)R_3/R_1]e_i$. With increasingly positive inputs, the signal is applied through D_2 in a similar manner.

The threshold voltage may be determined using Eq. (5-2). Thus, at the limits of the dead zone,

$$e_i = \frac{kE_R + E_B}{1 - k} \qquad (5\text{-}5)$$

Since the two potentiometers are adjusted independently, the dead zone need not be symmetrical about zero input.

On occasion it is necessary to obtain the *absolute value* of a quantity. To provide an absolute value, a computing circuit must have a positive output voltage for both positive and negative inputs. A precision absolute-value circuit and its output characteristic are shown in Fig. 5-13.

The operation of the circuit is straightforward. When the input e_i is negative, diode D_2 is reverse biased and voltage e_1 is zero. Since only the input $-e_i$ is applied to amplifier 2, the output e_o is positive and equals e_i. For e_i positive, diode D_2 conducts and voltage e_1 is equal to $-e_i$. Both e_i and e_1 are summed in amplifier 2 and the output e_o is now equal to $-[2(-e_i) + e_i] = e_i$. Thus the circuit functions such that $e_o = |e_i|$.

The circuits which have been described in this section illustrate the manner in which common non-linearities are simulated. A complete tabula-

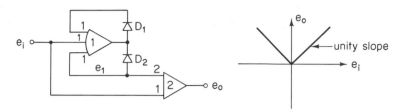

FIGURE 5–13   Absolute value circuit and output characteristic.

tion of the non-linearities occurring in nature would be extensive. In some cases two or more non-linearities may be present, such as when combined static and coulomb friction or hysteresis occur with a dead zone. Fortunately most non-linear functions may be adequately represented on the analog computer by using various diode circuits singly or in combination.

5-3   VARIABLE FUNCTION GENERATORS

Section 4-5 pointed out that a need frequently exists in analog computation to provide a non-linear function of a variable. Since the number of possible non-linear functions is almost without limit, function generators of a variable nature are widely used. The most common approach to generating non-linear functions involves approximating the function by a consecutive series of straight-line segments. This approach was illustrated in Fig. 4-12, and a device using a tapped servo potentiometer was described. In this section, we shall consider purely electronic methods for generating non-linear functions.

When the non-linear function may be approximated by straight lines, biased diodes are almost invariably used to generate the linear segments. A device of this type is generally known as a *variable-diode function generator* (VDFG). Variable diode function generators are popular for a number of reasons. These include the ease and speed with which a specific function may be set up, good frequency response, relatively low cost, and applicability to almost all functions. A number of VDFG circuits have been devised, generally differing in detail rather than in principle. Two of the more common circuits will be described in this section. The first uses diodes in a series-limiter arrangement while the second is a shunt-limiter type of circuit.

The manner by which a single straight-line segment is generated by a biased diode is shown in Fig. 5-14. The input diode D_1 is biased by a series emf E_1. If we assume an ideal diode, then, for e_i less than E_1, no input current will flow and the output of the operational amplifier is zero. When e_i becomes greater than E_1, the diode conducts, and the output is given by

$$e_o = -(e_i - E_1)\frac{R_f}{R_1} \qquad (5\text{-}6)$$

The output characteristic of the circuit is shown in Fig. 5-14. The point of intersection of the two straight-line segments is referred to as the *breakpoint*. The location of the breakpoint is determined by the magnitude of E_1, and the slope of the segment beyond the breakpoint is determined by the ratio of the feedback and input resistors.

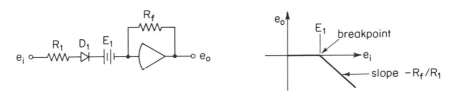

FIGURE 5–14 Biased diode circuit and characteristic.

The single segment may be extended to the generation of a non-linear function by providing additional diode input circuits as shown in Fig. 5-15. This circuit may be analyzed by separately considering each input circuit. When e_i exceeds E_1, diode D_1 conducts and segment 1 of the characteristic is generated at the amplifier output. When e_i exceeds E_2, diode D_2 conducts and a second segment is generated. Since the two input resistors are now effectively in parallel, the actual output voltage is the sum of the two segments, as shown by the composite curve of Fig. 5-15. As other diode circuits are added, additional straight-line segments are generated which extend the function beyond the two segments shown in the figure. The breakpoint of each added segment is set by the corresponding diode bias voltage and the slope is determined by the parallel combination of the resistors in the conducting input circuits.

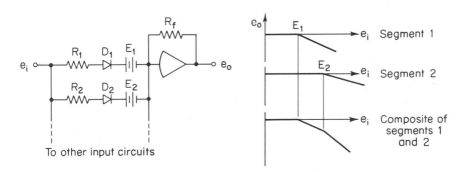

FIGURE 5–15 Simplified diode function generator circuit and characteristic.

It should be apparent that the use of a number of series emf's for diode biasing is impractical. Consequently, a biasing circuit such as shown in Fig. 5-16 is generally used. The voltage divider composed of R_1 and R_2 provides a negative bias to the anode of D_1. As the anode becomes positive with increasing input voltage, conduction occurs and an output voltage is generated. The breakpoint occurs when

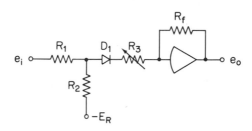

FIGURE 5–16   Practical biasing circuit.

$$\frac{(e_i + E_R)R_2}{R_1 + R_2} - E_R = 0$$

or, in terms of the input voltage,

$$e_i = \frac{R_1}{R_2} E_R \tag{5-7}$$

In order that the slope of a straight-line segment will conform to the function, an adjustable resistor R_3 is included in the input circuit. As the value of R_3 is made less, the slope is increased.

The segments that are generated by the circuit in Fig. 5-16 can only represent a function whose slope is continually increasing in one direction. Such a function is known as a *monotonic* function. A *non-monotonic* function may be generated by providing a means whereby the slope of a given segment may be either positive or negative in direction as desired. One such circuit is shown in Fig. 5-17. Two operational amplifiers are used with the biased diode networks. When e_i exceeds the breakpoint voltage, the diode conducts and the input signal is applied to the wiper of a potentiometer identified as the SLOPE control. This potentiometer determines the magnitude and direction of the slope of the corresponding segment. Its setting controls the ratio of two signal levels, one of which is applied directly to the output amplifier (2) and the second applied through an inverter amplifier (1). If the wiper is in the upper half of the resistance element, the (directly) applied signal is larger than the inverted signal and the output is a negative-going segment. If the wiper is in the lower portion, the condition is reversed and a positive

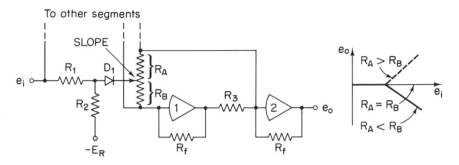

FIGURE 5–17   Circuit for generating non-monotonic functions.

slope results. When the wiper is at its midpoint, signals of equal magnitude are applied and the net output is zero.

In the circuit shown in Fig. 5-17, the breakpoints are determined by the values of R_1 and R_2 in each input circuit. In this case the breakpoints are distributed at fixed increments of the input variable. However, a better approximation of a function is generally possible if the location of the points is based on the rate of change of slope of the curve. If the slope changes rapidly, the points should be located fairly close together. For gradually changing slopes, fewer intermediate points are needed. Variable spacing of the breakpoints can be provided by adding a BREAKPOINT potentiometer to each input circuit, as shown in Fig. 5-18. This potentiometer

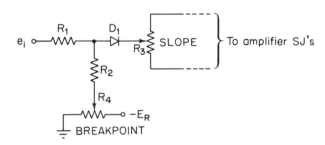

FIGURE 5–18   Variable breakpoint circuit.

allows the diode bias voltage to be adjusted to provide a breakpoint at an optimum location for the function being generated.

A second form of VDFG employs diodes as shunt elements, as shown in Fig. 5-19. In this circuit, the diode D_1 is back biased according to the condition

$$V_1 > \frac{R_2}{R_1 + R_2} e_i \qquad (5\text{-}8)$$

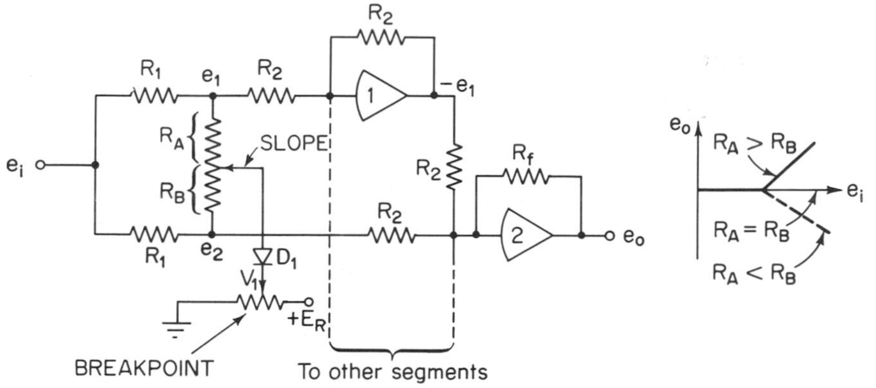

FIGURE 5–19   Alternate form of diode function generator.

For D_1 nonconducting, the voltages e_1 and e_2 are equal and the output voltage is zero. When e_i becomes sufficiently large, D_1 will conduct. If the wiper of the SLOPE potentiometer is not centered, the voltages e_1 and e_2 are unequal and the output will increase linearly with e_i. The slope and polarity of the output will depend on the wiper position, as indicated in Fig. 5-19. Additional input circuits connected to the amplifiers generate a series of segments which approximate the desired function.

The procedure for setting diode function generators is relatively simple. Although commercially available generators differ somewhat in their detailed set-up procedure, the same basic approach is generally followed.

The usual practice is to first draw the graph of the function to be generated. A series of straight-line segments which approximate the function are then superimposed on the graph and labelled. For a generator with *fixed* breakpoints, the segments must conform to equal increments of the input variable. A table may be prepared showing the desired output at each breakpoint. All segments of the function generator are initially set to zero. The input voltage is then set at the first breakpoint and the slope potentiometer of segment 1 is adjusted for the desired output. This procedure is sequentially repeated at the remaining breakpoints until the complete function is approximated and set up. Some smoothing or rounding of the function occurs at the breakpoints due to the diode characteristics. This effect generally improves the representation of the function, although trimming of the adjustments may be required to obtain optimum conformity.

The procedure for setting a *variable* breakpoint generator is somewhat more involved since both slope and breakpoint potentiometers must be adjusted. The function is now approximated by straight-line segments whose breakpoints provide a best fit. To minimize interaction during setting, the adjacent breakpoints should be at least several tenths of a volt apart.

In adjusting the potentiometers at a particular breakpoint, the slope of the preceding segment is set first. The breakpoint of the next segment is then adjusted until the slope value previously set is offset by approximately 0.1 volt.

In addition to the BREAKPOINT and SLOPE adjustments, a PARALLAX potentiometer is also provided. This allows a constant voltage to be applied to the amplifier as a bias, which shifts or offsets the whole function along the output axis. Thus, an initial value of e_o corresponding to $e_i = 0$ can be set.

Commercially available function generators generally provide between 10 and 20 straight-line segments. The maximum slope of a given segment is from one to ten volts per volt, depending upon the manufacturer. For steeper changes of slope at any point, two or more networks of a variable break-point generator can be operated in parallel by shifting to the same breakpoint. As has been pointed out, the frequency response of diode function generators is quite good. Typically, only several degrees of phase shift occur at frequencies to 1 kHz and the amplitude errors over this range are negligible.

EXAMPLE 5-2

It is desired to generate the function $y = \cos x$ for $0° \leq x \leq 90°$ using a VDFG having 6 segments with variable breakpoints. Prepare a table of values for the function assuming the range of computer voltages is ± 10 volts.

SOLUTION:

As a first step, we must relate the variables x and y to the computer voltages. For maximum accuracy, the input and output voltage ranges should be as large as possible; hence, we will choose an x scale factor of 1 volt $= 10°$ and a y scale factor of 10 volts $= 1.00$ (cosine of zero degrees). Figure 5-20 then shows the graphed function together with the straight-line approximations which we shall use.

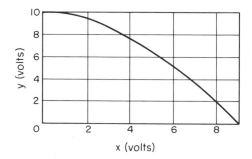

FIGURE 5-20   Function $y = \cos x$ for Example 5-2.

The following table provides data for setting the function $y = \cos x$.

| x | | y | | Adjustments | |
Degrees	Volts	Cosine	Volts	Breakpoint	Slope
0	0.0	1.000	10.00	Parallax	
10	1.0	0.985	9.85	2	1
20	2.0	0.940	9.40	3	2
30	3.0	0.866	8.66	4	3
45	4.5	0.707	7.07	5	4
60	6.0	0.500	5.00	6	5
90	9.0	0.000	0.00		6

The arrows in the right-hand column of the table indicate the sequence of adjustments. At $x = 0$, the parallax is set for $y = 10$ volts. At $x = 1$ volt, the slope of segment 1 is set for $y = 9.85$ volts and the breakpoint of segment 2 is adjusted. The remaining slope and breakpoint potentiometers are set alternately as shown.

Various other forms of electronic function generators have been devised and used in analog computation. One type, which has some advantages, is the *photoelectric-mask function generator*, or *photoformer* as it is usually called. This device permits the direct generation of a function to an accuracy of about one per cent without a straight-line approximation.

The principle of the photoformer is shown in the block diagram of Fig. 5-21. The device consists of: an ordinary cathode-ray tube, the face of

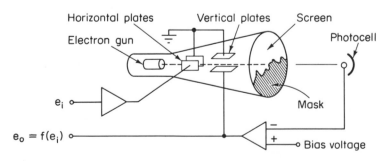

FIGURE 5–21   Block diagram of photoformer.

which is partially covered by an opaque mask whose shape conforms to the desired function; a photocell; and deflection amplifiers for the horizontal and vertical plates.

The input voltage e_i is applied to the horizontal plates and moves the electron beam horizontally across the screen. A feedback loop consisting of the photocell and vertical-deflection amplifier forces the beam to follow the upper edge of the mask in the following manner. A bias voltage applied to the vertical amplifier causes upward deflection of the beam (away from the mask). However, as the spot emerges from behind the mask, light strikes the photocell and an error signal is generated which forces the beam downward. As a result, the feedback loop tends to keep the spot positioned at the edge of the mask. As the spot is moved horizontally by the input voltage, it follows the edge of the mask and the vertical deflection voltage e_o then represents the desired function.

Useful frequency response up to 100kHz is possible with photoformers. Generally speaking, diode function generators are easier and less expensive to construct than generators using cathode-ray tubes. However, the latter permit convenient and rapid function changes if a number of stored function masks are available.

5-4 QUARTER-SQUARE MULTIPLIER

Although the multiplication of variable quantities is an elementary mathematical operation, it is one of the more difficult to implement by electronic circuitry. Paradoxically, an operational amplifier circuit to perform the more sophisticated operation of integration is quite simple in comparison to multiplying circuits.

A number of analog multiplication schemes have been devised and applied to some degree. One device, the servomultiplier, was described in Section 4-3. Of the various electronic approaches to multiplication, the one which has found widest acceptance is the *quarter-square multiplier*. This approach combines adequate accuracy with extremely good bandwidth and does not require overly complex or extensive circuitry.

Electronic quarter-square multipliers derive their name from the equation that is mechanized in performing the multiplication. The algebraic relation that is implemented is

$$\tfrac{1}{4}[(x + y)^2 - (x - y)^2] \tag{5-9}$$

in which x and y are the variables whose product xy is desired. That this is the case is seen by expanding Eq. (5-9) giving

$$\tfrac{1}{4}[(x^2 + 2xy + y^2) - (x^2 - 2xy + y^2)] = xy \tag{5-10}$$

Figure 5-22 shows a block diagram representation of the quarter-square multiplier. Input voltages proportional to x and y are applied to amplifiers 1 and 2, which form the quantities $(x + y)$ and $(x - y)$, respectively. These voltages are then squared in squaring circuits and the difference in the squared values is obtained at the output of amplifier 4. This output voltage is proportional to the product xy.

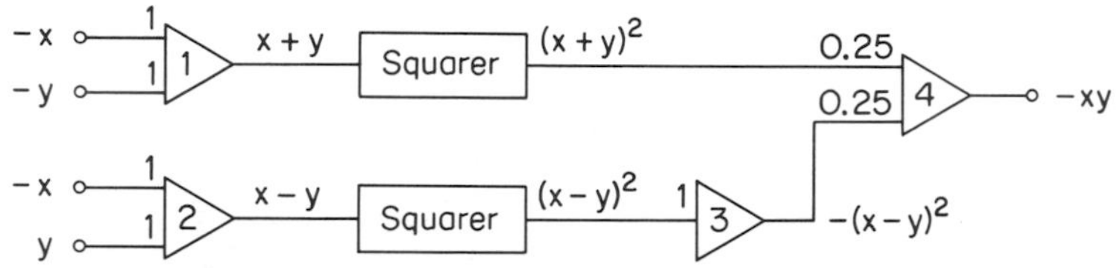

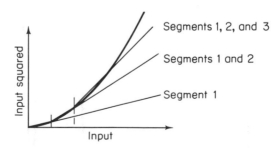

FIGURE 5-22   Block diagram of quarter-square multiplier.

Electronic squaring circuits based on the transfer characteristics of vacuum diodes and triodes, special vacuum tubes, and semiconductor diodes have been used in multipliers. These multipliers yield static accuracies within about two per cent of full-scale output and are useful at frequencies up to approximately 100kHz. However, circuits of this type may require frequent readjustments to maintain their calibration.

Substantially better performance has been obtained from squaring circuits based on special diode function generators; most of the practical quarter-square multipliers use this method. These circuits approximate the desired squaring characteristic by straight-line segments, as shown in Fig. 5-23. The accuracy of the squaring depends upon the number of segments used to approximate the function. Seven to ten segments are generally found to be adequate in quarter-square multipliers.

The diode circuits are similar to those described in the preceding section; however, since they generate only a single fixed monotonic function, the circuits generally require fewer components.

FIGURE 5-23   Straight-line approximation of squaring characteristic.

It is possible to perform both the summing and squaring operations in the diode function circuit, and thus to eliminate summing amplifiers 1 and 2 of Fig. 5-22. This is illustrated in Fig. 5-24(a), which shows a diode network with two inputs. The summing property of this circuit becomes evident if we replace the two input voltages and resistors with a Thévenin equivalent circuit as shown in Fig. 5-24(b).

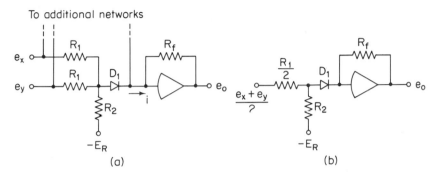

FIGURE 5–24   (a) Diode network and (b) equivalent circuit for quarter-square multiplier.

The diode network will generate a straight-line segment whose break-point and slope are determined by the relative values of resistors R_1, R_2, and R_f. By adding other networks in parallel with the one shown, a series of segments may be generated. A function generator is thus formed that accepts input voltages e_x and e_y and provides a current i to the amplifier summing junction proportional to $[(x + y)/2]^2$.

For proper operation of the circuit shown in Fig. 5-24, $(e_x + e_y)$ must be a positive voltage. By reversing the diode direction and bias voltage polarity, an input current in the opposite direction is obtained if $(e_x + e_y)$ is a negative voltage. We shall refer to the first connection as a "plus" squaring circuit and to the second as a "minus" squaring circuit.

Since either x or y or both may change sign during computation, it is necessary to provide a multiplier function in all four quadrants (for any combination of input polarities). This is accomplished by combining two plus and two minus squaring circuits as shown in Fig. 5-25. In this circuit there will always be an output from one of the plus circuits and from one of the minus circuits. (Recall that if x is negative, then $-x$ is a positive quantity.)

The multiplier output voltage cannot exceed the computer reference. Hence, to accommodate maximum values of the input voltages, the choice of resistor values in the circuit provides a scaling such that the output is given by

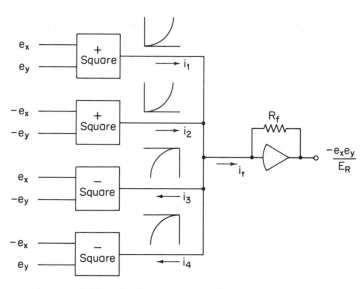

FIGURE 5–25   Circuit arrangement of four-quadrant multiplier.

$$e_o = -\frac{e_x e_y}{E_R} \tag{5-11}$$

The current into the amplifier summing junction is then

$$i_t = i_1 + i_2 + i_3 + i_4 = \frac{e_o}{R_f} = -\frac{e_x e_y}{R_f E_R} \tag{5-12}$$

The currents from the squaring circuits are subject to the following restraints
in order to satisfy Eq. (5-9) in all four quadrants.

$$i_1 = \begin{cases} 0 & x + y < 0 \\ \dfrac{1}{E_R R_f}\left(\dfrac{x+y}{2}\right)^2 & x + y > 0 \end{cases}$$

$$i_2 = \begin{cases} \dfrac{1}{E_R R_f}\left(\dfrac{x+y}{2}\right)^2 & x + y < 0 \\ 0 & x + y > 0 \end{cases}$$

$$i_3 = \begin{cases} 0 & x - y > 0 \\ \dfrac{1}{E_R R_f}\left(\dfrac{x-y}{2}\right)^2 & x - y < 0 \end{cases} \tag{5-13}$$

$$i_4 = \begin{cases} \dfrac{1}{E_R R_f}\left(\dfrac{x-y}{2}\right)^2 & x - y > 0 \\ 0 & x - y < 0 \end{cases}$$

Voltages proportional to $-x$ and $-y$ may be available from the computer set up; if not, inverters are required to provide these inputs to the multiplier.

Some manufacturers associate an absolute-value network with the squaring circuits, as shown in Fig. 5-26. In this case, only two function cir-

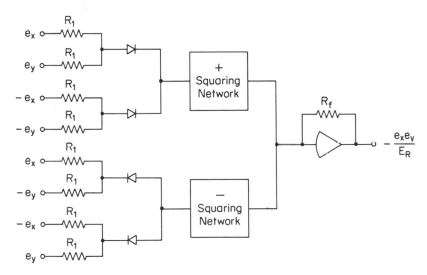

FIGURE 5–26 Alternate circuit arrangement of quarter-square multiplier.

cuits are required, one plus and one minus. The two voltages representing x and y are made available to the input summing resistors (R_1) in two polarities. The voltage polarities applied to the plus squaring network result in a voltage proportional to $(x + y)$, regardless of whether x and y are positive or negative. Those applied to the minus summing network result in $(x - y)$ for any input polarities. Thus the diodes in the input summing network form absolute value circuits which limit each resultant voltage to positive only for the upper channel and negative only for the lower channel.

The static accuracy of commercially available quarter-square multipliers is typically 0.5% of full scale for a ± 10-volt maximum output and 0.1% for a ± 100-volt maximum output. Their bandwidth is such that the phase shift is less than 1° at 1kHz and the output is typically -3dB at 20kHz. The diodes and resistors used in the squaring networks must be well matched to obtain good accuracy. In addition, the diode networks are often temperature compensated by adding temperature-sensitive resistors or diodes.

In a general-purpose computer, the diode squaring networks are generally provided as a separate unit or module which can be patched to any convenient operational amplifier. The correct amplifier feedback resistor is also included with the squaring circuits. A programming diagram which may be used for a quarter-square multiplier of this type is shown in Fig. 5-27.

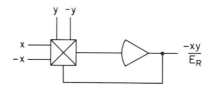

FIGURE 5–27   Programming   diagram for quarter-square multiplier.

5-5   TIME-DIVISION MULTIPLIER

Another all-electronic multiplying device which is employed in analog computation is the so-called *time-division multiplier*. These multipliers generally yield high static accuracy and fair frequency response. Although the design of the various time-division multipliers differs in detail, the principle on which they all operate is much the same.

A time-division multiplier forms the algebraic product of two variables by producing rectangular pulses proportional in amplitude to one variable and proportional in duration to the other. To understand the principle of operation of this multiplier, it is convenient to describe the multiplication of unvarying quantities rather than variables.

Consider a pulse waveform of voltage as shown in Fig. 5-28 whose amplitude $k_1 X$ is proportional to a quantity X which is to be multiplied. The net area of one cycle of the waveform is

$$A = A_1 - A_2 = k_1 X t_1 + (-k_1 X)t_2$$

where t_1 and t_2 are the widths of the positive and negative portions respectively. The average value of the waveform over one cycle is

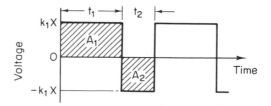

FIGURE 5–28   Rectangular pulse waveform.

$$E = \frac{A}{t_1 + t_2} = \frac{k_1 X(t_1 - t_2)}{t_1 + t_2} \tag{5-14}$$

Let us make the assumption that t_1 and t_2 are defined by the identities

$$t_1 = \frac{k_2}{Z - Y} \qquad t_2 = \frac{k_2}{Z + Y} \tag{5-15}$$

where Y is the second multiplier input and k_2 and Z are constants. Substituting for t_1 and t_2 in Eq. (5-14), we obtain the result

$$E = \frac{k_1 X \left(\dfrac{k_2}{Z - Y} - \dfrac{k_2}{Z + Y} \right)}{\dfrac{k_2}{Z - Y} + \dfrac{k_2}{Z + Y}} = \frac{k_1 XY}{Z} = kXY \tag{5-16}$$

where $k = k_1/Z$. Thus, we see that the average value of the rectangular wave is proportional to the product of the quantities X and Y.

To implement this multiplier, we must generate time periods t_1 and t_2 according to Eq. (5-15). This may be done by means of an integrator as shown in Fig. 5-29. If Y and Z are dc input voltages, then the equation for the integrator output is

$$e_o = -\frac{1}{RC} \int_0^t (Z + Y)\, dt = -\frac{(Z + Y)t}{RC} \tag{5-17}$$

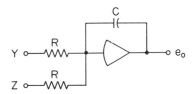

FIGURE 5–29   Integrator circuit.

Let us assume that Z is a negative reference voltage such that $(-Z + Y)$ is negative for any value of the input Y. The time to integrate to a specified output voltage E_o is then

$$t_1 = -\frac{RCE_o}{Y - Z} = \frac{RCE_o}{Z - Y} = \frac{k_2}{Z - Y} \tag{5-18}$$

where $k_2 = RCE_o$. For Z positive such that $(Z + Y)$ is always positive, the time to integrate to $-E_o$ is

$$t_2 = -\frac{RC(-E_o)}{Z + Y} = \frac{RCE_o}{Z + Y} = \frac{k_2}{Z + Y} \tag{5-19}$$

Note that Eqs. (5-18) and (5-19) express t_1 and t_2 in the desired form.

Figure 5-30 shows the circuit arrangement of a typical time-division multiplier. It is composed of an integrator, comparator, electronic switches, and output amplifier and filter. Amplifiers 1 and 2 and switch 1 form a multivibrator which oscillates due to a positive feedback voltage from the switch. To describe the operation of the multivibrator, assume that Y is a positive voltage such that $Y < Z$ and switch 1 is initially in the position shown. Thus $(-Z + Y)$ is a small negative quantity as shown in Fig. 5-31(a). As amplifier 1 integrates this input voltage, its output increases linearly with time, as shown in waveform (b). When it equals the magnitude of Z, the comparator (amplifier 2) changes state causing switch 1 to transfer to the $+Z$ input. When the switch output is changed in sign, the integrator input is a large positive quantity and the output now goes in a negative direction at a rate proportional to $(Z + Y)$. When the output reaches $-Z$, the com-

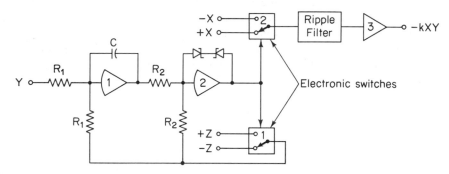

FIGURE 5–30   Time-division multiplier circuit.

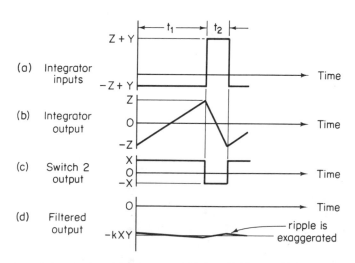

FIGURE 5–31   Waveforms in the time-division multiplier.

parator again changes state, restoring the circuit to the original condition and beginning another cycle of operation. The duty cycle of the waveform generated by the circuit is dependent upon the magnitude of Y. As Y decreases in value, t_1 decreases and t_2 increases. For increasing Y, the times are inversely affected.

A second electronic switch with inputs $+X$ and $-X$ is operated by the comparator in synchronism with switch 1. The output of switch 2, shown in waveform (c), is of the form shown in Fig. 5-28. The average or dc value of this waveform may be obtained by filtering its ripple frequencies. The output of amplifier 3 is then proportional to the product XY as given by Eq. (5-16).

In deriving Eq. (5-16), we assumed a rectangular waveform whose amplitude is proportional to one multiplier input and whose duty cycle is related to the second input. To satisfy this requirement when the inputs are variable quantities x and y, it is necessary that the frequency of the waveform be sufficiently high to ensure that x and y are essentially constant over several cycles of operation. In this case, the waveform is identified as *quasi-rectangular* and its average value kxy is a very close approximation of the desired product. The waveforms shown in Fig. 5-32 illustrate the operation of the time-division multiplier with variable inputs x and y.

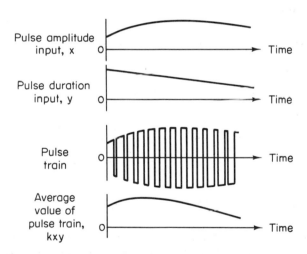

FIGURE 5–32   Time-division multiplier waveforms with variable inputs.

In designing a time-division multiplier, a compromise must be made between static accuracy and bandwidth. To obtain adequate attenuation of the ripple frequencies as well as uniform response over the signal frequency range, the filter bandwidth is invariably limited to frequencies at least two decades below the pulse-train frequency. Thus, operation at high pulse frequencies is indicated. However, errors caused by imperfect switch timing and switching spikes increase as the multivibrator frequency is increased; hence low-frequency operation is desired for high static accuracy.

In general, time-division multipliers operate at switching frequencies between 1kHz and 100kHz and yield static accuracies on the order of 0.01 to 0.1 per cent of full-scale output. A typical multiplier, operating at a 50kHz switching frequency, can provide static accuracy of 0.02 per cent of full scale, attenuation of ripple frequencies to less than 0.1 per cent of full scale, and phase shift of 0.5 degree at a signal frequency of 100Hz.

An added feature of the time-division multiplier is that other independent products of the input y may be generated with little increase in complexity or cost. Additional switches, which have other problem variables as their inputs, may be driven synchronously by the comparator. After filtering, the outputs of these switches yield other products of y. The multivibrator producing the switch drive waveforms is common to a number of multipliers.

5-6 HALL EFFECT MULTIPLIER

A phenomenon which occurs in semiconductor materials, known as the *Hall effect*, provides a simple and compact means of analog multiplication. The Hall effect may be described with the aid of Fig. 5-33. When a magnetic

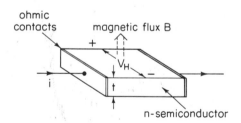

FIGURE 5–33   Hall effect.

field is applied to a current-carrying n- or p-semiconductor of rectangular shape, a voltage develops across the two faces that are mutually perpendicular to the current and magnetic flux. The magnitude of this voltage is given by

$$V_H = \frac{R_H i B}{t} \tag{5-20}$$

where

V_H = Hall voltage

R_H = Hall coefficient (related to material)

$i = $ current

$B = $ magnetic flux density.

$t = $ thickness of material

By suitably arranging the Hall element in a magnetic field so that the current through the element is proportional to one variable to be multiplied and the flux density is proportional to the other variable, the Hall voltage is made proportional to the product of the variables. This is accomplished by placing the Hall element in the airgap of a magnetic iron core, as shown in Fig. 5-34. In typical Hall effect multipliers, the element and core will occupy only several cubic inches of space.

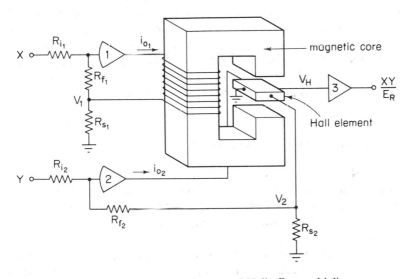

FIGURE 5–34   Schematic diagram of Hall effect multiplier.

Amplifiers 1 and 2 operate as current generators in the following manner. A small resistor R_s placed in series with the load (core winding or semiconductor element) develops a voltage given by

$$V = i_o\left(\frac{R_s R_f}{R_s + R_f}\right) \tag{5-21}$$

where i_o is the load current. The usual operational amplifier relationship holds so that

$$V = -\frac{R_f}{R_i}e_i$$

or

$$i_o = -\left(\frac{R_s + R_f}{R_s R_i}\right)e_i \qquad (5\text{-}22)$$

Hence the amplifier output current is proportional to the input voltage to the amplifier.

Amplifier 3 accepts the Hall voltage, which is typically on the order of millivolts, and provides amplification so that the multiplier output is correctly scaled.

By the inclusion of special drive circuits and error compensation, the static accuracy of Hall effect multipliers can be made comparable to that of other electronic multipliers. However, Hall effect multipliers are more commonly used as coarse, inexpensive multipliers (also as wattmeters) where static accuracies on the order of one or two per cent of full scale are acceptable. The frequency response of the Hall channel is quite good and the useable bandwidth extends to 10kHz or higher. On the other hand, the inductance associated with the magnetic channel limits its response and the bandwidth here is generally limited to several hundred hertz.

5-7 DIVISION AND SQUARE ROOT

In Section 4-4 we saw that a servomultiplier could be used in circuits to perform division, squaring, and extraction of a square root. The functioning of these circuits does not depend upon a particular multiplier type; as we shall now see, electronic multipliers may be used in a like manner for these operations.

As before, two-quadrant division may be accomplished by placing the multiplier in the feedback circuit of an operational amplifier, as shown in Fig. 5-35. We may analyze this division circuit by applying Kirchhoff's current law at the summing junction of amplifier 1. Assuming a sign inver-

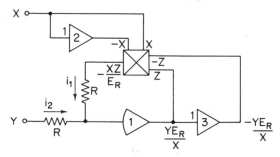

FIGURE 5–35   Division circuit.

sion is associated with the multiplier, we have

$$i_1 + i_2 = \frac{Y}{R} + \left(\frac{-XZ}{E_R R}\right) = 0 \qquad (5\text{-}23)$$

Solving Eq. (5-23) for the output of amplifier 1 gives

$$Z = \frac{YE_R}{X} \qquad (5\text{-}24)$$

Amplifiers 2 and 3 are inverters which provide the negative inputs required by the multiplier.

For stable operation, the voltage feedback to the amplifier summing junction must be of the same polarity as the amplifier output voltage. This occurs only when the voltage X is negative. The voltage Y may be either positive or negative; hence, division in two quadrants is possible with this circuit. If X is always a positive quantity, the X and $-X$ multiplier connections may be interchanged for proper operation.

An additional restriction is that the absolute value of the divisor X must be greater than or equal to the absolute value of the dividend Y to ensure that the output does not exceed the voltage limit of the amplifier.

Finally, the divisor Y cannot go to zero, because this implies an infinite quotient. Fortunately, the simulation of actual physical systems very seldom involves division by zero, since infinite quotients are usually not encountered in phenomena related to our physical world.

The analysis for the division circuit also applies, in general, to the square root operation. To obtain the square root of a voltage X, the multiplier is connected in the feedback path of an operational amplifier as shown in Fig. 5-36. Summing the currents at the input junction gives

$$i_1 + i_2 = \frac{X}{R} + \left(\frac{-Z^2}{E_R R}\right) = 0 \qquad (5\text{-}25)$$

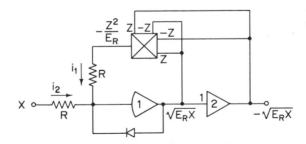

FIGURE 5–36 Square-root circuit.

from which

$$Z = \sqrt{E_R X}$$

The input voltage X must always be positive for stable operation of the circuit, since the circuit cannot generate imaginary solutions. The diode placed around amplifier 1 ensures that the circuit will not saturate in the wrong direction if X inadvertently goes negative.

PROBLEMS FOR CHAPTER 5

Unless otherwise specified, assume ideal diodes in the following problems.

1. Sketch the input-output characteristic (e_i vs e_o) for each of the circuits below for $-10\text{V} \leq e_i \leq 10\text{V}$.

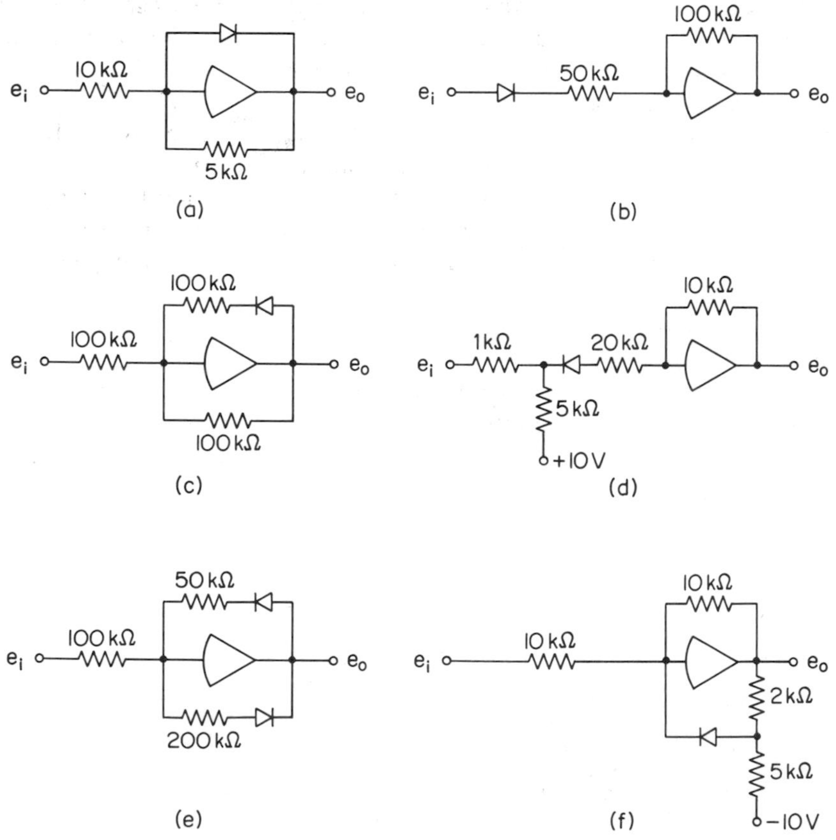

(a)

(b)

(c)

(d)

(e)

(f)

2. Sketch the input-output characteristic of the circuit below. What computing function could this circuit perform? What limitation would the circuit have when practical diodes are used?

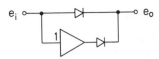

3. Graph the input-output characteristic of the circuit below for $-100\text{V} \le e_i \le 100\text{V}$. Assume E_b of D_1 and D_2 is 0.7V.

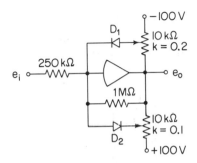

4. Develop a computing circuit to provide the following non-linear function. Assume computer reference voltages of $\pm 10\text{V}$.

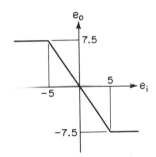

5. In the circuit below, D_1 and D_2 have breakdown voltages of 10V. Determine the potentiometer settings to produce the indicated non-linear function.

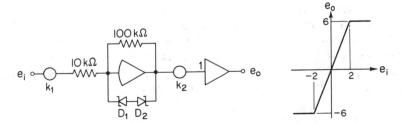

6. In the circuit below, determine the input gain G_1 and the potentiometer settings k_1 and k_2 to produce the indicated non-linear function.

7. Sketch the input-output characteristic for the circuit below for $-10V \leq e_i \leq 10V$. Assume E_b of D_1 and D_2 is 0.5V.

8. Sketch the input-output characteristic for the circuit below for $0 \leq e_i \leq 10V$.

9. The function $Y = 10 \sin X$ is to be approximated to within $\pm\frac{1}{10}$ unit by straight-line segments for $0 \leq X \leq 180°$. What is the minimum number of segments required? Determine the coordinates of the breakpoints of the function. (*Hint:* Use a graphic solution and plot the upper and lower error limits.)

10. Develop an electronic computing circuit for taking the cube root of a variable.

11. What would be the result of interchanging the X and $-X$ inputs to the multiplier shown in Fig. 5-27? Of interchanging both the X and $-X$ and the Y and $-Y$ inputs?

12. Sketch waveforms of the time-division multiplier like those shown in Fig. 5-31, using the other three polarity combinations of X and Y, in order to verify that the device is a four-quadrant multiplier.

13. What is the output voltage from the circuit below if the computer reference is 10 volts? If it is 100 volts?

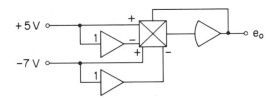

14. A logarithmic multiplier implementing the relation

$$\log X + \log Y = \log (XY)$$

can be constructed using networks whose output current is proportional to the logarithm of the input voltage. Develop a simple circuit suitable for one-quadrant multiplication which incorporates log networks.

15. The circuit below is a constant-current source whose output current i is proportional to the input voltage e_i. Determine values of R_1, R_2, and R_3 so that $i_{max} = 20mA$ for $e_i = 10V$.

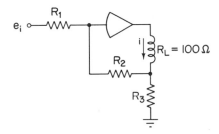

6

CONTROL
AND
AUXILIARY
DEVICES

6-1 INTRODUCTION

So far we have studied the electronic circuits and devices which are used to perform analog computing operations. A number of computing elements must be interconnected in an appropriate manner to solve a problem with the computer. The operation of these elements must then be controlled in some fashion. Finally, means must be provided to obtain the output information from the computer. It is the purpose of this chapter to consider these requirements and describe the equipment by which they are satisfied.

Analog computers vary from small table-top units to relatively large facilities which have a hybrid capability. The essential differences are due to the number of available computing elements, the features provided for operator convenience, and the ease of problem set up. In general our discussion will be limited to those features and equipment which are common to most smaller analog computers.

General-purpose analog computers are usually constructed so that the computing elements are available on plug-in chassis or modules. The front of the chassis provides the necessary input and output terminals for the unit. The chassis are mounted in an appropriate cabinet or rack and connected to the necessary power supplies and control circuitry. The exact configuration as to number and types of computing elements is more or less at the discretion of the user.

Figure 6-1 shows a front or panel view of a typical small analog computer. The various items which will be discussed in this chapter are shown on the figure.

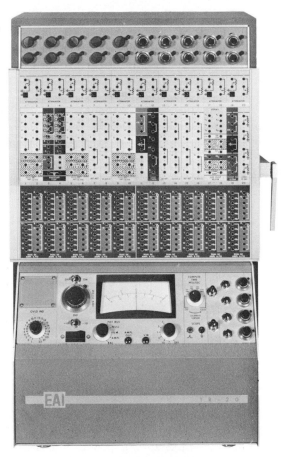

FIGURE 6–1   Typical desk-top analog computer showing control features. (Electronic Associates, Inc.)

6-2   PATCHING SYSTEMS

The equipment that has been described in the preceding chapters must be interconnected to perform useful computations. Several different interconnection schemes are available. The choice depends on the use to be made of the equipment as well as on operator convenience and cost. Since the exact method of interconnection is unique to a given computer, we will not attempt to discuss the subject in other than general terms.

In special-purpose computers designed for a particular application, the computing elements may be mounted in an appropriate-size cabinet and permanently wired together. This is perhaps the most straightforward method of interconnection but it lacks flexibility.

A simple method of interconnection used in some general-purpose computers is a terminal board or panel to which the terminals of the various computing units are brought by means of cables. *Patch cords*, which are simply short wires with plugs on each end, interconnect the computing equipment. Thus, if we want to connect the output of a summer to an integrator input, we plug one end of a patch cord into the jack connected to the summer output and the other end into a jack which connects to an input resistor. The other resistor terminal connects to the integrator amplifier summing junction. The computing resistors and capacitors are mounted on plugs which are also inserted in the terminal board. By choosing appropriate plug-in components, an amplifier can be set up to perform a desired operation. Although this method provides a great deal of versatility in component-value selection, it suffers from the fact that the precision resistors and capacitors are exposed to the adverse effects of handling. Also, a rather large terminal board is required to hold the components. Consequently, this scheme is generally used only in smaller, less expensive computers.

The interconnection system most commonly used in general-purpose computers involves a removable terminal board, or *patch board*. All problem wiring is done on the patch board by means of patch cords. The patch board, in turn, plugs into a matching terminal board on the console of the computer called the *patch bay*. The computing resistors and capacitors are part of the computer modules and their terminals are brought to the patch bay. This arrangement allows a higher concentration of jacks on the patch board.

The primary advantage of the patch-board system is that it permits patching to be done away from the computer and avoids holding up use of the computer while the program wiring is being prepared. A further benefit of the removable patch board is that a problem or particular patching configuration can be stored (in the form of a wired patch board) so that the problem can be repeated at a later date.

Although patch boards of various computers differ in detail, they have certain features in common. Patch boards are usually modular to facilitate wiring. A portion of a typical patch board is reproduced in Fig. 6-2. Interconnection terminals for operational amplifiers, integrator networks, coefficient potentiometers, and reference voltages are shown. The operational amplifiers have inputs providing fixed gains of 1 and 10. When used as a summer, the amplifier input is jumpered to the summing junction (SJ) and the amplifier output is connected to any one of the inputs. For integration, the amplifier is interconnected with an integrating network. Non-linear

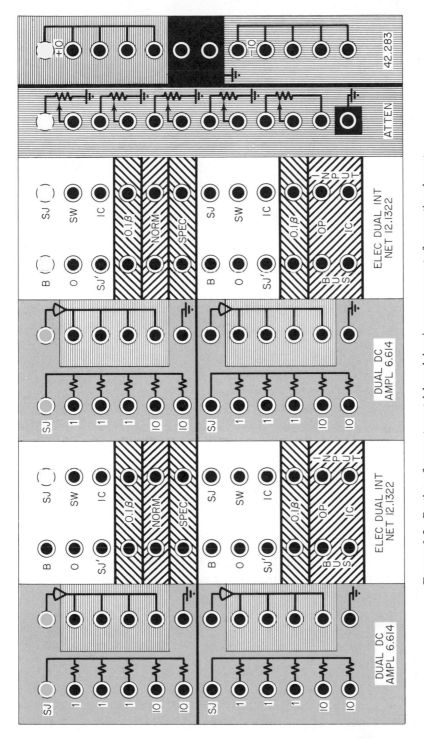

FIGURE 6-2 Portion of computer patch board showing arrangement of computing element terminals. (Electronic Associates, Inc.)

167

devices, such as electronic multipliers and function generators, generally incorporate patch-board operational amplifiers for best equipment utilization.

6-3 CONTROL SYSTEMS

To permit the starting and stopping of a problem, a *control system* is necessary on any computer. The basic operating control is known as the *mode control*. It is a selector switch with positions corresponding to the operating modes of the computer.

Every analog computer has at least two modes: the RESET (or IC) mode and the COMPUTE (or OPERATE) mode. In addition, most computers have a third mode known as the HOLD mode. All computing elements except the integrators are active in all three modes. Hence, the mode control only involves the integrators in the following manner.

RESET: The output voltages of the integrators are set to the values specified by the initial conditions of the problem. This mode provides the starting point for a solution.

OPERATE: The integrator accepts inputs and integrates them with respect to time.

HOLD: The inputs are disconnected from the integrators and the integrator maintains or *holds* the voltage attained at the time that the computer was switched into HOLD.

Control of the three basic modes of computer operation is accomplished by switching the integrator circuitry. The connection of an integrator in each of these modes is shown by the simplified schematic diagrams in Fig. 6-3. Two relays, identified as RESET and HOLD, are used to control the mode of an integrator.

In the OPERATE mode, the input resistors are connected to the amplifier and the integrator functions in the normal manner. The IC input is grounded during OPERATE and does not affect the circuit.

During HOLD operation, the input resistors are disconnected from the amplifier. With no input current, the capacitor current is zero (disregarding the extremely small input offset current) so that the output voltage remains constant.

In the RESET mode, a resistor is connected in parallel with the integrating capacitor and an additional resistor, equal in value to the first, is connected from the IC terminal to the amplifier input. Since the resistors are equal, the output voltage will be the negative of the IC input voltage. In resetting

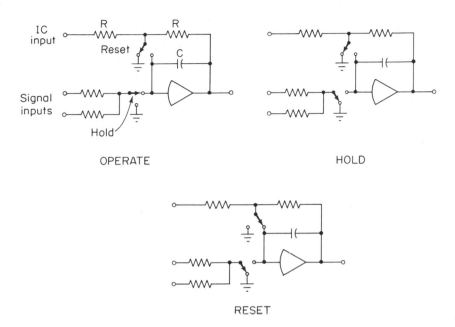

FIGURE 6-3   Integrator control modes.

the circuit, sufficient time must be allowed for the capacitor to charge. This is generally taken as ten times the *RC* time constant of the circuit. For example, if the *RC* product is 0.1 second, then at least one second should be allowed for the reset operation.

If no IC voltage is applied to the integrator, the capacitor discharges through the shunt resistor during RESET and the problem starts with zero output from the integrator.

Normally the Reset and Hold relays for all integrators are connected to common RESET and HOLD lines so that the integrators can be switched simultaneously by the operator.

Various other operating modes are useful and are provided on some computers. A PATCH or STANDBY mode disconnects the reference voltages from the patch board as a safeguard while plugging and unplugging patch cords. On larger and more complex computers, a CHECK mode facilitates the check-out of a problem after it has been patched.

In setting coefficient potentiometers, it is necessary that amplifier input resistors be connected to the potentiometers so that potentiometer loading will be compensated. If the resistors also connect to the amplifier summing junction, the reference voltage which is applied to the potentiometer during the setting procedure described in Section 2-5 may cause the amplifier to overload. To avoid this condition, some computers provide a POT SET mode in which the input resistors are switched from the summing junction to ground. On computers that do not have a POT SET mode, the potentiometer setting is done in the RESET mode following the same procedure as outlined before. Some computers also provide a BALANCE mode wherein the amplifiers may be manually balanced prior to commencing operations. In most cases, however, balancing is infrequent and is performed in the RESET mode.

6-4   REPETITIVE OPERATION

In many problems solved by an analog computer, we wish to investigate the different behavior resulting from a change in the parameters and/or initial conditions of a system. This is especially true when we are using the simulation to optimize the design of a system. In such cases, a trial and error adjustment of the parameters may be made until the desired behavior is attained. Investigations of this kind could be made by switching the computer from RESET to OPERATE and back again as frequently as desired with a change in parameter setting in between. Obviously, this procedure would be quite time-consuming if a large number of parameters are involved.

Experiments of this kind are greatly facilitated by the use of high-speed *repetitive-operation* (REP-OP) and this is commonly made available as an operating mode. In the REP-OP mode, the gains of the integrators are increased so that the time of solution is decreased by a factor of 100 or more. By automatically cycling the computer at a high rate between the OPERATE and RESET modes, a continuous trace of the results can be displayed on an instrument such as an oscilloscope. If the parameter or initial-condition setting is continuously and slowly adjusted, the effects of the change can be immediately observed.

Figure 6-4 shows the circuit arrangement of an integrator in the REP-OP mode. The $10 \mu F$ capacitor is the feedback element used for normal "slow" operation. The smaller $0.1 \mu F$ capacitor used in the REP-OP mode speeds up the integration by a factor of 100. The integrator is rapidly cycled between the OPERATE and RESET modes by a high-speed relay driven by an oscillator circuit. For very high speeds, an electronic switch must be used. The oscillator has two synchronized outputs; a rectangular wave to drive the switches, and a sawtooth wave to drive the horizontal axis of the display oscilloscope. The reset time must be long enough to allow the integrators to return to their initial values. This is determined by the time constant of the initial-condition network; this time constant is 1 millisecond in the circuit of Fig. 6-4. The length of the OPERATE time is generally adjusted by the operator for a suitable value. Obviously, in the REP-OP mode only electronic computing elements can be used, since electromechanical components are too slow.

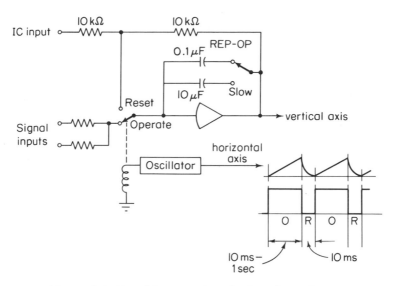

FIGURE 6–4   Repetitive operation circuit and waveforms.

6-5   OVERLOAD ALARM

An analog simulation may require dozens of operational amplifiers. To achieve satisfactory results, it is necessary to know if an amplifier output exceeds its operating range during the solution of a problem. This condition is referred to as an *amplifier overload.*

An overload is generally caused by excessive input voltage as a result of improper scaling of the problem. It can also occur as a result of component malfunction, patching errors, or excessive output current. Since the operator cannot observe the output of every amplifier, an automatic means of detecting and indicating an overload becomes essential. Consequently, some form of overload alarm system is provided in all but the most simple computers.

In computers using stabilized amplifiers, a reliable means of overload detection is readily available. During normal operation, the summing junction of an amplifier is very near zero voltage. If the amplifier output cannot respond to the demand of the input signal(s), the summing-point voltage will immediately increase by a significant amount. This causes the output of the stabilizing amplifier to rise from its normal millivolt level to several volts or higher. This change in stabilizer output voltage is used to trigger an alarm which alerts the operator to the overload condition.

Figure 6-5 shows an overload alarm system for use with computers having ±100 volt amplifiers. The individual outputs of the stabilizer ampli-

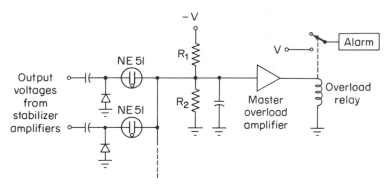

FIGURE 6–5   Overload alarm system.

fiers are rectified and applied to neon lamps. An overloaded amplifier develops a stabilizer output sufficient to fire the lamp associated with that amplifier. The master overload amplifier is biased through R_1 so that the overload relay is normally de-energized. Should any lamp fire, the current through R_2 overcomes this bias and operates the overload relay. This energizes an overload alarm which may be either an audible signal or a readily visible lamp. The exact location of the overload can be pinpointed by the glowing neon lamp.

The voltage levels in computers using lower output amplifiers (such as ±10 volts) are insufficient to operate neon glow lamps. In this case, incandescent lamps are used in a circuit of the type illustrated in Fig. 6-6. As in

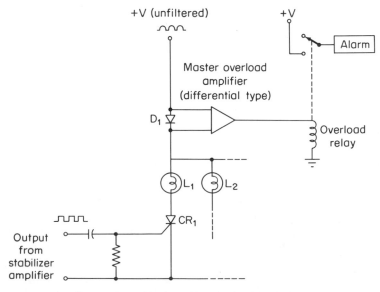

FIGURE 6–6   Alternate form of overload system.

the previous circuit, a large square wave appears at the stabilizer output of an overloaded amplifier. This signal is differentiated and applied to the control gate of silicon-controlled rectifier CR_1. The rectifier then conducts and its anode current illuminates the lamp. Once a controlled rectifier conducts, the gate loses control. In order to extinguish the lamp, the anode-to-cathode voltage must be reduced to a point insufficient to cause conduction. A common turn-off technique is to use an unfiltered dc supply so that the anode voltage falls to zero during each cycle of the supply frequency. This permits the lamp to go out when the overload is removed.

A number of indicator circuits are connected in parallel through diode D_1 to the anode supply. If one or more overloads occur, the resultant lamp current develops a small voltage across the diode. This voltage drop may be applied to a master overload amplifier and will activate an alarm as was described before.

6-6 READOUT EQUIPMENT

In Chapter 1, it was pointed out that an analog computer solves problems by establishing an electronic circuit whose behavior is analogous to the system under study. Thus, the information about a problem, i.e., about its solution, is in the form of continuously varying voltages. Therefore, a means must be provided to present these voltage variations in a form suitable for study and interpretation. Readout devices which can provide a visible display of the computer voltages include voltmeters, recorders, and oscilloscopes.

The simplest form of readout device is a voltmeter of the conventional D'Arsonval type. A meter is invariably made available as an integral part of the computer. This meter may be used for the direct reading of voltages with an accuracy of several per cent. For more precise measurements the meter may be used with a null potentiometer, as described in Section 2-6. A digital voltmeter is frequently used for increased accuracy and speed of readout. These meters usually display 3 or 4 significant figures and provide a voltage reading within a fraction of a second. For convenience, the computer may provide a selector switch which permits the voltmeter to be connected to the output of any amplifier. In addition, the meter terminals are available on the control panel or patch board.

A voltmeter is suitable only for measuring voltages that do not change with time; its indication is of little value in interpreting the behavior of a variable quantity. Consequently, it is used almost exclusively for setting potentiometers and for making static checks during problem set up.

The principal means of computer readout is the *strip-chart recorder* shown in two of its forms in Figs. 6-7 and 6-8. This instrument overcomes the readout limitations of a voltmeter.

In a strip-chart recorder, paper on a roll is drawn at a constant speed past one or more pens. The paper movement represents the independent

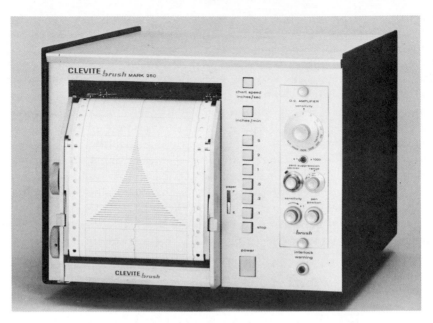

FIGURE 6–7 Single-channel strip-chart recorder showing chart speed and amplifier controls. (Clevite Corporation, Brush Instruments Division)

FIGURE 6–8 Eight-channel strip-chart recorder for use with large analog computer. (Clevite Corporation, Brush Instruments Division)

variable, time. The pen moves at right angles to the direction of paper travel with a deflection proportional to the dependent variable being recorded. Permanent traces are produced either with ink fed through special light-weight pens by gravity or pressure, or on heat-sensitive paper by a hot-wire stylus. The resultant trace gives a record of the behavior of a problem variable as a function of time.

In most recorders, the deflection principle of the pen arm is the same as in the D'Arsonval meter movement. However, if we visualize the tip of a meter needle as drawing a trace, the result is an arc of a circle rather than a straight line. This means that the trace is in *curvilinear coordinates* which leads to some difficulty in interpreting the results; a sine wave does not appear sinusoidal but is somewhat distorted. In ink recorders, the curvilinear motion is frequently translated into *rectilinear coordinates* by a special mechanical linkage system. In the hot-wire recorder, the "pen" contacts the paper along a raised straight edge perpendicular to the paper travel; this feature inherently produces a trace in rectilinear coordinates.

As shown in the illustrations, strip-chart recorders include a control unit as well as electronic amplifiers for the input voltages. The amplifiers provide good linearity and frequency response from the recording pens, as well as sensitivity and offset adjustments for the operator. A typical strip-chart recorder has a static accuracy of 0.5 to 1 per cent of full scale and is useable at frequencies up to 100Hz. To cover a variety of recording uses, the motorized paper drive system provides selectable chart speeds ranging from 0.1 inch per minute to about 5 inches per second.

Strip-chart recorders are available as single-channel or multi-channel instruments. The latter type are ideal for computer readout because a number of variables can be simultaneously recorded to aid in analyzing the results. Additional pens, called *event markers*, are sometimes provided at the edge of the chart paper to produce timing marks.

Another widely used form of readout device is the *X-Y recorder*, also known as a plotting board. It is used to record two variables simultaneously in the form of a rectangular-coordinate graph. As an example, we might wish to record the velocity of some object as a function of its displacement. By providing a linearly increasing voltage to one axis of the recorder, graphs of variables as a function of time may be obtained. An *X-Y* recorder is particularly useful where a family of computed curves is desired, since they may be sequentially plotted on the same graph paper.

A typical recorder is shown in Fig. 6-9. It consists of a fixed bed and a moving arm which holds the marking pen. The pen moves in both the horizontal and vertical directions (hence, the designation *X-Y*) when signal voltages are coupled to the respective drive circuits. Unlike the strip-chart recorder, the pen is positioned by two servo systems. Each servo consists of an amplifier, servo motor and pen drive cable, and feedback potentiometer (see Section 4-2 for a description of servomechanism operation). The station-

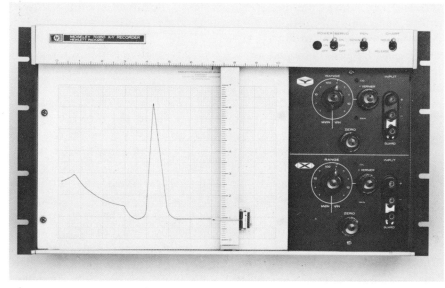

FIGURE 6–9   *X-Y* recorder. (Hewlett-Packard Corporation,
Moseley Division)

ary graph paper is held onto the flat bed either by clips, with a vacuum
created by a small suction pump, or by electrostatic attraction. Like the
strip-chart recorder, the *X-Y* recorder is a slow-speed device. Its speed of
response is limited by the servo systems which drive the pen; typically this
speed is about 20 inches per second maximum. This is not necessarily a serious limitation, but it must be kept in mind when the recorder is used. Because
of the closed-loop nature of the pen-positioning system, the recorder is
capable of quite high static accuracy. Specifications of 0.1 and 0.25 per cent
of full scale are typical.

   In addition to its readout function, an *X-Y* recorder is sometimes supplied with an attachment so that it can be used to generate a non-linear
function of a variable. The device in this case is known as a *curve follower*.
The principle of operation is shown in Fig. 6-10.

   The ink pen is replaced by a head containing a high-frequency resonant
circuit. The function for which a voltage is to be generated is drawn on
paper with conductive ink. The drawn line is excited by a high frequency
voltage (100–500kHz) which makes it act as an antenna. If the head is near
the curve, an ac voltage is induced in the resonant circuit. The magnitude of
the voltage is proportional to the distance of the center of the head to the
line and the phase depends upon which side of the line the head is on. A
phase-sensitive detector can derive an error signal from the head as shown in
Fig. 6-10(b). This error is applied to the *Y* servo amplifier and causes the

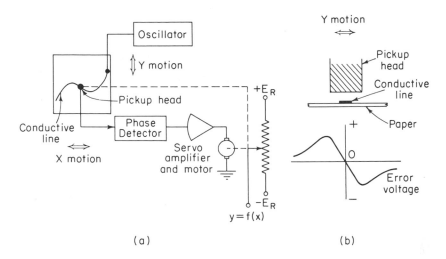

FIGURE 6–10   Block diagram of curve follower.

head to position itself directly above the curve. If the head is now driven along the X axis by an independent variable, the Y servo system will cause the head to follow the curve. Since the Y-axis potentiometer is not needed for feedback, its wiper voltage, which is proportional to the Y displacement, can be used to provide an output voltage. The function to be generated must be continuous and the speed of the curve follower is subject to the same limits as when recording. The primary advantages of the curve follower are the ease of setting up a function and storing it for use at some later time.

Cathode-ray oscilloscopes (CRO's) are familiar instruments which are used to observe voltage waveforms. Since a CRO possesses the same two-way movement as an X-Y recorder, it can serve as a useful computer read-out device. The low-inertia electronic beam is capable of writing much faster than the computing equipment, so that no speed limitation is imposed by the readout equipment. For computer work, the deflection amplifiers must be dc coupled.

The primary limitation in using a CRO is the short persistence of the cathode-ray tubes commonly used in oscilloscopes. By using long-persistence phosphors, traces can be observed for several seconds. The advent of storage-type cathode-ray tubes provides a means of holding a trace indefinitely. A permanent record of a solution may be obtained by photographing the trace.

The primary use of CRO's is in the repetitive mode of computer operation, when computing speeds are high enough for solutions to be conveniently displayed. In some problems, it is desirable to display simultaneously a number of variables. In the REP-OP mode of operation, this can be done by electronic switching of the various signal inputs to the CRO.

CRO's are more difficult to calibrate, and their displays are usually not as accurate as those of recorders. Special CRO's used for computer readout incorporate voltage-reference or coordinate lines on the screen of the cathode-ray tube. Since both the signals and the "electronic grid" undergo the same distortion, the accuracy of the readout is improved.

6-7 POWER SUPPLIES

DC power supplies provide operating voltages for amplifiers and other circuits in the computer, as well as the computer reference voltages. These power supplies, particularly the reference supplies, must maintain a constant voltage in spite of variations of the power line voltage to the computer and the amount of current drawn from the supply. In addition the source impedance of the power supply must be low to prevent undesired interaction between the computing elements. Power supplies which meet requirements of this type are known as *regulated supplies*.

The most common design of a regulated supply employs a series regulator element as shown in the simplified circuit in Fig. 6-11. Basically, this circuit functions as a feedback amplifier in the following manner. One input to the differential amplifier is a reference voltage; in this case, the Zener voltage V_z of diode D_1. The other input is a fraction V_1 of the regulated output voltage as determined by voltage divider R_1 and R_2. The output of the differential amplifier controls the series transistor which is connected as an emitter-follower to drive the load. The closed-loop action of the circuit maintains (or regulates) the output voltage so that $V_1 = V_z$. For example, should the output voltage tend to increase as load current is reduced, an error voltage $V_1 - V_z$ will be developed. This voltage is amplified and biases the series transistor to restore the output voltage to its proper value.

The specifications for regulated power supplies depend upon the size and precision of the computer. DC voltages to operate the equipment are

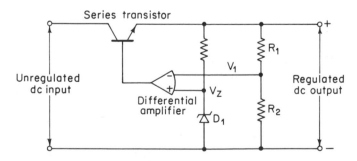

FIGURE 6–11   Simplified circuit of series regulator.

generally regulated to within 0.1 to 1.0 per cent of their nominal value for anticipated variations in line voltages and load current. Computer reference voltages are usually regulated to within 0.01 to 0.1 per cent. More important than their absolute values are close matching between the positive and negative reference voltages. This is usually obtained by slaving one reference supply to the other.

In addition to temperature-compensated Zener diodes, gas-filled regulator tubes are used as the reference element in regulated supplies. For the most accurate reference supplies, mercury batteries or standard cells may be used.

PROBLEMS FOR CHAPTER 6

1. Describe three methods of interconnecting analog computer elements.

2. A patch board arrangement for an operational amplifier is shown below. With patch cords inserted as shown, what computing function is provided by the amplifier?

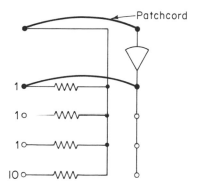

3. An alternate patch board arrangement for an operational amplifier is shown below. With patch cords as shown, what computing function is provided?

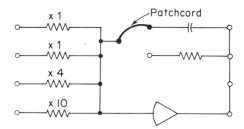

4. Below, at left, are the patch board connections for two coefficient potentiometers. How could each be used?

5. Referring to the patch board shown in Fig. 6-2, trace out the patch cord connections for the circuit shown below, at right.

6. What modes of operation does a typical analog computer have? For what purpose is each mode used?

7. Suggest why one would wish to temporarily halt a problem solution on an analog computer.

8. Describe the circuit operation of an integrator in each of the computing modes identified in Problem 6.

9. It can be shown that the decay of an integrator output voltage e_o in HOLD is given by the equation

$$e_o = E_o \epsilon^{-t/AR_{in}C}$$

where E_o is the output at time of switching into HOLD, A is the amplifier open-loop gain, R_{in} is its input resistance, and C is the feedback capacitance. For $E_o = 1V$, $A = 10,000$, $R_{in} = 100,000k\Omega$, and $C = 10\mu F$, determine e_o after 100 seconds in HOLD.

10. What is meant by repetitive operation? Explain how it is achieved in an analog computer.

11. Why is it important to detect an intermittent overload condition in an analog computer?

12. What is meant by curvilinear and rectilinear recording? Give two methods by which the latter may be obtained on a strip-chart recorder.

13. An X-Y recorder has an X-axis sensitivy of 0.5 volt per inch. Using computer elements, design an X-axis drive such that the pen will move linearly at a rate of 1 inch per second.

14. The circuit below uses a mercury battery and operational amplifier to provide a precision reference voltage. What is the magnitude of the voltage? What determines the battery current drain?

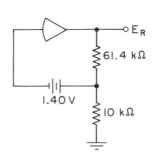

7-1 INTRODUCTION

The behavior of a physical phenomenon or system can be defined by natural laws expressed in the form of mathematical equations. An equation expresses the relationship of at least two variables. These include one or more dependent variables whose behavior is of interest, and one or more independent variables which determine this behavior. A mathematical equation containing only the variables is an algebraic equation. An equation which contains not only the variables themselves, but also the rates of change or derivatives of these variables, is known as a *differential equation*. To solve a differential equation is to find an equation expressing the relationship between the variables with no derivatives occurring.

In many engineering and scientific problems, we are interested in the behavior of some physical system as a function of an independent variable such as time. The behavior of this system can, of course, be observed by constructing a physical model. However, it cannot be analyzed without an understanding of the applicable differential equation and its solution. An ability to formulate and solve differential equations is therefore invaluable in investigating the dynamic behavior of diverse phenomena such as electrical currents, heat conduction, the bending of a beam, or the motion of a rotating shaft.

As we have learned, the elec-

7

DIFFERENTIAL EQUATIONS

tronic analog computer is a device well suited to the solution of differential equations in which time is the independent variable. To this point, our study has been primarily concerned with the circuits and equipment used in analog computation. We will now turn our attention to the manner in which analog computers are used in solving problems of a dynamic nature. This requires that we have some knowledge of differential equations and their solution. Therefore, the purpose of this chapter is to introduce the subject of differential equations to the reader who has not yet acquired a familiarity with this topic.

The subject of differential equations is one of wide scope, and is treated exhaustively in many texts. We will confine ourselves to the most basic types of differential equations, and will illustrate their application with several simple, yet familiar, problems.

7-2 DEFINITIONS

As we stated above, a mathematical relationship involving one or more derivatives is called a differential equation. If the problem involves only one independent variable (such as time), the derivatives are called ordinary derivatives and the equation is called an *ordinary differential equation.* When there is more than one independent variable (such as both time and distance), the derivatives which are present are partial derivatives. The equation is then said to be a *partial differential equation.* Since the solution of partial equations is more difficult, we will limit our study to ordinary differential equations.

The *order* of a differential equation is the order of the highest *derivative* that occurs in the equation. Thus Eq. (7-1) is a first-order ordinary differential equation and Eq. (7-2) is a second-order equation.

$$\frac{dy}{dx} + y = x \tag{7-1}$$

$$L\frac{d^2q}{dt^2} + R\frac{dq}{dt} + \frac{q}{C} = E \tag{7-2}$$

The *degree* of a differential equation is the power to which the highest derivative is raised. Thus Eq. (7-1) and Eq. (7-2) are both *first* degree while Eq. (7-3) is third order and second degree

$$\left(\frac{d^3y}{dx^3}\right)^2 - \left(\frac{dy}{dx}\right)^4 - y = 0 \tag{7-3}$$

Any equation (regardless of order) of the first degree of the dependent variable, and all its derivatives, is called a *linear differential equation.* All others are called *non-linear differential equations*. Because of their relative simplicity, only linear equations will be considered in our discussion.

7-3 SOLUTIONS

A *solution* of a differential equation is any relation between the variables which does not contain derivatives and which satisfies the differential equation. That an equation is a solution may be shown by differentiating the equation and substituting the derivatives in the given differential equation with a resulting identity.

EXAMPLE 7-1

Show that $y = x^2 + C$ is a solution of the differential equation $(dy/dx) = 2x$ where C is an arbitrary constant.

SOLUTION:

The derivative of $y = x^2 + C$ is $(dy/dx) = 2x$, which is the given differential equation. Thus $y = x^2 + C$ is a solution.

EXAMPLE 7-2

Show that $i = C \sin(\omega t + \phi)$ is a solution of the second-order differential equation $(d^2i/dt^2) + \omega^2 i = 0$.

SOLUTION:

The second derivative (d^2i/dt^2) may be found by differentiating the solution twice. Thus

$$\frac{di}{dt} = \omega C \cos(\omega t + \phi) \quad \text{and} \quad \frac{d^2i}{dt^2} = -\omega^2 C \sin(\omega t + \phi) = -\omega^2 i$$

Substituting for the second derivative in the differential equation, we obtain

$$-\omega^2 i + \omega^2 i = 0$$

which verifies the solution.

In the above examples, the solution to the first-order differential equation contains a single arbitrary constant C, and the solution of the second-order equation contains two constants, C and ϕ. This is a consequence of the fact that solving a differential equation involves the process of integration, which introduces constants of integration. The foregoing examples illustrate one characteristic of all differential equations, namely, that a differential equation of any order n will have a solution containing n arbitrary constants. The solution containing these arbitrary constants is called the *general solution* of the differential equation.

When specific values are assigned to the arbitrary constants in the general solution, the resulting expression is called a *particular solution* of the differential equation.

To arrive at a particular solution, additional information is required concerning the system described by the differential equation. The additional information, which allows values to be assigned to the arbitrary constants, is generally known as *boundary conditions*.

In physical problems where time is the independent variable, the additional information is frequently the initial values of the quantities involved in the equation. In this case, the boundary conditions are known at time $t = 0$, and are referred to as *initial conditions*.

At this point we should distinguish between initial conditions which lead to the particular solution, and those problem constants which define the general solution. Constants, which describe a system and are known quantities in the original differential equation, are referred to as problem *parameters*. As an example, consider a differential equation which shows how the current in an electrical circuit varies with time, starting when $t = 0$. The initial conditions might involve such factors as: (a) the quantities of charge on the various capacitors when $t = 0$; (b) the rates of change of current when $t = 0$; and (c) the amounts of current flowing when $t = 0$. The parameters would be the values of the resistors, capacitors, and inductors which make up the circuit.

EXAMPLE 7-3

Find the particular solution of $(dy/dx) = 2x$, given the boundary conditions that at $x = 1$, $y = -3$.

SOLUTION:

From Example 7-1, the general solution of this equation is

$$y = x^2 + C \tag{1}$$

Substituting the boundary conditions in Eq. (1) gives

$$-3 = 1 + C$$

Therefore

$$C = -4$$

Hence the particular solution is

$$y = x^2 - 4$$

EXAMPLE 7-4

From Example 7-2, the general solution of the differential equation (d^2i/dt^2) $+ 4i = 0$ is $i = C \sin(2t + \phi)$. Find the particular solution for the initial conditions $i = 2$ amp and $(di/dt) = 0$.

SOLUTION:

Substituting the initial conditions at $t = 0$, we obtain the equations

$$i = 2 = \quad C \sin(2t + \phi) = \quad C \sin \phi \tag{1}$$

$$\frac{di}{dt} = 0 = 2C \cos(2t + \phi) = 2C \cos \phi \tag{2}$$

For Eq. (1) to be valid, $C \neq 0$. Therefore, in Eq. (2), $\cos \phi = 0$ and $\phi = \pi/2$. Applying this result in Eq. (1), we have

$$2 = C \sin \pi/2 = C$$

Hence, we obtain the particular solution

$$i = 2 \sin(2t + \pi/2) = 2 \cos 2t \quad \text{amperes}$$

The result is a cosine wave whose peak amplitude is 2 amperes and whose angular velocity is 2 rad/sec.

7-4 METHODS OF SOLUTION

The solution of differential equations by analytical means is an arduous task for other than the simplest equations. Any one of a number of methods may be employed, depending upon the form and complexity of the equation. Moreover, the problem of solution is compounded when the physical system is described by a *set* of differential equations rather than by a single equation. In this case the equations must be solved simultaneously, just as a set of algebraic equations are solved in a simultaneous manner.

In addition to the classic methods of solution, techniques known as *transform methods* are commonly employed in solving differential equations. The most common of these is based upon a mathematical relationship, the Laplace transformation, by which a differential equation may be *transformed* into an algebraic equation. This algebraic equation is solved for the desired variables and its solution is then *inversely transformed* to provide the desired differential equation solution. Although the Laplace transformation is an extremely powerful method for solving differential equations, its application becomes laborious in very complex problems.

In lieu of analytical methods, the general-purpose analog computer provides a rapid and effective means of solving differential equations. In the following chapter, we shall see how a computer is programmed and used for this purpose.

For some types of lower-order differential equations, the classic methods of solution are relatively simple and straightforward. Several of these methods will be described in order that the student may have some insight into the technique of solving differential equations.

7-5 DIRECT INTEGRATION

Consider a first-order differential equation of the form

$$\frac{dy}{dx} = F(x) \tag{7-4}$$

in which $F(x)$ is a function of x only. Here we must find a function y whose derivative equals the given function F. This problem can be solved immediately by ordinary integration and the general solution can be written as

$$y = \int F(x)dx + C \tag{7-5}$$

where C is an arbitrary constant. Solution by direct integration is possible where only one derivative is involved and the dependent variable does not occur in the equation.

EXAMPLE 7-5

Solve the equation

$$\frac{dy}{dx} = 3x^2 + 6$$

SOLUTION:

By direct integration, the general solution is

$$y = \int (3x^2 + 6)\, dx = x^3 + 6x + C$$

EXAMPLE 7-6

Find an expression for e which satisfies the equation

$$\frac{de}{dt} = \cos t$$

and is such that $e = 1$ when $t = 0$.

SOLUTION:

We may write the general solution as

$$e = \int \cos t\, dt = \sin t + C$$

Substituting the initial conditions in the general solution gives

$$1 = 0 + C$$

The appropriate expression (particular solution) for e is

$$e = \sin t + 1$$

7-6 SEPARATION OF VARIABLES

The method of separation of the variables is a means of solution applicable to first-order, first-degree equations. Consider the equation

$$\frac{dy}{dx} = \frac{F(x)}{G(y)} \tag{7-6}$$

where F is a function of x alone and G is a function of y alone. From elementary calculus, we know that a derivative may be regarded as the ratio of the differential of the dependent variable to the differential of the independent variable.

As a consequence, the form of Eq. (7-6) may be changed from a derivative to the differential form

$$F(x)dx - G(y)dy = 0 \tag{7-7}$$

where dx and dy are the differentials of x and y respectively. The solution of Eq. (7-7) may be obtained by direct integration of each term with respect to its own variable. Thus

$$\int F(x)dx - \int G(y)dy = C \tag{7-8}$$

where C is the constant of integration.

The following steps summarize the method of separation of the variables. Its success depends on two techniques: first, the ability to separate the variables algebraically; and second, the ability to integrate the expressions obtained.

    1. Determine whether the equation is in the form of Eq. (7-7). If not, transform it to this form by algebraic manipulation.

2. Obtain the *general* solution by direct integration of each term *separately*. The general solution will contain a constant of integration.
3. If a *particular* solution is required, solve for the particular value of the constant of integration by substituting the *initial conditions* in the *general* solution.
4. The particular solution is obtained from the general solution when the particular value of the constant of integration is substituted in the expression.

This method of solving first-order differential equations is illustrated in the following examples.

EXAMPLE 7-7

Solve the equation $(dy/dx) = x^2/y$.

SOLUTION:

Separating the variables, we obtain

$$y \, dy = x^2 \, dx$$

By integration

$$\int y \, dy = \int x^2 \, dx$$
$$\frac{y^2}{2} = \frac{x^3}{3} + C$$

EXAMPLE 7-8

Find the general solution of the equation $(dy/dx) = e^{(2y-4x)}$ and the particular solution for the boundary conditions $x = 0, y = 0$.

SOLUTION:

By separating the variables

$$e^{-2y} \, dy = e^{-4x} \, dx$$

By integration, we obtain the general solution

$$\int e^{-2y} dy = \int e^{-4x} \, dx$$
$$-\tfrac{1}{2} e^{-2y} = -\tfrac{1}{4} e^{-4x} + C_1$$
$$e^{-4x} - 2e^{-2y} = C_2$$

where $C_2 = 4C_1$. Substituting the boundary conditions and solving for C_2

$$e^o - 2e^o = C_2$$
$$C_2 = -1$$

The particular solution is the expression

$$2e^{-2y} - e^{-4x} = 1$$

EXAMPLE 7-9

Find the general solution of the equation $(dy/dt) = 2yt$.

SOLUTION:

Separating the variables gives the equation

$$\frac{dy}{y} = 2t \, dt$$

Integrating, we have

$$\ln y + C_1 = \frac{2t^2}{2}$$

or

$$\ln y + \ln C_2 = t^2$$

where $C_1 = \ln C_2$. Combining terms gives

$$\ln (C_2 y) = t^2$$

Putting this result in exponential form, we obtain

$$C_2 y = e^{t^2}$$

or

$$y = C_3 e^{t^2}$$

where

$$C_3 = \frac{1}{C_2}$$

7-7 ELECTRICAL CIRCUITS

Simple electrical circuits consisting of either a resistance and inductance or a resistance and capacitance provide examples of first-order differential equations and their solutions. The opening or closing of a switch in such a circuit will usually cause a change in the voltages and currents. If the circuit contains an energy-storage element, such as an inductor or capacitor, the changes are not instantaneous. Rather, some period of time is required for the values to change from their sustained conditions before switching to the final sustained conditions after switching. The behavior of the variables during the transition time may be determined through the solution of the applicable differential equation in which time is the independent variable.

Consider the series RL circuit shown in Fig. 7-1 in which it is desired to find the current i as a function of time after the switch is closed. Applying Kirchhoff's voltage law, the differential equation for the circuit is

$$L\frac{di}{dt} + Ri = E \tag{7-9}$$

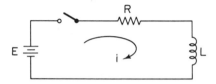

FIGURE 7-1   Series RL circuit.

This equation may be solved by separating the variables as follows

$$\frac{L}{R}di = \left(\frac{E}{R} - i\right)dt$$

or

$$\frac{di}{(E/R) - i} = \frac{R}{L}dt \tag{7-10}$$

By direct integration, we obtain the general solution as

$$-\ln\left(\frac{E}{R} - i\right) = \frac{Rt}{L} - \ln K$$

or

$$\ln\left(\frac{E}{R} - i\right) = -\frac{Rt}{L} + \ln K \tag{7-11}$$

where $\ln K$ represents the constant of integration. Placing this result in exponential form and solving for the current, we obtain

$$\frac{E}{R} - i = Ke^{-Rt/L}$$

$$i = \frac{E}{R} - Ke^{-Rt/L} \tag{7-12}$$

With the switch open, we have the initial condition $i = 0$ at $t = 0$. The particular solution may then be found as follows

$$0 = \frac{E}{R} - Ke^0$$

$$K = \frac{E}{R}$$

from which

$$i = \frac{E}{R}(1 - e^{-Rt/L}) \tag{7-13}$$

The general solution for the current contains two terms: E/R and $-Ke^{-Rt/L}$. The first term is the steady-state dc current, the current which would flow if there were no inductance in the circuit. This current value is approached as time increases; it is referred to as the *steady-state solution* of the problem. The second (exponential) term, which decreases as time goes on, represents the deviation from the final value approached by the current; it is known as the *transient solution*.

We have selected a familiar electrical circuit to illustrate the solution of a first-order differential equation. The response of simple circuits of this type is characterized by variables which either increase or decrease in an exponential manner. Other simple physical devices behave similarly. Their behavior (and that of Fig. 7-1) may be described by a first-order equation for which their transient response exhibits exponential growth or decay. Such examples include the cooling of a heated body, motion with resistance proportional to velocity, mixing of solutions, and radioactive decay.

EXAMPLE 7-10

Determine the current equation in the series RL circuit of Fig. 7-1 when $R = 10$ ohms, $L = 1$ henry, and $E = 1$ volt.

SOLUTION:

From Eq. (7-13), the current is

$$i = \frac{E}{R}(1 - e^{-Rt/L})$$

Substituting values, we have

$$i = 0.1\,(1 - e^{-10t})\quad \text{amperes}$$

The current shown in Fig. 7-2 exhibits the exponential rise character-istic of an inductive circuit.

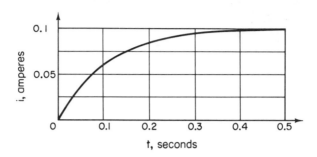

FIGURE 7–2   Current rise for *RL* circuit of Example 7-10.

7-8 OPERATOR NOTATION

The writing of differential equations containing derivatives and integrals often leads to unwieldy expressions. To simplify writing these equations, the use of operator notation has been widely adopted in engineering work. With operator notation, the derivatives and integrals are replaced by symbols known as *differential operators*.

The symbol D is frequently used as a differential operator; it indicates the differentiation of a function or dependent variable with respect to an independent variable. When placed to the left of any function, for example $Df(x)$, the symbol D indicates that the function $f(x)$ is to be differentiated with respect to the variable x. Thus, the differential operator D is defined by the expression

$$D \equiv \frac{d}{dx} \tag{7-14}$$

where x is the independent variable.

The concept of the differential operator may be extended to include multiple differentiation. For example

$$DD = D^2 = D\frac{d}{dx} = \frac{d}{dx}\left(\frac{d}{dx}\right) = \frac{d^2}{dx^2} \tag{7-15}$$

In general, for the nth derivative of a function, we may use

$$D^n = \frac{d^n}{dx^n} \tag{7-16}$$

The D operator is also used to represent the operation of integration. In this case

$$\int (\quad) \, dx = \frac{1}{D} = D^{-1} \tag{7-17}$$

Here the term contained within the parentheses is being integrated with respect to the independent variable x. For multiple integrations, the operator becomes (in the case of the second integral)

$$\int\int (\quad) \, dxdx = \frac{1}{D^2} = D^{-2} \tag{7-18}$$

It should be noted that D is not an algebraic quantity but denotes an *operation* to be performed on the variable following it. However, the D operator can be shown to satisfy the usual algebraic laws relating to addition, subtraction, and multiplication. Thus, the D operator can be manipulated algebraically, and a differential equation in operator notation is essentially algebraic in nature. Hence, the use of operators is a useful tool that permits certain higher-order differential equations to be replaced by algebraic equations which are more easily handled.

EXAMPLE 7-11

Express the equation $(d^2y/dx^2) + 5(dy/dx) + 6y = 0$ in D operator notation.

SOLUTION:

Substituting according to Eq. (7-16), we have

$$D^2y + 5Dy + 6y = 0$$

This may be written in factored form as

$$(D^2 + 5D + 6)y = 0$$

The expression within the parentheses, $D^2 + 5D + 6$, may be regarded as a differential operator which is applied to the dependent variable y.

EXAMPLE 7-12

Express the equation $3(dy/dx) + 4y - \int ydx = 0$ in operator form.

SOLUTION:

Substituting the differential operator gives

$$3Dy + 4y - \frac{y}{D} = 0$$

$$\left(3D + 4 - \frac{1}{D}\right)y = 0$$

The operator term may be simplified algebraically giving the result

$$(3D^2 + 4D - 1)y = 0$$

7-9 SECOND-ORDER EQUATIONS WITH CONSTANT COEFFICIENTS

Many differential equations in science and engineering are second- or higher-order equations with *constant coefficients*. For example, a second-order linear differential equation with constant coefficients has the form

$$\frac{d^2 y}{dx^2} + p \frac{dy}{dx} + qy = f(x) \tag{7-19}$$

where p and q are constants and $f(x)$ is either a constant or a function of the independent variable x. When the right side of such an equation is equal to zero, the equation is referred to as *homogeneous* and, using operator notation, is written as

$$(D^2 + pD + q)y = 0 \tag{7-20}$$

To develop a method for solving homogeneous equations, let us consider an equation similar to Eq. (7-20) but of the first order.

$$\frac{dy}{dx} + py = 0 \tag{7-21}$$

By the method of separable variables, we may obtain the solution to Eq. (7-21) as

$$y = Ce^{-px} \tag{7-22}$$

where C is an arbitrary constant.

This result suggests that we try an exponential relation of similar form

$$y = Ce^{mx} \tag{7-23}$$

as a solution of Eq. (7-20). The quantity C is again an arbitrary constant of integration, while m is a constant which is evaluated in obtaining the general solution. If Eq. (7-23) is indeed a solution of Eq. (7-20), the expression Ce^{mx} and its derivatives must satisfy Eq. (7-20) when they are substituted in it. Taking successive derivatives of Eq. (7-23), we obtain

$$\frac{dy}{dx} = Cme^{mx} \qquad \frac{d^2y}{dx^2} = Cm^2e^{mx} \qquad (7\text{-}24)$$

Substituting these expressions in Eq. (7-20), we have

$$Cm^2e^{mx} + Cpme^{mx} + Cqe^{mx} = 0 \qquad (7\text{-}25)$$

Factoring Eq. (7-25) gives

$$Ce^{mx}(m^2 + pm + q) = 0 \qquad (7\text{-}26)$$

Since our assumed solution is Ce^{mx}, then e^{mx} must be other than zero. Hence, for Eq. (7-26) to be an identity, it follows that

$$m^2 + pm + q = 0 \qquad (7\text{-}27)$$

Equation (7-27) is called the *auxiliary equation* and may be solved by ordinary algebraic means to yield the values of the two roots, m_1 and m_2. Substituting m_1 and m_2 in Eq. (7-23), we obtain two solutions of Eq. (7-20) as follows:

$$y = C_1e^{m_1x} \quad \text{and} \quad y = C_2e^{m_2x} \qquad (7\text{-}28)$$

It is a general property of homogeneous differential equations that the sum of the solutions of Eq. (7-28) is also a solution. Therefore

$$y = C_1e^{m_1x} + C_2e^{m_2x} \qquad (7\text{-}29)$$

is a general solution of Eq. (7-20). Note that Eq. (7-29) contains two arbitrary constants as required by the solution of a second-order equation.

The method of solving second-order homogeneous equations which has been developed may be extended to higher-order equations of this type. In general, the procedure for solving homogeneous differential equations is as follows.

1. Write the auxiliary equation by equating to zero the expression obtained by writing m in place of D in the given equation.
2. Solve the auxiliary equation for its roots, obtaining

$$m_1, m_2, m_3, \text{ etc.}$$

3. Write the general solution as

$$y = C_1e^{m_1x} + C_2e^{m_2x} + \cdots + C_ne^{m_nx}$$

4. If a particular solution is required, solve for the arbitrary constants by substituting the appropriate boundary conditions in the general solution and its derivatives.

EXAMPLE 7-13

Find the particular solution for the differential equation

$$2\frac{d^2 i}{dt^2} + 8\frac{di}{dt} + 6i = 0$$

given the initial conditions $i = 10$ and $di/dt = 0$ at $t = 0$.

SOLUTION:

After dividing by 2, the equation may be written in operator form as

$$(D^2 + 4D + 3)i = 0$$

The corresponding auxiliary equation is

$$m^2 + 4m + 3 = 0$$

The roots of this quadratic equation are

$$m_1 = \frac{-4 + \sqrt{16 - 12}}{2} = -1$$

$$m_2 = \frac{-4 - \sqrt{16 - 12}}{2} = -3$$

The general solution is then

$$i = C_1 e^{-t} + C_2 e^{-3t}$$

To evaluate C_1 and C_2, we substitute $i = 10$ and $t = 0$ in the general solution. Then

$$10 = C_1 + C_2$$

The first derivative of the general solution is

$$\frac{di}{dt} = -C_1 e^{-t} - 3C_2 e^{-3t}$$

Applying the second initial condition, we have

$$0 = -C_1 - 3C_2$$
$$C_1 = -3C_2$$

Hence

$$10 = -3C_2 + C_2$$
$$C_2 = -5$$
$$C_1 = 15$$

Thus, the particular solution is

$$i = 15e^{-t} - 5e^{-3t}$$

EXAMPLE 7-14

Find the general solution for the differential equation

$$(D^3 + 3D^2 - D - 3)y = 0$$

SOLUTION:

The corresponding auxiliary equation is

$$m^3 + 3m^2 - m - 3 = 0$$

By factoring, the roots of the auxiliary equation are

$$m = 1, -1, -3$$

The general solution is then

$$y = C_1e^x + C_2e^{-x} + C_3e^{-3x}$$

We may verify by differentiation and substitution that the above is indeed a solution of the given differential equation.

7-10   EQUAL ROOTS

In some homogeneous equations, the auxiliary equation will have two or more equal roots (as well as possibly other single roots). If a second-order equation has two equal roots $m_1 = m_2$, then, according to Eq. (7-29), the general solution with its two arbitrary constants has the form

$$y = C_1e^{m_1x} + C_2e^{m_2x}$$

Since $m_1 = m_2$, then

$$y = (C_1 + C_2)e^{m_1x}$$
$$= C_3e^{m_1x} \qquad\qquad (7\text{-}30)$$

where $C_3 = C_1 + C_2$. However, Eq. (7-30) no longer represents the general solution since the general solution of a second-order equation must contain two arbitrary constants.

If we have equal roots, the auxiliary equation is of the form

$$m^2 - 2m_1 m + m_1^2 = 0 \qquad (7\text{-}31)$$

Factoring Eq. (7-31) yields two equal roots $m = m_1$. This implies that the original differential equation is

$$(D^2 - 2m_1 D + m_1^2)y = 0 \qquad (7\text{-}32)$$

It can be shown by rigorous methods that a general solution involving equal roots is obtained by multiplying the repeating terms of the solution by successively higher powers of the independent variables. Thus, the solution of Eq. (7-32) is

$$y = C_1 e^{m_1 x} + C_2 x e^{m_2 x} \qquad (7\text{-}33)$$

That (7-33) is the general solution may be verified by differentiating and substituting in Eq. (7-32).

EXAMPLE 7-15

Find the general solution of the equation

$$(D^2 + 6D + 9)y = 0$$

SOLUTION:

The corresponding auxiliary equation is

$$m^2 + 6m + 9 = 0$$

By factoring, the roots of the auxiliary equation are

$$m_{1,2} = -3, -3$$

From Eq. (7-33), the general solution is

$$y = C_1 e^{-3x} + C_2 x e^{-3x}$$

7-11   COMPLEX ROOTS

In some homogeneous equations, the auxiliary equation will have roots which are complex quantities. If the coefficients p and q in Eq. (7-20) are real numbers (as is invariably the case in practical problems), then the complex roots m_1 and m_2 will occur in conjugate pairs. Thus

$$m_1 = a + jb \qquad m_2 = a - jb \tag{7-34}$$

The general solution of a homogeneous equation given by Eq. (7-29) is applicable in this case. Therefore, we can write the solution

$$
\begin{aligned}
y &= C_1 e^{(a+jb)x} + C_2 e^{(a-jb)x} \\
&= e^{ax}(C_1 e^{jbx} + C_2 e^{-jbx})
\end{aligned}
\tag{7-35}
$$

The solution given by Eq. (7-35) contains imaginary quantities and is difficult to interpret. Since this type of solution frequently occurs in actual problems, it is desirable to arrange the result in a form which does not involve imaginary terms. This can be done by means of mathematical relationships known as *Euler's identities*. These identities are

$$e^{jbx} = \cos bx + j \sin bx \tag{7-36}$$

$$e^{-jbx} = \cos bx - j \sin bx \tag{7-37}$$

Substituting Eqs. (7-36) and (7-37) in Eq. (7-35), the solution becomes

$$
\begin{aligned}
y &= e^{ax}[C_1(\cos bx + j \sin bx) + C_2(\cos bx - j \sin bx)] \\
&= e^{ax}[(C_1 + C_2) \cos bx + j(C_1 - C_2) \sin bx]
\end{aligned}
\tag{7-38}
$$

Since the constants C_1 and C_2 are arbitrary, they need not necessarily be real. If we should let $C_1 = \frac{1}{2}(A - jB)$ and $C_2 = \frac{1}{2}(A + jB)$, then the solution reduces to

$$y = e^{ax}(A \cos bx + B \sin bx) \tag{7-39}$$

Therefore, when a pair of complex roots appears in the solution of the auxiliary equation, the corresponding part of the solution of the differential equation may be immediately written in the form given by Eq. (7-39).

Alternately, we may express Eq. (7-39) as a single sinusoid having some initial phase angle. Referring to the phasor diagram in Fig. 7-3, we see that

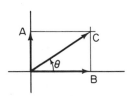

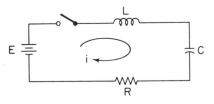

FIGURE 7-3   Phasor diagram.   FIGURE 7-4   Series *RLC* circuit.

the two terms of Eq. (7-39) may be combined vectorially, and Eq. (7-39) may then be written in the form

$$y = Ce^{ax} \sin(bx + \theta) \qquad (7\text{-}40)$$

where

$$C = \sqrt{A^2 + B^2} \qquad \theta = \arctan(A/B) \qquad (7\text{-}41)$$

In the solution given by Eq. (7-40), C and θ are the arbitrary constants which must be evaluated to obtain a particular solution.

EXAMPLE 7-16

Find the general solution of the differential equation

$$\frac{d^2y}{dx^2} + 4\frac{dy}{dx} + 13y = 0$$

SOLUTION:

The corresponding auxiliary equation is

$$m^2 + 4m + 13 = 0$$

Using the quadratic formula, the roots of the auxiliary equation are

$$m = \frac{-4 \pm \sqrt{4^2 - (4)(13)}}{2} = -2 \pm j3$$

From Eq. (7-35), the general solution is

$$y = e^{-2x}(C_1 e^{j3x} + C_2 e^{-j3x})$$

Using Eqs. (7-39) and (7-40), the solution may be written as either

$$y = e^{-2x}(A \cos 3x + B \sin 3x)$$

or

$$y = Ce^{-2x} \sin(3x + \theta)$$

In Eq. (7-20), it is possible for the coefficient p of the first derivative to be zero. In this special case, the auxiliary equation reduces to $m^2 + q = 0$. The roots are now imaginary numbers and we may write them as $m_{1,2} = \pm jb$ where $b = \sqrt{q}$. The solution given by Eq. (7-39) may be applied by setting the real part a of the complex root equal to zero. Thus, for imaginary roots, we have as the general solution

$$y = A \cos bx + B \sin bx \qquad (7\text{-}42)$$

7-12 SECOND-ORDER SYSTEMS

The behavior of a number of simple physical systems can be described by *second-order* homogeneous equations. Systems of this type are characterized by elements that can store energy in two different forms and are known as *second-order systems*. Examples are a mechanical system possessing both potential and kinetic energies, and a resonant electrical network with energy contained in both magnetic and electric fields.

In the discussion of second-order equations in Sections 7-9, 7-10, and 7-11, we observed that a second-order system can exhibit various forms of behavior depending upon the relative values of its parameters. In order to better understand second-order equations and their solution, two familiar systems will be studied in detail. These system are a simple series electrical circuit and a vibrating mass–spring system. In the following sections the differential equations describing these systems will be formulated from known physical laws, and particular solutions will be obtained illustrating the various forms of behavior.

7-13 SERIES *RLC* CIRCUIT

Figure 7-4 shows a circuit containing a resistor, a capacitor, and an inductor which are connected in series to a dc voltage E at a time $t = 0$. We are interested in determining the general equation for current in the circuit immediately after the switch is closed. Applying Kirchhoff's voltage law, the voltages around the circuit with the switch closed are related by the equation

$$L\frac{di}{dt} + Ri + \frac{1}{C}\int i\,dt = E \qquad (7\text{-}43)$$

Differentiating both sides of Eq. (7-43) and dividing each term by L gives the second-order homogeneous equation

$$\frac{d^2i}{dt^2} + \frac{R}{L}\frac{di}{dt} + \frac{i}{LC} = 0 \qquad (7\text{-}44)$$

The corresponding auxiliary equation is

$$m^2 + \frac{R}{L}m + \frac{1}{LC} = 0 \qquad (7\text{-}45)$$

The roots of the auxiliary equation may be written as

$$m_{1,2} = \frac{-R}{2L} \pm \sqrt{\left(\frac{R}{2L}\right)^2 - \frac{1}{LC}} \tag{7-46}$$

The general solution of the differential equation of the current is

$$i = C_1 e^{m_1 t} + C_2 e^{m_2 t} \tag{7-47}$$

The arbitrary constants C_1 and C_2 may be evaluated through a knowledge of the circuit conditions when $t = 0$. At the instant the switch is closed there can be no current, since the inductor prevents any instantaneous increase in current. If the capacitor is initially uncharged, then we have the conditions

$$i = 0 \qquad q = \int i\,dt = 0 \tag{7-48}$$

at $t = 0$. Substituting the initial conditions into Eq. (7-43), we obtain the added condition

$$\frac{di}{dt} = \frac{E}{L} \quad \text{at} \quad t = 0 \tag{7-49}$$

Applying the initial condition $i = 0$ at $t = 0$ to Eq. (7-47), we obtain $C_1 = -C_2$. Therefore, Eq. (7-47) becomes

$$i = C_1(e^{m_1 t} - e^{m_2 t}) \tag{7-50}$$

The constant C_1 may be evaluated by differentiating Eq. (7-50) and applying the initial condition of Eq. (7-49). Thus

$$\frac{di}{dt} = C_1(m_1 e^{m_1 t} - m_2 e^{m_2 t})$$

Then, at $t = 0$

$$\frac{E}{L} = C_1(m_1 - m_2) \tag{7-51}$$

Substituting the values of m_1 and m_2 given in Eq. (7-46) into Eq. (7-51) gives the result

$$C_1 = \frac{E}{\sqrt{R^2 - 4L/C}} \tag{7-52}$$

Substituting Eq. (7-52) into Eq. (7-50), we obtain the desired current as

$$i = \frac{E}{\sqrt{R^2 - 4L/C}}(e^{m_1 t} - e^{m_2 t}) \tag{7-53}$$

where m_1 and m_2 are defined by Eq. (7-46). The nature of the current depends on whether the roots m_1 and m_2 are: I—real and unequal; II—complex; III —imaginary; or IV—real and equal.

CASE I: ROOTS REAL AND UNEQUAL

When the components of the circuit have values such that

$$\left(\frac{R}{2L}\right)^2 > \frac{1}{LC}$$

the values of m_1 and m_2 are *real negative* numbers. Upon closing the switch, there will be a single surge of current which will rise and then decrease as the capacitor voltage approaches the applied voltage. This is referred to as the *overdamped case*, since the current decreases rather slowly to its final value.

EXAMPLE 7-17

Determine the current i in the series RLC circuit of Fig. 7-4 when $R = 8$ ohms, $L = 1$ henry, $C = 0.5$ farad, and $E = 1$ volt.

SOLUTION:

Using Eq. (7-44), the differential equation describing the current is

$$\frac{d^2 i}{dt^2} + 8\frac{di}{dt} + 2i = 0$$

The corresponding auxiliary equation is

$$m^2 + 8m + 2 = 0$$

This equation has roots $m_1 = -0.26$ and $m_2 = -7.74$. The general solution as given by Eq. (7-50) is

$$i = C_1(e^{-0.26t} - e^{-7.74t})$$

Evaluating C_1 according to Eq. (7-52), the particular solution is

$$i = 0.134(e^{-0.26t} - e^{-7.74t}) \quad \text{amperes}$$

A plot of the two components of the current and their combination is shown in Fig. 7-5.

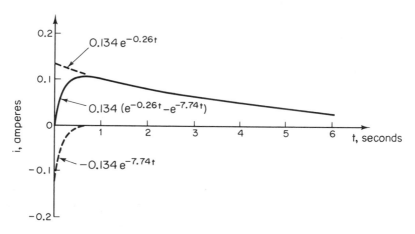

FIGURE 7–5   Current in Example 7-17 (overdamped case).

CASE II: ROOTS COMPLEX

If the series RLC circuit has components such that

$$\left(\frac{R}{2L}\right)^2 < \frac{1}{LC},$$

then the roots of the auxiliary equations are *complex* and may be written as

$$m_{1,2} = -\frac{R}{2L} \pm j\sqrt{\frac{1}{LC} - \left(\frac{R}{2L}\right)^2} \tag{7-54}$$

These roots may be substituted in Eq. (7-53) and the equation written in factored form as

$$i = \frac{E}{\sqrt{4L/C - R^2}} e^{-Rt/2L} \left[\exp\left(j\sqrt{1/LC - (R/2L)^2}\right) \right.$$
$$\left. -\exp\left(-j\sqrt{1/LC - (R/2L)^2}\right) \right] \tag{7-55}$$

The current may also be expressed in the form given by Eq. (7-39), in which case

$$i = e^{-Rt/2L}\left(A \cos\sqrt{1/LC - (R/2L)^2}\, t + B \sin\sqrt{1/LC - (R/2L)^2}\, t\right)$$
$$\tag{7-56}$$

Applying the initial condition $i = 0$ at $t = 0$, Eq. (7-56) becomes

$$i = Be^{-Rt/2L} \sin \sqrt{1/LC - (R/2L)^2}\, t \qquad (7\text{-}57)$$

Differentiating Eq. (7-57) and applying the initial condition $(di/dt) = E/L$ at $t = 0$, the arbitrary constant B becomes

$$B = \frac{2E}{\sqrt{4L/C - R^2}} \qquad (7\text{-}58)$$

The equation for the current is then

$$i = \frac{2E}{\sqrt{4L/C - R^2}} \, e^{-Rt/2L} \sin \sqrt{1/LC - (R/2L)^2}\, t \qquad (7\text{-}59)$$

This expression is the product of three factors: a *constant*; a decreasing exponential called the *damping factor*; and a *sinusoidal oscillation*. The result is a current function which approaches zero in an oscillatory manner. This is the *underdamped case* and the result is called a *damped oscillation*.

EXAMPLE 7-18

Determine the current i in the series RLC circuit of Fig. 7-4 when $R = 1$ ohm, $L = 1$ henry, $C = 0.5$ farad, and $E = 1$ volt.

SOLUTION:

Substituting the above values in Eq. (7-59), the differential equation describing the current is

$$\frac{d^2 i}{dt^2} + \frac{di}{dt} + 2i = 0$$

The corresponding auxiliary equation is

$$m^2 + m + 2 = 0$$

which has roots $m_1 = -0.5 + j1.32$ and $m_2 = -0.5 - j1.32$. From Eq. (7-55) the particular solution is

$$i = 0.755\, e^{-0.5t} \sin 1.32\, t \quad \text{amperes}$$

A plot of the factors in the solution and their product is shown in Fig. 7-6. This result is typical of the response of an underdamped system.

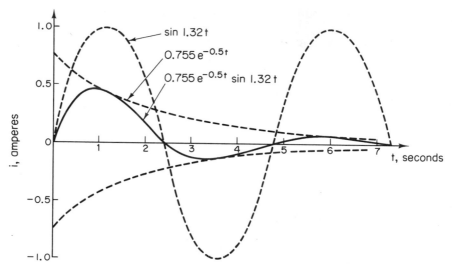

FIGURE 7-6 Current in Example 7-18 (underdamped case).

CASE III: ROOTS IMAGINARY

If the series circuit consists only of an inductor and a capacitor, the Case II analysis may be applied by taking $R = 0$. In this case, the roots of the auxiliary equation do not contain a real part and are imaginary numbers. Thus, from Eq. (7-46)

$$m_{1,2} = \pm j \sqrt{\frac{1}{LC}} \tag{7-60}$$

If Eq. (7-59) is simplified by setting $R = 0$, the resulting current is a sinusoid

$$i = \frac{E}{\sqrt{L/C}} \sin \frac{t}{\sqrt{LC}} \tag{7-61}$$

This result represents the *undamped case*. When the circuit is shock-excited by the suddenly applied voltage, it will oscillate indefinitely at a frequency $(1/\sqrt{LC})$ rad/second. Obviously this case is hypothetical since some resistance is always present in a passive network. In practice, a circuit of this type would exhibit a slight damping and the oscillations would gradually decay in amplitude.

CASE IV: ROOTS REAL AND EQUAL

If the circuit has component values such that

$$\left(\frac{R}{2L}\right)^2 = \frac{1}{LC},$$

then the roots of the auxiliary equation will be *real* and *equal* since the radical term of Eq. (7-46) equals zero. Thus

$$m_1 = m_2 = -\frac{R}{2L} \tag{7-62}$$

Using Eq. (7-33), the general solution for the current is

$$i = C_1 e^{m_1 t} + C_2 t e^{m_1 t} \tag{7-63}$$

Applying the initial condition $i = 0$ at $t = 0$, C_1 is found to be zero. Therefore

$$i = C_2 t e^{m_1 t} \tag{7-64}$$

Differentiating Eq. (7-64) and applying the condition $di/dt = E/L$ at $t = 0$ gives

$$\frac{di}{dt} = C_2(e^{m_1 t} + m_1 t e^{m_1 t}) = \frac{E}{L} \tag{7-65}$$

The constant C_2 is evaluated by substituting $-R/2L$ for m_1 and letting $t = 0$, which gives

$$C_2 = \frac{E}{L} \tag{7-66}$$

The particular solution is then

$$i = \frac{E}{L} t e^{-Rt/2L} \tag{7-67}$$

With this circuit condition, an arbitrarily small change (in the proper direction) of the circuit parameters will cause the response to become a damped oscillation. This borderline condition is called *critical damping* and represents the transition point between the overdamped and underdamped cases.

EXAMPLE 7-19

Determine the current in the series *RLC* circuit of Fig. 7-4 when $R = 2\sqrt{2}$ ohms, $L = 1$ henry, $C = 0.5$ farad, and $E = 1$ volt.

SOLUTION:

The differential equation describing the current is

$$\frac{d^2 i}{dt^2} + 2\sqrt{2}\frac{di}{dt} + 2i = 0$$

The corresponding auxiliary equation is

$$m^2 + 2\sqrt{2}\, m + 2 = 0$$

The roots are $m_1 = m_2 = -\sqrt{2}$. Since the roots are real and equal, the particular solution is given by Eq. (7-67). Therefore

$$i = te^{-\sqrt{2}t} \text{ amperes}$$

The response, shown in Fig. 7-7, represents the critically damped case.

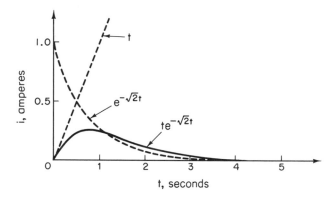

FIGURE 7-7   Current in Example 7-19 (critically damped case).

A comparison of the results of Examples 7-17, 7-18, and 7-19 shows the effect of various degrees of damping on the circuit response.

7-14 VIBRATING SPRING

There is a mechanical analogy to the *RLC* circuit which we have just considered: simple harmonic motion with a damping force. Consider the simple mass–spring–damper system shown in Fig. 7-8 in which a weight, W, is suspended on a spring from a rigid frame. The spring will obey Hooke's law: if it is stretched or compressed, its change in length is proportional to the force exerted upon the spring. The so-called "stiffness" of the spring is represented by a spring constant, k, defined as the ratio of the force exerted to the displacement produced by the force. Thus

$$f_s = -kx \tag{7-68}$$

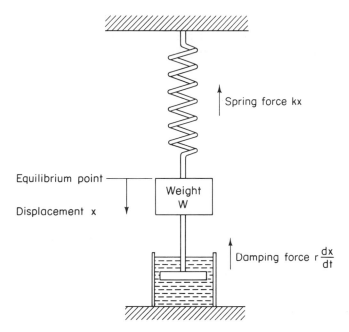

FIGURE 7–8   Vibrating spring system.

where

$$f_s = \text{spring force, lb}$$
$$x = \text{displacement, ft}$$
$$k = \text{spring constant, lb/ft}$$

Since the force f_s tends to oppose the displacement, it is opposite in sign to x.

The vibration of a spring with a suspended weight is retarded by damping forces, such as air resistance. The damping force, represented by the dashpot in Fig. 7-8, does not act on the weight as long as the weight is not in motion. However, as soon as the weight moves, the damping force is proportional to the velocity. The damping force is also negative because it acts against the velocity. Therefore

$$f_d = -r\frac{dx}{dt} \qquad (7\text{-}69)$$

where

$$f_d = \text{damping force, lb}$$
$$r = \text{damping constant, lb/ft/s}$$
$$\frac{dx}{dt} = \text{velocity, ft/s}$$

Assume that the weight in Fig. 7-8 is initially at rest in a static equilibrium state. The weight is then displaced a distance x from the equilibrium point and then released. According to Newton's Second Law of Motion, the sum of the external forces applied to a free body must equal the product of the mass of the body and its acceleration. Therefore, we may write a force–balance equation around the equilibrium point as

$$f_s + f_d = \frac{W}{g}\frac{d^2x}{dt^2} \tag{7-70}$$

where

$$\frac{d^2x}{dt^2} = \text{acceleration, ft/s}^2$$

Substituting Eqs. (7-68) and (7-69) into Eq. (7-70), we have

$$-kx - r\frac{dx}{dt} = \frac{W}{g}\frac{d^2x}{dt^2} \tag{7-71}$$

Rearranging Eq. (7-71), we obtain

$$\frac{d^2x}{dt^2} + \frac{rg}{W}\frac{dx}{dt} + \frac{kg}{W}x = 0 \tag{7-72}$$

Equation (7-72) is the differential equation of motion. It is a linear, second-order homogeneous equation whose solution will be an expression for the instantaneous displacement of the weight as a function of time.

If Eq. (7-72) is compared with Eq. (7-44), which is the differential equation for the current in the series RLC circuit, we note that the equations are both second-order and homogeneous, and that they differ only in the dependent variable and the equation parameters. Hence the solutions of Eq. (7-72) will be of the same form as the solutions of Eq. (7-44).

The roots of the auxiliary equation of Eq. (7-72) are found to be

$$m_{1,2} = -\frac{rg}{2W} \pm \sqrt{\left(\frac{rg}{2W}\right)^2 - \frac{kg}{W}} \tag{7-73}$$

The general solution of the differential equation of motion is

$$x = C_1 e^{m_1 t} + C_2 e^{m_2 t} \tag{7-74}$$

As in the previous example, the arbitrary constants C_1 and C_2 are evaluated through a knowledge of the initial conditions of the system. The behavior of the system may be overdamped, underdamped, or critically damped depending upon the relative values of the parameters W, k, and r.

EXAMPLE 7-20

The spring shown in Fig. 7-8 is such that it is stretched 3 inches by a 6-pound weight. A 12-pound weight is attached to the spring and pulled down 4 inches below the equilibrium point. If the weight is started upward with a velocity of 2 feet per second, describe its ensuing motion.

SOLUTION:

Assume the system damping, r, is negligible. The spring constant k is found using Eq. (7-68)

$$k = \frac{f_s}{x} = \frac{6}{1/4} = 24 \text{ lb/ft}$$

Substituting the system parameters in Eq. (7-72) with $r = 0$, the differential equation of motion is

$$\frac{d^2x}{dt^2} + \frac{(24)(32)}{12}x = 0$$

The auxiliary equation is

$$m^2 + 64 = 0$$

This equation has roots $m_1 = j8$ and $m_2 = -j8$. Since the roots are imaginary, the motion is an undamped oscillation. In this case Eq. (7-39) is used without the exponential term and the equation of motion is

$$x = A \cos 8t + B \sin 8t$$

Applying the initial condition $x = -4$ inches at $t = 0$, the arbitrary constant A is evaluated as -4 inches. To apply the initial condition, $(dx/dt) = 2$ ft/s at $t - 0$, the general solution is differentiated giving

$$\frac{dx}{dt} = 2 = -8A \sin 8t + 8B \cos 8t$$

Evaluating the above equation at $t = 0$ yields

$$8B = 2$$
$$B = \tfrac{1}{4} \text{ ft} = 3 \text{ inches}$$

Substituting the values of A and B, the particular solution is

$$x = -4 \cos 8t + 3 \sin 8t \text{ inches}$$

Using Eq. (7-40), the motion may be expressed as a single sinusoid

$$x = C \sin (bx + \theta)$$

where

$$C = \sqrt{A^2 + B^2} = \sqrt{4^2 + 3^2} = 5 \text{ inches}$$

and

$$\theta = \arctan \frac{-4}{3} = \arctan(-1.33) = -53° = -0.925 \text{ rad}$$

Substituting the values of C and θ, the solution is

$$x = 5 \sin(8t - 0.925) \text{ inches}$$

The motion of the weight is therefore a sine wave having peak amplitudes of 5 inches above and below the equilibrium point, a frequency of 8 rad/s (1.27 Hz), and a lagging phase angle of 53°. The graph of the motion is shown in Fig. 7-9.

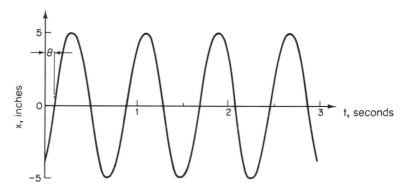

FIGURE 7-9   Vibration of spring and weight in Example 7-20.

EXAMPLE 7-21

A dashpot having a damping coefficient $r = 0.6$ lb/ft/s is added to the spring and mass in Ex. 7-20. Describe the motion if the initial displacement and velocity are as before.

SOLUTION:

The differential equation of motion is

$$\frac{d^2x}{dt^2} + 1.6 \frac{dx}{dt} + 64x = 0$$

The auxiliary equation is

$$m^2 + 1.6m + 64 = 0$$

This equation has roots $m_{1,2} = -0.8 \pm j7.97$ which, for convenience, are taken as approximately $-0.8 \pm j8$. From Eq. (7-39), the general solution is

$$x = e^{-0.8t}(A \cos 8t + B \sin 8t)$$

Applying the initial conditions in the same manner as in Ex. 7-20, the value of the arbitrary constant A remains -4 inches. Differentiating the general solution yields

$$\frac{dx}{dt} = -0.8e^{-0.8t} A \cos 8t - 8Ae^{-0.8t} \sin 8t$$

$$-0.8e^{-0.8t} B \sin 8t + 8Be^{-0.8t} \cos 8t$$

Using the initial condition $(dx/dt) = 2$ at $t = 0$ gives

$$2 = -0.8A + 8B = -0.8(-\tfrac{1}{3}) + 8B$$

$$B = 0.216 \text{ ft} = 2.6 \text{ inches}$$

The particular solution is then

$$x = e^{-0.8t}(-4 \cos 8t + 2.6 \sin 8t) \text{ inches}$$

Using the form of Eq. (7-40) and solving for C and θ, the solution is

$$x = 4.78e^{-0.8t} \sin (8t - 0.995) \text{ inches}$$

In this example the system is underdamped and the motion is the damped oscillation shown in Fig. 7-10.

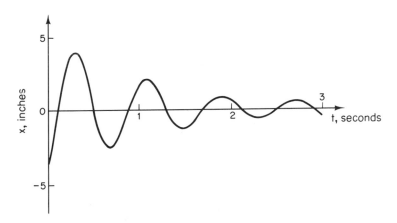

FIGURE 7–10   Vibration of spring and weight in Example 7-21.

7-15 NONHOMOGENEOUS EQUATIONS

In the preceding sections, we have considered differential equations in which a summation of terms containing the dependent variable and its derivatives is equated to zero. If the summation is not equal to zero, the differential equation is known as a *nonhomogeneous equation*. For example, the second-order equation

$$a\frac{d^2x}{dt^2} + b\frac{dx}{dt} + cx = f(t) \tag{7-75}$$

is nonhomogeneous. If the independent variable t represents time, then the dependent variable x varies with time. The right side of the equation represents an external energy source that is applied to the system represented by the differential equation. For this reason, $f(t)$ is commonly referred to as a *forcing function*.

Although a forcing function may conceivably be any arbitrary function of time, certain easily described functions are frequently of interest in the study of engineering problems. These functions are the sine wave, square wave, triangular wave, and a step input. Figure 7-11 illustrates these waveforms.

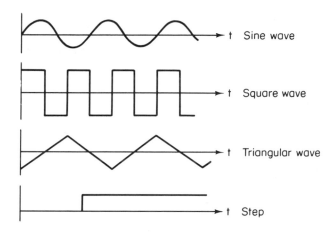

FIGURE 7–11   Common forcing functions.

As we have seen, the solution of a *homogeneous* differential equation is *independent* of any forcing function, and gives zero when substituted into the equation. If the real parts of the roots of the auxiliary equation are negative, the solution approaches zero as the independent variable tends to infinity. Thus, the solution is entirely transient in nature.

The presence of a forcing function in the *nonhomogeneous* equation causes an *additional* solution to exist. This solution is present after the transient solution has vanished and is the steady-state solution. By superposition, the total solution is the sum of the transient and steady-state solutions.

Solving nonhomogeneous equations requires determining both the transient and steady-state solutions. The transient solution is obtained by treating the equation as homogeneous. The steady-state solution requires an expression which, when substituted into the left side of the differential equation, will produce the expression of the right side.

Referring to the series RL circuit in Section 7-7, we see that the switched battery voltage represents a forcing function and the solution given by Eq. (7-13) contains both transient and steady-state components. Thus, the differential equation in this example is a first-order nonhomogeneous equation which was solved completely by simply separating the variables. In general, obtaining the steady-state solution of a differential equation is a complicated process and the methods are beyond our objectives in this chapter. As we shall see in the next two chapters, the analog-computer solution of a nonhomogeneous equation differs little from the solution of a homogeneous equation. In neither case is it necessary to know analytic methods of solution in order to apply the analog computer.

However, we can illustrate the solution of a nonhomogeneous equation by an intuitive approach incorporating elementary ac circuit theory. A series RL circuit excited by a sinusoidal voltage $E \sin \omega t$ is shown in Fig. 7-12. The voltage equation after the switch is closed is

$$L\frac{di}{dt} + Ri = E \sin \omega t \tag{7-76}$$

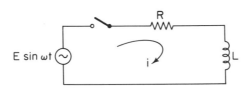

FIGURE 7–12   Series RL circuit with sinusoidal voltage source.

The current i is composed of two components: a transient current i_t and the steady-state current i_s. To solve for the transient current, we substitute zero for the excitation in Eq. (7-76). The result is a first-order homogeneous equation which, in operator notation, is

$$\left(D + \frac{R}{L}\right)i_t = 0 \tag{7-77}$$

The root of the corresponding auxiliary equation is $m = -R/L$ and the solution of Eq. (7-77) is

$$i_t = Ke^{-Rt/L}$$

From ac circuit theory, the steady-state current in a series circuit excited by a sine wave of voltage $E \sin \omega t$ is

$$i_s = \frac{E}{Z} \sin (\omega t - \phi) \tag{7-78}$$

where Z is the circuit impedance and ϕ is the phase angle by which the current lags the applied voltage. Drawing an impedance triangle, we have

$$Z = \sqrt{R^2 + (\omega L)^2} \quad \text{ohms} \tag{7-79}$$

and

$$\phi = \arctan (\omega L / R) \quad \text{radians} \tag{7-80}$$

The complete general solution may be written as

$$i = i_t + i_s = K e^{-Rt/L} + \frac{E}{Z} \sin (\omega t - \phi) \tag{7-81}$$

To find the value of the arbitrary constant K, we must consider the initial conditions at the instant when the switch closes. If it is assumed that both the applied voltage and current are zero at the time of closure, then at $t = 0$

$$i = 0 = K e^0 + \frac{E}{Z} \sin (-\phi)$$

$$K = -\frac{E}{Z} \sin (-\phi) = \frac{E}{Z} \sin \phi = \frac{E \omega L}{Z^2} \tag{7-82}$$

where $\sin \phi = \omega L / Z$. The particular solution of Eq. (7-76) may now be written. Thus

$$i = \frac{E \omega L}{Z^2} e^{-Rt/L} + \frac{E}{Z} \sin (\omega t - \phi) \tag{7-83}$$

Equation (7-83) reveals that the current is a sinusoidal function superimposed on an exponential transient.

We should note that the form of the transient response of a system is independent of the type of forcing function and is determined entirely from the system parameters. The initial magnitude of the transient response is affected by the initial conditions. On the other hand, the steady-state response is determined by the form of the input as well as the system parameters.

EXAMPLE 7-22

Determine the current in the series RL circuit of Fig. 7-12 when $R = 100$ ohms, $L = 0.1$ henry, and the applied voltage is 10 sin 628t volts.

SOLUTION:

$$Z = \sqrt{100^2 + (62.8)^2} = 118 \text{ ohms}$$

$$\phi = \arctan \frac{62.8}{100} = 32.1° = 0.561 \text{ radian}$$

Substituting in Eq. (7-83), we obtain the result

$$i = 45.1e^{-1000t} + 84.8 \sin(628t - 0.561) \quad \text{milliamperes}$$

The variation of total current with time is shown in Fig. 7-13, together with the contributions due to the transient and steady-state currents.

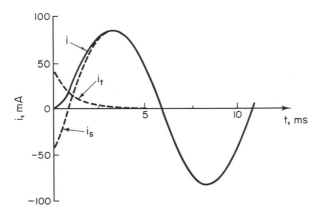

FIGURE 7–13   Current for *RL* circuit of Example 7-22.

PROBLEMS FOR CHAPTER 7

1. What is a differential equation?
2. What is an ordinary differential equation? A partial differential equation?
3. What is the order of a differential equation? The degree of a differential equation?
4. What is the solution of a differential equation?
5. Distinguish between the general solution and the particular solution of a differential equation.

In Problems 6 through 11 show that each equation is a solution of the indicated differential equation.

6. $y = x^2 + 3x$, $\dfrac{dy}{dx} = 2x + 3$

7. $y = \dfrac{t^3}{6} + 10$, $\dfrac{d^2 y}{dt^2} = t$

8. $\theta = 2e^{-t}$, $\dfrac{d\theta}{dt} + \theta = 0$

9. $y = 3e^{-x} + 5e^{2x}$, $\dfrac{d^2y}{dx^2} - \dfrac{dy}{dx} = 2y$

10. $i = C_1 \sin t + C_2 \cos t$, $\dfrac{d^2i}{dt^2} + i = 0$

11. $y = e^{x^2/2}$, $\dfrac{dy}{dx} = xy$

12. If the general solution of $\dfrac{dy}{dx} = x$ is $y = \dfrac{x^2}{2} + C$, find the value of C if $y = 3$ when $x = 2$.

Find the general solution of the equations in Problems 13 through 22.

13. $\dfrac{dy}{dx} = x$ **14.** $\dfrac{dy}{dx} = y$

15. $\dfrac{dy}{dt} = t^3$ **16.** $\dfrac{dy}{dx} = e^x$

17. $\dfrac{dy}{dx} = \dfrac{x}{y}$ **18.** $dy = e^{x+y}\,dx$

19. $4y\,dx = 3x\,dy$ **20.** $\dfrac{1}{2x}\left(\dfrac{dy}{dx}\right) - 2 = 0$

21. $(1 - x)\,y\,dx + (1 + y)x\,dy = 0$ **22.** $\dfrac{dv}{dt} = \sqrt{1 - t}$

Solve the equations in Problems 23 and 24 and sketch the systems of curves represented by the general solutions.

23. $\dfrac{dy}{dx} = \dfrac{1}{2}$ **24.** $\dfrac{d\theta}{dt} = \sin t$

Find the particular solution of the differential equations in Problems 25 through 28 for the indicated boundary conditions.

25. $\dfrac{dy}{dx} = 2x + 4$, $y = 3$ when $x = 0$

26. $\dfrac{dy}{dt} = 1 + \sin t$, $y = 2$ when $t = 0$

27. $e^x \dfrac{dy}{dx} + 1 = 0$, $y \longrightarrow 10$ when $x \longrightarrow \infty$

28. $\dfrac{dq}{dt} + t^2 = 0$, $q = 4$ when $t = 0$

29. A circuit carries a current $i = 6t^2$ amperes. What is the equation of the charge transferred if the current is initiated at time $t = 0$? Make a rough graph showing charge transferred for $0 \le t \le 2$ seconds.

30. A rod is actuated by a motor such that its acceleration over a portion of its path is $2t$ inches/second^2. If the rod starts from rest, what is the equation of its velocity? Make a rough graph showing the acceleration and velocity for $0 \leq t \leq 5$ seconds.

31. The mass shown in Fig. 7-8, page 209, is vibrating such that its velocity is given by $(dx/dt) = 2 \sin 2t$ inches/second. If $x = 1$ inch when $t = \pi/4$ seconds, what is the position when $t = \pi/2$ seconds?

32. The number n of bacteria in a certain culture grows at a rate proportional to n. Derive an equation for n as a function of time, assuming an initial number N_0.

33. If the rate of increase in Problem 32 is 0.5/hour, and N_0 is 100, what is the value of n after 2 hours?

34. Sugar in solution dissolves at a rate proportional to the amount of sugar remaining undissolved. If one pound of undissolved sugar reduces to one-half pound of undissolved sugar in 30 minutes, how much sugar is undissolved at the end of one hour?

35. For the circuit below, at left, derive the equation for the voltage across the capacitor following closing of the switch. Assume that the capacitor is initially uncharged.

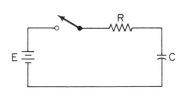 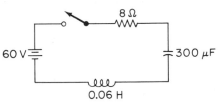

36. An object of weight W is acted upon by a steady force F. If the particle experiences a retarding force proportional to its velocity v, derive an equation for v as a function of time. (*Hint:* Recall Newton's Second Law of Motion.)

37. Make a rough graph of the velocity of the weight in Problem 36 if $W = 32$ pounds, $F = 10$ pounds, and the object starts from rest with a retarding force in pounds equal to 0.1 times the velocity. Assume $0 \leq t \leq 100$ seconds.

Find the general solution of the differential equations in Problems 38 through 46.

38. $\dfrac{d^2 y}{dx^2} - 5\dfrac{dy}{dx} + 6y = 0$

39. $2\dfrac{d^2 x}{dt^2} - 4\dfrac{dx}{dt} + x = 0$

40. $\dfrac{d^2 y}{dx^2} - 4\dfrac{dy}{dx} + 4y = 0$

41. $\dfrac{d^3 y}{dw^3} - 5\dfrac{d^2 y}{dw^2} + 8\dfrac{dy}{dw} - 4y = 0$

42. $\dfrac{d^2 i}{dt^2} + 4i = 0$

43. $\dfrac{d^2 y}{dx^2} - 2\dfrac{dy}{dx} + 2y = 0$

In Problems 44, 45, and 46, assume $y = f(t)$.

44. $(3D^2 + 8D - 3)y = 0$

45. $(D^2 - D + 1)y = 0$

46. $(D^2 + 2D + 10)y = 0$

Find the particular solution of the differential equations in Problems 47, 48, and 49 for the indicated boundary conditions.

47. $\dfrac{d^2 y}{dx^2} - \dfrac{dy}{dx} - 6y = 0,$ $\dfrac{dy}{dx} = 0$ and $y = 5$ when $x = 0$

48. $\dfrac{d^2 q}{dt^2} + \dfrac{dq}{dt} + q = 0,$ $\dfrac{dq}{dt} = 1$ and $q = 2$ when $t = 0$

49. $2\dfrac{d^2 y}{dx^2} + 4\dfrac{dy}{dx} + 4y = 0,$ $\dfrac{dy}{dx} = 3$ and $y = 0$ when $x = 0$

50. For the circuit on p. 219, at right, state the equation for the current after the switch is closed at time $t = 0$. Assume the capacitor is completely discharged prior to closing the switch. Make a rough graph of current versus time.

51. A 4-pound weight stretches a certain spring 1.5 inches. The weight is pulled three inches below its equilibrium point and released. Find the equation of the resulting motion, assuming no damping, and make a rough sketch of the resulting curve.

52. Repeat Problem 51 if a damping force numerically equal to the velocity is present.

53. What must be the value of the coefficient b so that the motion described by the equation

$$\frac{d^2 y}{dt^2} + b\frac{dy}{dt} + 36y = 0$$

is critically damped.

54. An LC series circuit is connected to a 6-volt battery. If $L = 0.01$ henry and $C = 400\mu F$, find the charge q as a function of time. Assume that the capacitor is initially uncharged.

55. In the circuit of Fig. 7-12, find the expression for i for the following conditions: $L = 0.1$ henry, $R = 100$ ohms, $e = 10 \cos 628t$ volts, and $i = 0$ and $e = 10$ at $t = 0$. Plot the current waveform for the first cycle after the switch is closed.

56. Show that the current in the RC series circuit below, left, is given by the expression

$$i = -\frac{\omega CE}{1 + (\omega CR)^2} e^{-t/RC} + \frac{\omega CE}{\sqrt{1 + (\omega CR)^2}} \sin(\omega t + \theta)$$

where $\theta = \arctan 1/\omega CR$. Assume $i = 0$ and $e = 0$ at $t = 0$.

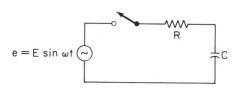

$e = E \sin \omega t$

R

C

θ

57. A circular disk is suspended by a wire as shown in the figure above, at right.

If the disk is twisted through an angle θ and released, it will oscillate with a rotary motion. The differential equation for this motion (neglecting damping) is

$$J\frac{d^2\theta}{dt^2} = -k\theta$$

where J is the moment of inertia of the disk and k is the torsion spring constant of the wire. Derive the equation of motion if $\theta = \theta_o$ and $d\theta/dt = \omega_o$ at time $t = 0$.

8-1 INTRODUCTION

Chapter 7 introduced differential equations as a mathematical means of representing physical systems and of analyzing their dynamic behavior.

In the preceding chapters, we covered linear and non-linear elements which are used in analog computing, and we saw that various mathematical operations such as addition, subtraction, integration, and multiplication are performed by these elements.

In this chapter, the analog computer method is used to solve differential equations. Obviously, certain steps are required before a computer can be switched into COMPUTE and problem solutions obtained in the form of graphs of the variables plotted against time. The operation of preparing a problem for computer solution is known as *programming*. In this context, the programming of an analog computer is much akin to digital computer programming; however, the two operations differ greatly in detail.

Analog computer programming usually involves a series of steps which are listed below.

1. The system differential equations are modified so that they are compatible with the characteristics of the analog computer.
2. A diagram is prepared which shows the computer elements in symbolic form together with their interconnections.

8

PROGRAMMING

3. The elements are wired on the patch board in accord with the computer set up diagram (2 above).
4. The coefficient potentiometers are adjusted to their required settings.

In this chapter, the first two programming steps are considered, but in reverse order. We will assume initially that the equations are in suitable form for the computer, and will develop computer circuits for single first- and second-order equations, as well as the more general case of simultaneous equations. The modification of the problem equations is then taken up, and methods are described for making appropriate changes in the scales of the variables.

The final two steps in the programming procedure are essentially mechanical in nature. Since these procedures have already been described in previous chapters, they will not now be considered further.

8-2 FIRST-ORDER DIFFERENTIAL EQUATIONS

The first-order linear differential equation with constant coefficients has the form

$$a\frac{dx}{dt} + bx = f(t) \qquad (8\text{-}1)$$

where t is the independent variable, x is the dependent variable, a and b are constants, and $f(t)$ is the forcing function.

For the homogeneous case, $f(t) = 0$ and Eq. (8-1) may be written*

$$\frac{dx}{dt} = \dot{x} = -\frac{b}{a}x \qquad (8\text{-}2)$$

We now wish to solve this differential equation for the variable x by means of analog computation.

The two variables in Eq. (8-2) are x and $\dot{x}$. The relation between them can be represented on an analog computer by an integrator. If $\dot{x}$ is fed into an integrator having a gain of one, the integrator output will be $-x$. This is shown in Fig. 8-1.

But we are faced with the question, Where can $\dot{x}$ be obtained? From Eq. (8-2), it can be seen that $\dot{x}$ is simply $-(b/a)x$. Since $-x$ is assumed to be

---

*It is common practice in analog computer programming to use a notation wherein dots are placed above a dependent variable to indicate its derivative with respect to time. Thus $\dot{x} = \dfrac{dx}{dt}$, $\ddot{x} = \dfrac{d^2x}{dt^2}$, $\dddot{x} = \dfrac{d^3x}{dt^3}$, etc.

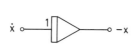

FIGURE 8–1   Integration of $\dot{x}$.

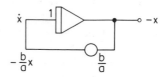

FIGURE 8–2   Computer circuit for solution of homogeneous first-order equations.

available at the integrator output, the output can be multiplied by b/a using a coefficient potentiometer (assuming $(b/a) \leq 1$). This produces $-(b/a)\,x$ at the potentiometer output. Since this is the value needed at the integrator input, the potentiometer output is connected to the integrator input as shown in Fig. 8-2.

If the circuit shown in Fig. 8-2 was set up on the computer and the machine placed in the COMPUTE mode, nothing would happen. This is due to the fact that the integrator output at $t = 0$ is zero, therefore $-x = 0$ and $\dot{x} = 0$. If, however, the integrator output at $t = 0$ were non-zero, that is, if x had some initial value $x(0)$, then a time variation of x and $\dot{x}$ would result. Actually, Eq. (8-2) has infinitely many solutions, since each value of the initial condition produces a unique solution. Referring to Eq. (7-22), we may write the solution of Eq. (8-2) as

$$x = x(0)e^{-(b/a)t} \tag{8-3}$$

where $x(0)$ is the initial value of x evaluated at $t = 0$. For the analog computer solution, $x(0)$ represents the initial-condition voltage applied to the integrator. With a positive initial-condition input, the circuit shown in Fig. 8-2 actually produces the output $-x$. If it is desired to generate $+x$, the initial-condition input voltage should be negative as shown in Figure 8-3.

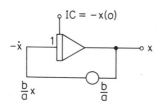

FIGURE 8–3   Computer circuit including initial-condition input.

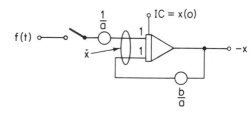

FIGURE 8–4   Computer circuit for solution of nonhomogeneous first-order equations.

The programming method described above is frequently called the *bootstrap technique*. The method assumes that the first derivative dx/dt of the function is available and, when integrated, produces the variable x at the integrator output. This integrator output is then used to generate the derivative with which we started.

As we shall see, this programming technique is not limited to first-order differential equations but is equally applicable to higher-order equations.

The nonhomogeneous first-order equation is programmed in a similar manner. Equation (8-1) is solved for the derivative giving

$$\frac{dx}{dt} = \dot{x} = -\frac{b}{a}x + \frac{1}{a}f(t) \tag{8-4}$$

The assumption is again made that dx/dt is available. The resulting computer circuit is shown in Fig. 8-4. Note that the right-hand side of Eq. (8-4) represents the sum of the two inputs to the integrator. The integrator input $f(t)$ is the forcing function and represents the excitation which is applied to the physical system described by the differential equation.

To illustrate the application of first-order programming, assume that we wish to simulate the behavior of the series RL circuit described in Section 7-7. The forcing function is a constant voltage E applied at the time of switch closure, $t = 0$. Solving the Kirchhoff voltage equation, Eq. (7-9), for the derivative gives

$$\frac{di}{dt} = -\frac{R}{L}i + \frac{E}{L}$$

To arrive at the computer circuit, the derivative di/dt is formed by summing the integrator output and the forcing function according to the right-hand side of the differential equation. The resulting circuit is shown in Fig. 8-5.

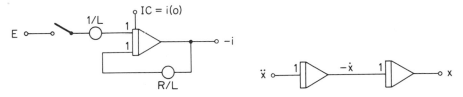

FIGURE 8-5 Computer circuit for solution of series RL circuit.

FIGURE 8-6 Circuit for obtaining x from $\ddot{x}$.

The integrator output simulates the current in the circuit after the switch is closed and will have the form

$$-i = \frac{E}{R}(1 - e^{-Rt/L})$$

In this example, there is no initial current flowing in the circuit and the integrator initial-condition voltage is, therefore, zero. At this point, we may note that the response of the circuit to other forcing functions can be readily determined by applying the appropriate input $f(t)$. For example, $f(t)$ might be a sinusoidal voltage, $E \sin \omega t$, or an input voltage which increases linearly with time. The latter case is known as a *ramp input*.

8-3 SECOND-ORDER DIFFERENTIAL EQUATIONS

A second-order homogeneous differential equation in which time t is the independent variable has the form

$$a\frac{d^2x}{dt^2} + b\frac{dx}{dt} + cx = 0$$

Using dot notation, this equation may be written as

$$a\ddot{x} + b\dot{x} + cx = 0 \tag{8-5}$$

The second-order equation is solved by the computer in essentially the same manner as the first-order equation. The three variables in this case are x, $\dot{x}$, and $\ddot{x}$, and these quantities may be related by two integrating amplifiers as shown in Fig. 8-6. In Fig. 8-6 we must have $\ddot{x}$ available as an input in order to generate the variable x. By solving Eq. (8-5) for the second derivative, we have

$$\ddot{x} = -\frac{b}{a}\dot{x} - \frac{c}{a}x \tag{8-6}$$

If the right-hand side of Eq. (8-6) can be formed, then an expression for $\ddot{x}$ is obtained. In Fig. 8-6 we note that both x and $\dot{x}$ are available as integrator outputs. Hence x can be formed by using a summing amplifier and two coefficient potentiometers as shown in Fig. 8-7a. The amplifier may be connected as an integrator having two unity-gain inputs, in which case its output is $\dot{x}$, as shown in Fig. 8-7b. Note that in this circuit the variable $\ddot{x}$ is not available as an output since it is formed at the summing point of the integrator.

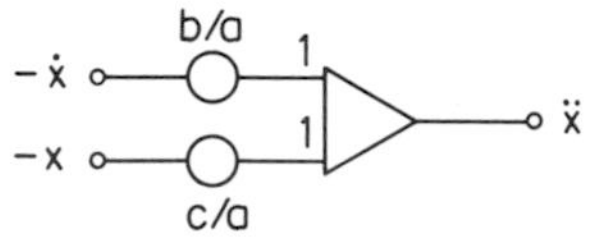

FIGURE 8–7a Circuit for forming $\ddot{x}$. 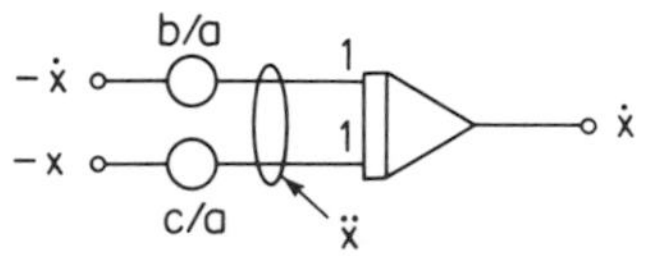 FIGURE 8–7b Circuit for forming $\dot{x}$.

The complete circuit for solving Eq. (8-6) is formed by adding a second integrator and closing the loop as shown in Fig. 8-8. Note that an inverter amplifier is added since $+x$ is available from the second integrator, while the equation calls for $-x$.

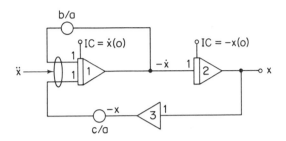

FIGURE 8–8   Complete circuit for solution of second-order equation.

Initial-condition voltages are shown applied to the integrators so that the circuit represents the general case. The initial-condition voltage to integrator 1 represents the value of $\dot{x}$ at $t = 0$. The voltage applied to integrator 2 represents the initial value of x.

The coefficient ratios in Fig. 8-8 are assumed to be less than one so that coefficient potentiometers are used in conjunction with the unity-gain inputs of integrator 1. If the ratios are greater than one, non-unity gains may be used in integrator 1.

When the computer is placed in COMPUTE, the simulation starts from the initial values of $\dot{x}$ and x, and moves toward the equilibrium or rest condition as the stored energy is dissipated. The exact form of the response of the variable x depends on the relative values of the coefficients a, b, and c in Eq. (8-5). As described in Sections 7-9, 7-10, and 7-11, the solution may be overdamped, underdamped, critically damped, or oscillatory.

In studying the second-order system described by Eq. (8-6), we may wish to investigate its behavior with various combinations of parameter values. This is readily accomplished by running a series of solutions having different settings of the coefficient potentiometers.

The computer circuit for solving a nonhomogeneous second-order equation is essentially the same as Fig. 8-8. If the nonhomogeneous equation is solved for the second derivative, we have

$$\ddot{x} = -\frac{b}{a}\dot{x} - \frac{c}{a}x + \frac{1}{a}f(t) \qquad (8\text{-}7)$$

Equation (8-7) requires an additional input to integrator 1 in Fig. 8-8 so that the forcing function may be introduced through a coefficient potentiometer set to $1/a$.

8-4 SUMMARY OF PROGRAMMING PROCEDURE

The steps in preparing a programming diagram for analog-computer solution of an ordinary differential equation are summarized as follows.

1. Solve the equation for the highest-order derivative that occurs in the equation.
2. Integrate the highest-order derivative to obtain the next lower derivative. Repeat the integration process until the variable itself is obtained.
3. Multiply the variable and its lower derivatives by the constants given in the equation.
4. Sum the terms produced by Step 3 as specified by the equation and introduce them as inputs to the first integrator.
5. Introduce required initial-condition voltages to the integrators.

EXAMPLE 8-1

A series RLC circuit is connected to a sinusoidal generator as shown in Fig. 8-9. Develop a computer circuit to simulate the behavior of the current after the switch is closed.

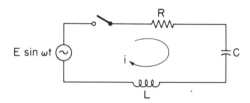

FIGURE 8–9   Circuit for Example 8-1.

SOLUTION:

The Kirchhoff voltage equation is

$$L\frac{di}{dt} + Ri + \frac{1}{C}\int i\,dt = E\sin\omega t$$

To develop the computer circuit, we follow the procedure just outlined. The voltage equation is differentiated and solved for the second derivative, giving

$$\frac{d^2i}{dt^2} = -\frac{R}{L}\frac{di}{dt} - \frac{1}{LC}i + \frac{E\omega}{L}\cos\omega t$$

The second derivative is obtained by forming the terms in the right-hand side of the equation and then closing the two loops. The resulting circuit is shown in Fig. 8-10.

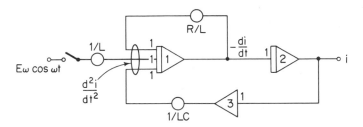

FIGURE 8–10   Computer circuit for solution of series *RLC* circuit.

Because no current is flowing in the circuit prior to closing the switch, no initial-condition voltages are applied to the integrators.

Since the differential equation of the circuit is nonhomogeneous, the current has both transient and steady-state components. The steady-state current is a sine wave of frequency ω having a phase angle and magnitude determined by the network parameters. The transient portion of the current is determined not only by the parameters but also depends upon the instant during a cycle when the switch is closed.

8-5 SIMULTANEOUS EQUATIONS

In the preceding sections, an analog computer was programmed to solve single first- and second-order linear differential equations. Although it is convenient to start with these simple equations in order to become familiar with analog methods, their solutions are well known and a computer would not generally be used to obtain them.

There are many physical systems whose equations are higher than second order. These equations could be solved using the procedure outlined in Sec. 8-4 in which the equation is solved for the highest-order derivative. However, since the manipulation of higher-order equations becomes rather complex, an alternate approach is commonly used in analog simulation. In this method the system is described by a set of simultaneous differential equations of either first or second order. This approach has the advantage that these equations are those which most naturally describe the system.

There are numerous instances of this type of physical system. For example, in analyzing a passive electrical network by means of Kirchhoff's Laws, a series of loop equations may be written. The equation describing each loop can be no higher than second order, no matter how complex the network may be. In a multi-loop network, coupling exists between loops because of common branches or mutual inductance. Since the current in one loop affects the current in other loops, the network represents what is known as a *coupled system.*

In the mechanical realm, an example of a coupled system would be two spring–mass systems in which there exists some type of mechanical coupling between the masses.

To simultaneously solve a set of second-order equations by analytic means requires considerable mathematical facility (as well as time). However, the simulation of simultaneous differential equations on an analog computer is no more difficult than the simulation of single differential equations. Each equation is represented by a computer circuit of the type previously described, and appropriate interconnections are made between the circuits to introduce the coupling effects.

EXAMPLE 8-2

To illustrate the computer analysis of a coupled system, consider the electrical network shown in Fig. 8-11. This circuit contains two loops which are coupled by the common capacitor.

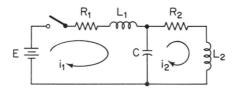

FIGURE 8–11   Coupled network.

SOLUTION:

The Kirchhoff voltage equations for the circuit are

$$E = R_1 i_1 + L_1 \frac{di_1}{dt} + \frac{1}{C} \int i_1\, dt - \frac{1}{C} \int i_2\, dt$$

$$0 = R_2 i_2 + L_2 \frac{di_2}{dt} + \frac{1}{C} \int i_2\, dt - \frac{1}{C} \int i_1\, dt$$

In this case, rather than differentiating the equations to eliminate the integral, we will find it more convenient to change the dependent variable from current to electric charge. Using the relationships

$$i = \frac{dq}{dt} \quad \text{and} \quad q = \int i\, dt$$

the equations may be written as

$$E = R_1\dot{q}_1 + L_1\ddot{q}_1 + \frac{1}{C}q_1 - \frac{1}{C}q_2$$

$$0 = R_2\dot{q}_2 + L_2\ddot{q}_2 + \frac{1}{C}q_2 - \frac{1}{C}q_1$$

Solving these equations for their highest derivatives, we have

$$\ddot{q}_1 = -\frac{R_1}{L_1}\dot{q}_1 - \frac{1}{L_1C}q_1 + \frac{1}{L_1C}q_2 + \frac{E}{L_1}$$

$$\ddot{q}_2 = -\frac{R_2}{L_2}\dot{q}_2 - \frac{1}{L_2C}q_2 + \frac{1}{L_2C}q_1$$

To develop a computer circuit for simulating this network, we apply the procedure outlined in Sec. 8-4 to each of the equations. However, to form the right-hand side of each equation, an additional input is required from the circuit simulating the other loop. It is these added inputs which introduce the coupling that exists between the two loops.

The complete computer set-up is shown in Fig. 8-12. The circuit interconnections, which represent the coupling between the loops, are shown in bold lines.

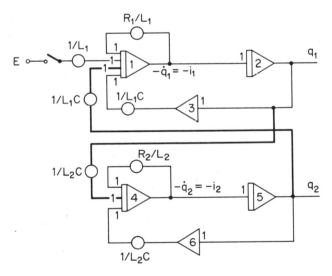

FIGURE 8–12   Computer simulation of coupled network of Figure 8–11.

The outputs of integrators 2 and 5 represent the charges q_1 and q_2 respectively. The loop currents i_1 and i_2 may be obtained at the outputs of integrators 1 and 4 respectively.

EXAMPLE 8-3

Develop a computer diagram for the mechanically coupled system shown in Fig. 8-13. The system consists of two spring–mass assemblies which are coupled

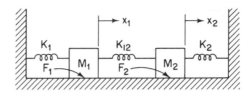

FIGURE 8–13   Mechanical system for Example 8-3.

together by a third spring. Sliding friction acts to oppose the movement of the masses.

SOLUTION:

Let us initially assume that the masses are not coupled together. Applying Newton's Second Law ($f = Ma$) to each mass, the differential equations of motion are found to be

$$M_1 \frac{d^2x_1}{dt^2} + F_1 \frac{dx_1}{dt} + K_1 x_1 = 0$$

$$M_2 \frac{d^2x_2}{dt^2} + F_2 \frac{dx_2}{dt} + K_2 x_2 = 0$$

where M is the mass, F is the coefficient of friction, and K is the spring constant. These two second-order equations may be solved independently since the masses are uncoupled. If the coupling spring K_{12} is added, an additional force is exerted on each mass. The differential equations of motion now become

$$M_1 \frac{d^2x_1}{dt^2} + F_1 \frac{dx_1}{dt} + K_1 x_1 + K_{12}(x_1 - x_2) = 0$$

$$M_2 \frac{d^2x_2}{dt^2} + F_2 \frac{dx_2}{dt} + K_2 x_2 + K_{12}(x_2 - x_1) = 0$$

Solving these equations for their second derivatives, we have

$$\ddot{x}_1 = -\frac{F_1}{M_1}\dot{x}_1 - \frac{K_1 + K_{12}}{M_1}x_1 + \frac{K_{12}}{M_1}x_2$$

$$\ddot{x}_2 = -\frac{F_2}{M_2}\dot{x}_1 - \frac{K_2 + K_{12}}{M_2}x_2 + \frac{K_{12}}{M_2}x_1$$

The computer circuit for simulating this system is shown in Fig. 8-14. The circuit interconnections which represent the coupling due to K_{12} are shown in bold lines.

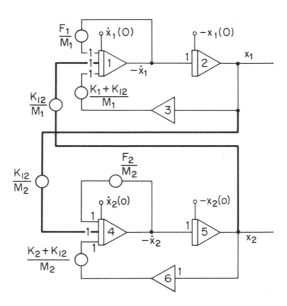

FIGURE 8–14   Computer circuit for simulating
mechanical system of Figure 8–13.

8-6 MAGNITUDE SCALE FACTORS

In electronic analog computers, physical quantities such as distance, temperature, flow rate, etc., are represented by voltages. The level of a particular
voltage must always represent a proportionate amount of its related quantity.
In other words, a consistent scale must be used to translate from a problem
variable to the computer voltage and vice versa. For example, if 100 volts
represent a distance of 500 feet, then 50 volts must represent 250 feet, and 10
volts must represent 50 feet.

The translation from the physical problem variables to the computer
or machine variables is made by multiplying the former by appropriate
constants called *magnitude scale factors*. A magnitude scale factor, therefore,
is a proportionality constant which relates the computer voltage to the
corresponding variable in the system under consideration. It is defined by
the relation

$$\text{magnitude scale factor} = \frac{\text{computer variable}}{\text{problem variable}}$$

Mathematically this is expressed as

$$a_x = \frac{e_x}{x} \tag{8-8}$$

where a_x is the magnitude scale factor and e_x is the analog voltage which represents the problem variable x.

From Eq. (8-8), the relation between a computer variable and a problem variable is $e_x = a_x x$. The computer variable is generally written in the form $(a_x x)$; the parentheses around the quantity indicate that it is a scaled problem variable.

The choice of scale factors is not completely arbitrary. For example, if variable $\dot{x}$ has a maximum value of 1000 ft/s, then an amplifier whose output is equal in magnitude to $\dot{x}$ would have to produce 1000 volts, which is highly impractical. Hence the scale factor must be chosen such that the computer variable never exceeds the available voltage range of the computer or overloads any of its components. For present solid-state computers, a voltage range from -10 to $+10$ volts is common, although -100 to $+100$ volts is also employed. The maximum voltage output is known as the *computer reference voltage*.

At the same time, the computer variable must be sufficiently large to be unaffected by noise, hum, or other stray voltages in the computer which might impair its accuracy. A variable with a maximum value of 0.002 lb cannot be accurately represented by an amplifier output whose maximum value is 0.002 volt, since this is of the same order of magnitude as the errors associated with the amplifier.

The approach to choosing computer scale factors is similar to the choice of scale factors in plotting data. The number of inches that will correspond to one unit of each variable being plotted is determined by noting the maximum value of the variable and comparing it with the size of the graph paper. Our object is to produce a graph large enough to use most of the paper, yet not so large that it runs off scale. Similarly, in analog computation we should use as much of the available voltage range as possible without exceeding the amplifier limits.

To determine an appropriate value for a scale factor, we need an estimate of the maximum value of the problem variable. When the problem variable reaches its maximum value, the amplifier output should be at or near its maximum value. Therefore, a simple procedure is to take the scale factor as the largest convenient number satisfying the relationship

$$a_x \leq \frac{computer\ reference\ voltage}{maximum\ absolute\ value\ of\ problem\ variable\ x} = \frac{E_r}{|x|_{max}} \qquad (8\text{-}9)$$

By a "convenient" number we mean such numbers as 0.1, 0.5, 1, 2, 10, etc.—numbers that are convenient to implement on the computer and that provide fairly simple interpretation of the results.

EXAMPLE 8-4

A problem variable x has a maximum value of 1000 ft. Determine the amplitude scale factor and computer variable for computers having (a) 10-volt reference, (b) 100-volt reference.

SOLUTION:

(a) $a_x = \dfrac{E_r}{x_{max}} = \dfrac{10}{1000} = 0.01$ V/ft

computer variable $= (0.01x)$

(b) $a_x = \dfrac{100}{1000} = 0.1$ V/ft

computer variable $= (0.1x)$

EXAMPLE 8-5

Scale the following variables for a computer whose reference is 10 volts.

Physical Variable	Range of Variable
Force (f)	0 to 1000 lb
Temperature (T)	-100 to $+200°C$
Current (i)	-1.5 to $+1A$
Velocity $(\dot{x})$	0 to 88 ft/s.

SOLUTION:

The scaling table below shows the scale factors and computer variables. Where appropriate, the scale factors are rounded downward to a convenient value.

Problem Variable	Estimated Maximum	Scale Factor	Computer Variable
f	1000 lb	$\dfrac{10}{1000} - 0.01$ V/lb	$(0.01f)$
T	200°C	$\dfrac{10}{200} = 0.05$ V/°C	$(0.05T)$
i	1.5 A	$\dfrac{10}{1.5} = 6.67$ round to 5 V/A	$(5i)$
$\dot{x}$	88 ft/s	$\dfrac{10}{88} = 0.114$ round to 0.1 V/ft/s	$(0.1\dot{x})$

8-7 SCALED EQUATIONS

When maximum values have been estimated and appropriate scale factors selected, the next step is to make the computer circuit consistent with the original problem equations. These equations contain problem variables such as x, $\dot{x}$, q, etc., while the computer variables appear as voltages from operational amplifiers. The original problem equations must therefore be translated into equations containing computer variables. The scale factors which have been selected may be incorporated into the problem equation by writing each term as

$$\frac{1}{a_x}(a_x x) \qquad\qquad (8\text{-}10)$$

We should note the above substitution maintains the equality of the equation since each term is multiplied and divided by the same factor.

The expression containing the computer variables is called a *scaled equation*. To prepare a scaled equation, the following sequence of steps may be followed.

1. Express the original problem equation in terms of the highest-order derivative and simplify.
2. Prepare a scaling table, listing every variable that appears in the problem equation.
3. Estimate the maximum value of each of the variables in the scaling table.
4. To obtain the scale factor for each variable, divide the computer reference voltage by the estimated maximum value of that variable and round the result downward to the nearest convenient number.
5. Substitute the computer variables into the original equation according to Eq. (8-10). The resulting equation is the scaled equation.

EXAMPLE 8-6

To illustrate the scaling process, we will develop a scaled equation for the following second-order differential equation describing a spring–mass system.

$$25\frac{d^2x}{dt^2} + 50\frac{dx}{dt} + 100x = 0$$

The initial conditions are

$$x(0) = 5 \quad \text{inches}$$

$$\frac{dx}{dt}(0) = 0$$

SOLUTION:

We will assume a 10-volt computer is being used. Rewriting the differential equation in terms of the highest derivative, we have

$$\ddot{x} + 2\dot{x} + 4x = 0$$

The next step is to prepare a scaling table for the variables. For the moment, we will arbitrarily assume maximum values for the problem variables.

Problem Variable	Estimated Maximum	Scale Factor	Computer Variable
x	5 in	2 V/in	$(2x)$
$\dot{x}$	10 in/s	1 V/in/s	$(\dot{x})$
$\ddot{x}$	50 in/s²	0.2 V/in/s²	$(0.2\ddot{x})$

Substituting the computer variables into the differential equation gives

$$5(0.2\ddot{x}) + 2(\dot{x}) + 4(0.5)(2x) = 0$$

This simplifies to

$$(0.2\ddot{x}) + 0.4(\dot{x}) + 0.4(2x) = 0$$

which is the final scaled equation. The scaled variables appear in parentheses to emphasize their relationship to the original problem variables.

The transformation from problem variables to computer variables will affect the gains of the integrators in the computer circuit. In the problem equation, a variable and its derivatives are related according to

$$x = \int \dot{x}\, dt \quad \text{and} \quad \dot{x} = \int \ddot{x}\, dt \tag{8-11}$$

in which case the integrator gains are unity.

If the scaled variables are substituted in Eq. (8-11), we have

$$\frac{1}{a_x}(a_x x) = \frac{1}{a_{\dot{x}}} \int (a_{\dot{x}} \dot{x})\, dt$$

$$\frac{1}{a_{\dot{x}}}(a_{\dot{x}} \dot{x}) = \frac{1}{a_{\ddot{x}}} \int (a_{\ddot{x}} \ddot{x})\, dt$$

or

$$(a_x x) = \frac{a_x}{a_{\dot{x}}} \int (a_{\dot{x}} \dot{x})\, dt$$

$$(a_{\dot{x}} \dot{x}) = \frac{a_{\dot{x}}}{a_{\ddot{x}}} \int (a_{\ddot{x}} \ddot{x})\, dt \tag{8-12}$$

Thus, for the scaled equation, the integrator gain is the ratio of the scale factor of the output variable to the scale factor of the input variable.

EXAMPLE 8-7

Develop a computer circuit for simulating the spring–mass system given in Example 8-6.

SOLUTION:

Using the scale factors given in the table, the gain of the first integrator is

$$\frac{a_{\dot{x}}}{a_{x}} = \frac{1}{0.2} = 5$$

and the gain of the second integrator is

$$\frac{a_{x}}{a_{\dot{x}}} = \frac{2}{1} = 2$$

Solving the scaled equation developed in Example 8-6 for the highest-order derivative, we obtain

$$(0.2\ddot{x}) = -0.4(\dot{x}) - 0.4(2x)$$

Combining this equation with the above integrator gains, we obtain the scaled computer diagram shown in Fig. 8-15. In actual practice, the two coefficient potentiometers could be deleted and integrator gains of $5 \times 0.4 = 2$ used with equivalent results. The outputs of the circuit are related to the problem variables by the scale factors. For example, assume that the output of integrator 2 equals 2.5 volts. Applying the a_x scale factor, the actual displacement is 1.25 inches.

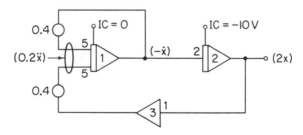

FIGURE 8–15   Computer circuit for Example 8–7.

8-8   ESTIMATING MAXIMUM VALUES

As we have seen, knowledge of the maximum values of the problem variables is necessary in order to determine magnitude scale factors. In this section we will briefly consider the matter of estimating maximum values of the problem variables. In general, two approaches are available. We may begin with rough estimates of the maximum values and then use one or more trial computer solutions to refine the scale factors. Alternatively, some formal approach may be employed to obtain more accurate estimates of the maximum values. For this purpose, a number of methods have been developed which involve the analysis of the differential equations to be solved. However, these techniques are generally of interest only to the specialist in analog-computer programming and will only be touched on here.

In following a "trial and error" approach, we can generally make reasonable estimates of the range of the variables from our prior knowledge of the physical system under study. The initial conditions in the system, as well as the forcing function (if any), can provide some insight into the values of the variables. After making estimates of the maximum values, or even "guesstimates" if that is the case, we can proceed to program the problem and observe the behavior of the simulation. If any of the scale factors are unsuitable, as indicated by amplifiers either saturating or using only a small part of their voltage range, then the scale factors can be changed accordingly. In setting the scale factors, the prime rule is to permit each amplifier to operate at the highest practicable voltage without overloading. After one or two trial runs of the problem, the scale factors can generally be set for satisfactory results.

For a majority of problems, this approach proves adequate. Obviously, the accuracy of the initial estimates of the maxima will depend on the programmer's experience and knowledge of the field with which the problem is concerned. Although it is generally possible to obtain a reasonable estimate of the maximum value of the dependent variable itself, estimates of the maximum values of the derivatives may be more difficult. For homogeneous equations, a simple method is available for analyzing the equations for their maxima.

A first-order homogeneous equation of the form

$$\dot{x} + ax = 0$$

has a solution

$$x = x(0)e^{-at} \tag{8-13}$$

The maximum value of the dependent variable x is the initial value $x(0)$ at $t = 0$. The first derivative may be found by differentiating Eq. (8-13), giving

$$\dot{x} = -ax(0)e^{-at} \tag{8-14}$$

The maximum value of $\dot{x}$ occurs at $t = 0$ and is

$$\dot{x}_{max} = -ax(0) = -ax_{max} \tag{8-15}$$

The general second-order homogeneous equation is of the form

$$a\ddot{x} + b\dot{x} + cx = 0 \tag{8-16}$$

In analyzing this equation, let us assume that the damping term $b\dot{x}$ is zero. The response of the system is then undamped and is of the form

$$x = K \sin \omega_n t \tag{8-17}$$

where K is the maximum amplitude of x and ω_n is the natural resonant frequency of the system equal to $\sqrt{c/a}$. By successive differentiation, we obtain

$$\dot{x} = K\omega_n \cos \omega_n t \quad \text{and} \quad \ddot{x} = -K\omega_n^2 \sin \omega_n t \tag{8-18}$$

The maximum values of these variables are then

$$\dot{x}_{max} = K\omega_n \quad \text{and} \quad \ddot{x}_{max} = K\omega_n^2 \tag{8-19}$$

Since the presence of damping in the system will decrease the value of ω_n, the maxima given by Eq. (8-19) represent conservative estimates.

EXAMPLE 8-8

In Example 8-6, we determined the scale factors using specified maximum values of the variables. We will now examine the basis for choosing these maximum values.

SOLUTION:

Since the differential equation is homogeneous, we will take the maximum value of x to be its initial value of 5 inches.

The natural resonant frequency of the system is determined from the undamped equation

$$\ddot{x} + 4x = 0$$

The value of ω_n is 2 rad/s.

Using Eq. (8-19), the maximum values of the derivatives are estimated as

$$\dot{x}_{max} = \omega_n x_{max} = 10 \quad \text{in/s}$$
$$\ddot{x}_{max} = \omega_n^2 x_{max} = 20 \quad \text{in/s}^2$$

In the scaling table in Example 8-6, the latter value is rounded up to provide a convenient scale factor.

8-9   COMPUTER TIME LIMITATIONS

In dynamic systems, time is the independent variable, and one is interested in studying the behavior of the system with respect to time. The length of time over which the system may display any given pattern of behavior may vary over extremely wide ranges, depending upon the type of system under study. Many physical systems, such as chemical reactions or inter-planetary flights, may take hours, days, or even longer for completion. On the other hand, systems such as electrical networks or ballistic projectiles may take only a fraction of a second to respond.

There are several factors which affect the length of time a computer may use in solving a problem. The minimum time is determined by the speed of response of the computer and its recording devices. That is, the equation frequencies must be suited to the range of frequencies which can be handled by the equipment being used.

Where electromechanical devices such as servomultipliers or X–Y plotters are used, the upper frequency limit is of the order of one to five cycles per second. By using only electronic computing elements together with a galvanometer-type recorder, the maximum frequencies may be on the order of 100 to 200 Hz. A cathode-ray oscilloscope may be used to monitor computer outputs over a frequency range from dc up to several hundred kilohertz, which is beyond the frequency range of most computer components.

There is also a maximum limit on computer solution time which is almost entirely determined by the drift and capacitor leakage of the integrators. Since integrator drift error is proportional to integration time, computer runs should not have a duration of more than several minutes under normal conditions. In addition, slow integration requires low input voltages and, as has been mentioned, low voltages are generally undesired in analog compu-tation.

In addition to the above limitations, it is difficult to obtain either very fast or very slow times using the nominal component values or input gains normally available with the computer.

8-10 TIME SCALE FACTORS

Because of the time limitations described above, it is frequently advantageous to either slow down or speed up the time of problem solution with respect to real time. Changing the time scale of the original problem to one suitable for the computer is referred to as *time scaling*. By slowing down time, rapidly occurring phenomena can be studied in sufficient detail; by speeding up time, very slow systems can be studied in a reasonable time interval.

We customarily distinguish between time in the original problem and time on the computer by using the letters t and τ respectively. Thus $t =$ "problem time" (the independent variable in the original problem statement), and $\tau =$ "computer time" (the independent variable on the computer). In time scaling, as in magnitude scaling, the computer variable is made proportional to the corresponding problem variable. This relationship may be expressed as

$$\tau = \beta t \tag{8-20}$$

where β is defined as the *time scale factor.**

The time scale factor has the units of computer time (which is usually seconds) divided by problem time. If the problem time is also measured in seconds, then β is dimensionless. In this case, the magnitude of β indicates the factor by which the problem is speeded up or slowed down. If $\beta > 1$, then the solution on the computer is slower than the original process; if $\beta < 1$, the computer solution is faster than the original process.

For example, assume $\beta = 10$. Then, from Eq. (8-20), we see that $\tau = 10t$. When $t = 1$ second, $\tau = 10$ seconds. Since an event that takes place in one second in the original problem would require 10 seconds on the computer, the system under study is effectively slowed down.

8-11   TIME SCALING PROCEDURE

Examination of the components of a standard analog computer indicates that only one component, the integrator, is related to time. For all of the other components, the relation between inputs and outputs does not involve time (if we ignore long-term drift effects). Therefore, only integrators are involved in the time scaling of the computer.

A change in time scale is made by changing the gains of all integrators according to the time scale factor β. The following example describes the way in which this is done. Assume that we apply a constant input of -1 volt to an integrator having unity gain. As shown in Fig. 8-16, the output voltage increases linearly at a rate of 1 volt per second, so that 10 seconds are required to reach 10 volts.

If the integrator gain is now increased to 10, the output rate of change will increase proportionately and only one second is needed to reach 10

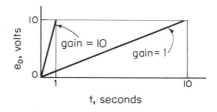

FIGURE 8–16   Effect of integrator gain change.

_____

*This designation of β should be distinguished from its use as feedback factor or transistor current gain.

volts. Thus, increasing the integrator gain by 10 reduces to 1/10 the time that is required to reach the same output voltage. Expressed in another way, the time scale has been speeded up by a factor of 10. Using Eq. (8-20), the time scale factor is

$$\beta = \frac{\tau}{t} = \frac{1}{10}$$

Thus, we see that a time scale factor of 1/10 is obtained by multiplying the integrator gain by $1/\beta$ or 10.

From this example, we can infer a general rule; the time scale of a problem can be changed by multiplying all integrator gains by the factor $1/\beta$. Thus, for $\beta > 1$, the gain is decreased and the integrator will operate at a slower rate. If $\beta < 1$, the gain is increased and the integrator operates faster. The change in gain may be accomplished by using an input with a different gain, by the use of a coefficient potentiometer, or by changing the value of the feedback capacitor.

We should again note that a time-scale change does not affect the magnitude scaling. All magnitude scale factors, all coefficient potentiometer settings, and all computer variables remain the same as before.

EXAMPLE 8-9

Referring to the spring–mass system of Examples 8-6 and 8-7, modify the simulation to slow the solution by a factor of 10.

SOLUTION:

Since the time scale factor β is 10, then the change of time scale is effected by multiplying the gain of each integrator by $1/\beta$ or, in this case, by 1/10. The gains of integrator 1 become 0.5 each and the gain of integrator 2 is 0.2. All other aspects of the circuit are unchanged. The computer set up for this example is shown in Fig. 8-17. In recording the behavior of the variables, 10 seconds of actual time correspond to one second in the problem.

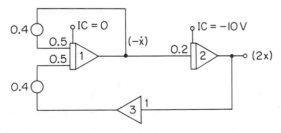

FIGURE 8–17   Scaled computer circuit for Example 8–9.
$\beta = 10$.

8-12   NON-LINEAR PROGRAMMING

It was pointed out in Chapter 4 that non-linear effects are frequently encountered in engineering work and non-linear differential equations are required to describe these effects. Non-linear differential equations have no standard form but generally involve powers of derivatives, products of derivatives, or functions of the dependent variable. Unfortunately, no general analytic method exists for handling non-linear equations; the methods used generally prove to be unique to the particular equation being solved. Approximation methods such as linearization around an operating point (see Section 4-1) are sometimes used with satisfactory results.

Analog computers are readily capable of solving many types of non-linear differential equations. One of the advantages of using a computer to study a non-linear system is that the operator does not need an extensive knowledge of analytic methods.

The basic approach to solving non-linear equations is the same as that applied to the linear equations. We assume the highest-order derivative is available, process it as necessary to develop the terms to which it is equal according to the equation, and then feed all of the terms back to the first integrator. The difference lies in the fact that non-linear equations require the use of non-linear computing elements. Common non-linear elements were described in Chapters 4 and 5; among them are included multipliers, various types of function generators, and diode circuits. As a general rule, specific non-linear elements are introduced into the simulation according to the non-linearities present in the system under study. For example, if a dead-zone exists at some particular point in a control system, then the simulation would include an appropriate diode circuit at a corresponding location.

Just as the subject of non-linear differential equations is beyond the scope of this text, so non-linear programming will not be described in any detail. The reader who wishes to acquire more knowledge in this area is referred to the bibliography. However, we will include a brief example of non-linear programming, primarily to point up its similarity to the linear procedure already studied.

EXAMPLE 8-10

Develop a programming diagram for the equation

$$\frac{d^2x}{dt^2} + ax\frac{dx}{dt} + bx = \sin \omega t$$

where a and b are arbitrary constants. Since the equation contains a term proportional to the product of two variables $\left(x \text{ and } \frac{dx}{dt}\right)$, it is a non-linear equation.

SOLUTION:

We will follow the same procedure as for linear equations and solve the given equation for the highest-order derivative. Thus

$$\ddot{x} = -ax\dot{x} - bx + \sin \omega t$$

The unscaled programming diagram is shown in Fig. 8-18. A multiplier of the quarter-square type is included to provide the product of x and $\dot{x}$. Note that the gain of integrator 1, which is associated with the multiplier output, must be increased to compensate for the attenuation constant $1/E_R$ of the multiplier.

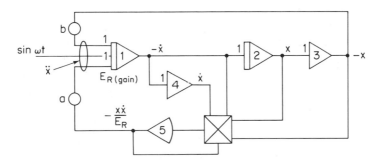

FIGURE 8–18   Programming diagram for Example 8–10.

8-13 PROBLEM CHECKING

In the process of programming, scaling, and patching a problem, numerous opportunities for errors arise. In addition, equipment malfunctions may occur, and one faulty component can nullify the entire simulation. Therefore, a discussion of analog-computer programming would not be complete without some mention of the procedures for detecting and correcting errors before actual computation begins.

Obviously, the probability of error is magnified as the size and complexity of the problem increase. For this reason, large computers frequently have special problem-check equipment and procedures built into the design. Since a detailed discussion of problem checking would be primarily of interest to a programming specialist, we will but briefly describe commonly accepted procedures which are applicable to all computers, large or small.

Problem checking should start with a review of the problem equations or mathematical model of the physical system under study. If the system is incorrectly represented, no amount of checking of the programming can produce satisfactory results. Next, the steps in preparing the equations for problem solution should be checked. The scaling should be verified and the programming diagram and table of potentiometer coefficients checked for errors in transcription.

The patching of the computer should be checked against the block diagram and the potentiometer settings verified. A systematic means of carrying out a patching check is to examine the inputs and outputs of each amplifier in turn.

Problem patching and checking are expedited if each amplifier and potentiometer are identified according to the patch-board nomenclature. If the programming is done by individuals working in pairs, the checking of the problem can best be performed by a person other than the one who actually executed the work.

After all of the programming checks have been completed, the actual operation of the computer should be verified. A static check may be made by calculating the dc voltages which appear in the computer in the RESET (or IC) mode. The calculations start with assumed values at the integrator outputs. Since the integrators are not in operation in the RESET mode, the assumed outputs are the initial-condition voltages. In cases where the initial condition of an integrator is zero, an appropriate voltage may be connected temporarily for test purposes.

Knowing the setting of each coefficient potentiometer and the gains through each amplifier or non-linear unit, we may calculate the voltage output of every amplifier in the circuit. After all of the voltages have been calculated, each of the amplifier outputs is successively measured and checked against the predetermined value. Any disagreement should be investigated for either a patching error or a component malfunction.

The procedures which we have described do not provide a check of integrator operation, since this requires a dynamic mode of computer operation. However, a partial integrator check may be made by measuring the inputs to the integrators, which represent the initial derivatives of their respective outputs. The value of a derivative can be readily calculated by summing the inputs to the integrator. Consider the integrator shown in Fig. 8-19. The derivative to the integrator is calculated as the sum of the two inputs. Thus, we have

$$\text{Derivative} = (1)(0.4)(1) + (2)(0.3)(2) = 1.6 \quad \text{volts}$$

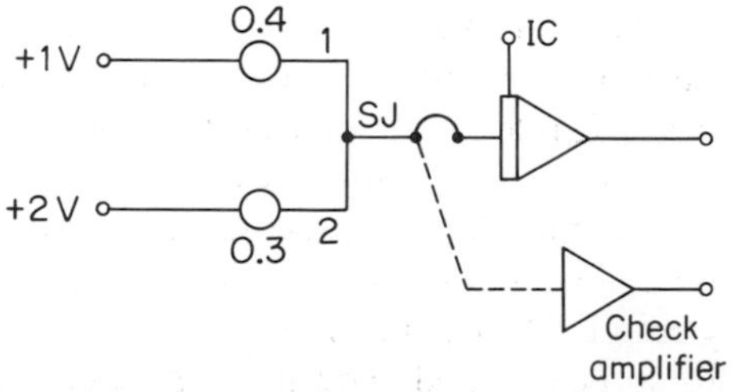

FIGURE 8–19   Integrator and check amplifier.

In general, the voltage representing a derivative exists at the integrator summing point and cannot be read directly. However, a derivative can be measured by momentarily disconnecting the summing junction from the integrator (this will not affect the integrator output in the RESET mode) and temporarily connecting the summing point to an auxiliary or check amplifier. As shown in Fig. 8-19, the output of this amplifier provides a direct reading of the derivative.

Of course, the most desirable check for analog-computer solutions is a comparison with an analytic solution, if this is available. This is usually possible for the beginner in programming, for a wide variety of less complex problems and their solutions are described in the literature.

EXAMPLE 8-11

The programming diagram shown in Fig. 8-20 simulates an automobile suspension system (a problem which we will discuss in detail in the next chapter). We will use this circuit to illustrate the calculation of problem-check voltages. For simplicity, the problem variables have not been included on the diagram.

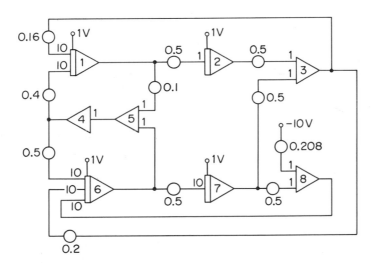

FIGURE 8-20   Programming diagram for Example 8-11.

SOLUTION:

A test voltage of $+1$ volt is applied to the initial-condition input of all four integrators in the RESET mode. The table shows the output voltage of each amplifier; these are calculated using the procedure described above. In addition, the calculated integrator inputs or derivatives are given for each of the four integrating amplifiers; these voltages may be measured by means of a check amplifier.

TABLE OF PROBLEM-CHECK VOLTAGES

Amplifier Number	Output Voltage	Derivative Voltage
1	−1.0	2.8
2	−1.0	0.50
3	1.0	
4	−1.1	
5	1.1	
6	−1.0	−22.3*
7	−1.0	5.0
8	2.58	

*This voltage exceeds the computer reference. It can be measured by reducing the gain of the check amplifier to 0.1 so that its output is −2.23 volts.

PROBLEMS FOR CHAPTER 8

1. Develop an unscaled computer diagram for solving the following differential equations. Assume the computer reference is 10 volts and the operational amplifiers have input gains of 1, 1, 1, 10, and 10.

(a) $\dot{x} - 3 = 0$ $x(0) = 5$

(b) $\dot{y} + 0.4y = 0$ $y(0) = -3$

(c) $2\dot{q} + 6q + 4 = 0$ $q(0) = 0$

(d) $\ddot{x} + 16x = 0$ $\dot{x}(0) = 0$ $x(0) = 10$

(e) $5\ddot{y} + 4\dot{y} + 6y = f(t)$ $\dot{y}(0) = 1$ $y(0) = -2$

(f) $\ddot{y} - 9\dot{y} + 3 = 0$ $\ddot{y}(0) = \dot{y}(0) = 0$ $y(0) = 10$

(g) $100\dot{h}_1 + 0.7h_1 - h_2 = 10$ $\dot{h}_1(0) = h_2(0) = 0$
   $10\dot{h}_2 + h_2 + 5h_1 = 50$

2. Determine the differential equation and initial conditions for the computer circuits shown below.

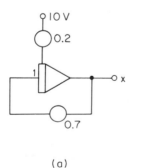

(a)

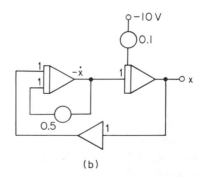

(b)

3. Devise a computer circuit for generating the following functions. (Hint: What are the differential equation and initial conditions which define each function?)

(a) $y = 10t$
(b) $x = 10 - 2t$
(c) $x = 10e^{-5t}$
(d) $\theta = 10 \sin 10t$

4. Select appropriate scale factors for the following variables. Assume that the computer reference is 100 volts.

Physical Variable	Range of Variable
Charge (q)	0 to 50 coulombs
Displacement (x)	-80 to $+50$ ft
Flow (Q)	0 to 140 gal/min
Pressure (q)	0 to 1800 psi
Voltage (v)	-45 to $+25$ volts

5. Fill in the missing terms in the following scaling table. Assume the computer reference is 10 volts.

Physical Variable	Estimated Maximum	Scale Factor	Computer Variable
x	15	————	————
$\dot{x}$	————	————	$(0.1\dot{x})$
y	————	20	————
$\dot{y}$	————	————	$(2\dot{y})$
$\sin x$	1	————	————

6. Given the differential equation

$$4\ddot{x} + 10\dot{x} + 20x = 0$$

and the computer variables $(2x)$, $(4\dot{x})$, and $(10\ddot{x})$, write the differential equation in scaled form.

In Problems 7, 8, and 9, determine the following for the given differential equation:
   (a) Estimated maximum values of variables.
   (b) Magnitude scale factors (assume 10-volt computer reference).
   (c) Scaled equation.
   (d) Scaled computer-programming diagram.

7. $50\dot{v} + 2v = 0$ $v(0) = 100$ volts $= v_{max}$
8. $\ddot{x} + 1.6\dot{x} + 16x = 0$ $x(0) = 45$ cm $= x_{max}$
                                             $\dot{x}(0) = 0$
9. $\ddot{q} + 40\dot{q} + 2500q = 0$ $q(0) = 5$ coulombs $= q_{max}$
                                             $\dot{q}(0) = 0$

10. In Problem 9 it is desired that the solution frequencies be in the range of 0.1

to 10 rad/s. Suggest an appropriate time-scale change. What changes must be made in the computer circuit?

11. The motion of a body is described by the non-linear differential equation

$$\ddot{y} + A|\dot{y}|\dot{y} = -B$$

Draw an unscaled computer diagram to obtain y. (*Hint:* See Section 5-2.)

12. Prepare a table of problem-check voltages for the following computing circuit.

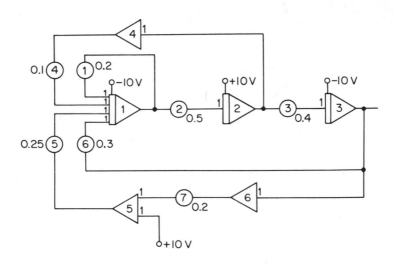

9-1 INTRODUCTION

Previous chapters have been concerned with analog-computing circuits and equipment, as well as with programming methods for solving linear mathematical models on an analog computer. Since illustrative examples tend to clarify principles and methods, this final chapter is devoted to describing computer application through problems selected from various engineering disciplines.

The scope and complexity of problems to which analog computers are applied is almost without limit. Numerous problems and their computer solution are described in texts, journal articles, and application notes from computer manufacturers. The latter source of information is especially good for one just beginning in the field of analog simulation. The examples presented in this chapter are relatively simple; their purpose is to show the function of the computer and to illustrate the programming procedures. The problems have been chosen to involve mechanical, electrical, and chemical principles, and are arranged roughly in order of increasing complexity. They are presented in sufficient detail to serve as beginning laboratory exercises using a small analog computer having approximately 10 amplifiers.

The focus of an engineering problem is some physical system that requires analysis. This analysis begins by completely defining the problem. Although this step may

9

ANALOG SIMULATION EXAMPLES

sound simple, it is often true in practice that the definition of a problem is more difficult than the actual solution of it. In defining a problem, the related physical phenomena must be identified to determine the principles which will form the basis of the analysis. The parameters of the problem must be determined, and simplifying assumptions applied wherever appropriate. Simplification must be judiciously made to avoid introducing errors into the analysis.

This analysis of the problem leads to a mathematical model of the system, which generally takes the form of a series of differential equations. Once a model is available, the analog computer can be applied to its solution, using the techniques which have been described. The response of the system to various inputs can be studied, and the effect of parameter changes on system behavior may be evaluated.

We shall generally follow the above procedure in the examples of this chapter. The analysis of each problem includes:

1. Definition of problem.
2. Formulation of mathematical model.
3. Programming and scaling of model.
4. Generation of solutions in the form of curves showing relationships between system variables.

9-2 SIMULATION OF FALLING BODY

Our first example is a familiar problem in physics, that of determining the trajectory of a body projected vertically upward. To simulate the behavior of this body, we must develop a differential equation which describes its motion. Let us define the vertical displacement y from the point of launch with the upward direction considered positive. We will initially simplify the problem by neglecting air resistance. Then the only force on the body is gravity, which acts in a downward direction. Considering Newton's Second Law, the equation of motion of the body is

$$f = Ma = -Mg \qquad (9\text{-}1)$$

where M is the mass of the body and g is the acceleration of gravity. The acceleration may be expressed as

$$a = \frac{d^2 y}{dt^2} = \ddot{y} = -g = -32 \text{ ft/s}^2 \qquad (9\text{-}2)$$

The displacement may be determined by integrating acceleration with respect to time. Using operator notation, we obtain for $\dot{y}$ and y

$$\dot{y} = \frac{\ddot{y}}{D} + \dot{y}(0) \tag{9-3}$$

and

$$y = \frac{\dot{y}}{D} + y(0) \tag{9-4}$$

where $\dot{y}(0)$ and $y(0)$ are the initial velocity and the displacement, respectively.

Figure 9-1 shows an unscaled computer diagram for obtaining $\dot{y}$ and y. The circuit consists simply of two integrators in cascade with acceleration as the input and $\dot{y}(0)$ and $y(0)$ as initial conditions.

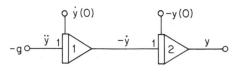

FIGURE 9-1   Unscaled computer diagram for falling body.

Let us assume that the output voltage of integrator 2 has a positive sign relationship; that is, when y is positive the voltage will be positive, and when y is negative the voltage will be negative. As we are aware, a polarity reversal is associated with an operational integrator. Therefore, the input voltage applied to integrator 2 must have a negative sign relationship; when $\dot{y}$ is positive, the voltage will be negative, and when $\dot{y}$ is negative, a positive voltage exists. Hence, the output of integrator 1 is designated $-y$. Since the input to integrator 1 ($\ddot{y}$) will have a positive sign relationship, a negative voltage representing $-g$ is applied. The polarities shown for the initial-condition inputs assume that these inputs are inverted at the outputs of the integrators.

To select amplitude scale factors, we must estimate the maximum values of the problem variables. The maximum value of the velocity will be the initial velocity, which we shall specify as 100 ft/sec. The maximum height y_m may be calculated from energy considerations. Thus, for conservation of energy, we have

$$\text{maximum kinetic energy} = \text{maximum potential energy}$$

$$\frac{1}{2}M[\dot{y}(0)]^2 = Mgy_m$$

from which

$$y_m = \frac{[\dot{y}(0)]^2}{2g} = 156 \text{ ft}$$

A scaling table for the problem based on a 10-volt reference is shown below. For convenience, the maximum values of the variables are rounded off to slightly higher values.

Problem Variable	Estimated Maximum	Scale Factor	Computer Variable
y	200 ft	0.05 V/ft	$(0.05y)$
$\dot{y}$	100 ft/s	0.1 V/ft/s	$(0.1\dot{y})$
$\ddot{y}$	50 ft/s²	0.2 V/ft/s²	$(0.2\ddot{y})$

Substituting the computer voltage corresponding to gravitational acceleration into Eq. (9-2) gives the scaled equation

$$(0.2\ddot{y}) = -32(0.2) = -6.4 \tag{9-5}$$

The initial-condition voltage corresponding to $\dot{y}(0) = 100$ ft/s is 10 volts. Since the point of launch is selected as our displacement reference, $y(0) = 0$.

The gains of the integrators are determined by taking the ratio of the scale factor of the output variable to the scale factor of the input variable. Thus the gain of integrator 1 is

$$\frac{a_{\dot{y}}}{a_{\ddot{y}}} = \frac{0.1}{0.2} = 0.5$$

and the gain of integrator 2 is

$$\frac{a_y}{a_{\dot{y}}} = \frac{0.05}{0.1} = 0.5$$

The scaled computer diagram is shown in Fig. 9-2. Amplifier 3 has been added to the circuit so that a positive velocity is available. The setting of potentiometer 1 incorporates both the scaling of the input voltage and the integrator gain of 0.5.

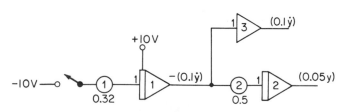

FIGURE 9-2   Scaled computer diagram of falling body.

The graphs of Fig. 9-4 show the displacement and velocity of the body as a function of time after launch. From these curves we might make the following observations: (1) the maximum height is the predicted 156 feet, (2) the time of flight is approximately 6.3 seconds, and (3) the velocity varies linearly between ± 100 ft/s.

To make the results more exact, we will introduce the effect of air resistance into the simulation. Let us assume that the drag force f_d on a body, owing to air resistance, is proportional to the velocity. For constant body cross-sectional area and atmospheric density, the drag force may be expressed as

$$f_d = Kv \qquad\qquad (9\text{-}6)$$

where

$v = $ velocity, ft/s

$K = $ coefficient of aerodynamic resistance, lb-s/ft

Although experiments have shown that drag force is approximately proportional to the square of the velocity, we have chosen to use the linear relationship of Eq. (9-6) because of its simplicity.

The equation of motion now becomes

$$Ma = -Mg - Kv$$

or

$$\ddot{y} = -g - \frac{K}{M}\dot{y} \qquad\qquad (9\text{-}7)$$

Using the previously developed scale factors, the scaled equation corresponding to Eq. (9-7) is

$$(0.2\ddot{y}) = -6.4 - 2\frac{K}{M}(0.1\dot{y}) \qquad\qquad (9\text{-}8)$$

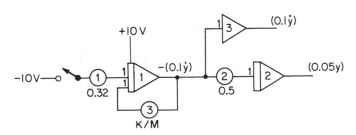

FIGURE 9-3   Scaled computer circuit for falling body including atmospheric drag.

The scaled computer diagram is shown in Fig. 9-3. The setting of potentiometer 3 incorporates both the ratio $2K/M$ and the integrator gain of 0.5.

The patching of this circuit may be checked using the procedure outlined in Section 8-13. The table of problem-check voltages is based on a setting of 0.2 for the ratio K/M and assumes that $+10V$ is temporarily connected to the initial-condition input of integrator 2.

PROBLEM-CHECK VOLTAGES

Amplifier Number	Output Voltage	Derivative Voltage
1	−10.0	5.2
2	−10.0	5.0
3	10.0	

The results of the simulation are included in Fig. 9-4 for a value of $K/M = 0.2$. We note that the maximum altitude is now 110 feet and the time of flight is 5.4 seconds. The velocity follows an exponentially decaying curve and reaches a value of about 70 ft/s at the time of impact.

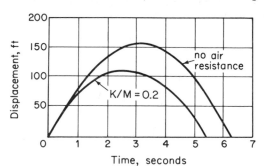

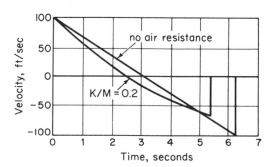

FIGURE 9-4   Velocity and displacement of falling body.

9-3 TRANSIENT RESPONSE OF
SERIES *RLC* CIRCUIT

In Section 7-13 we studied the behavior of a series circuit containing resistance, inductance, and capacitance when a dc voltage was applied to the circuit. A second-order differential equation was solved to obtain an equation for the current through the circuit. Depending upon the relative values of the components in the circuit, the response was either overdamped, underdamped, or critically damped.

As we have seen, this problem is simple enough to solve without a computer. However, it does provide an ideal simulation example, since we know how the circuit will behave. By using the parameter values given in Examples 7-17, 7-18, and 7-19, we may compare the computer results with those obtained from direct solution of the circuit equation.

The circuit to be simulated and the parameter values are given in Fig. 9-5.

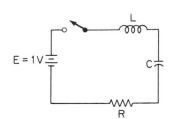

Parameter Values

Case	R, ohms	L, henrys	C, farads
I	8	1	0.5
II	1	1	0.5
III	$2\sqrt{2}$	1	0.5

FIGURE 9-5   Series *RLC* circuit and parameter values.

Using Kirchhoff's voltage law, the differential equation of the circuit is

$$L\frac{di}{dt} + Ri + \frac{1}{C}\int idt = E \qquad (9\text{-}9)$$

where i is the current after the switch is closed. Since $i = dq/dt$, we may remove the integral from Eq. (9-9) by using charge as the dependent variable. Thus

$$L\ddot{q} + R\dot{q} + \frac{q}{C} = E \qquad (9\text{-}10)$$

Solving Eq. (9-10) for the highest-order derivative gives

$$\ddot{q} = -\frac{R}{L}\dot{q} - \frac{1}{LC}q + \frac{E}{L} \qquad (9\text{-}11)$$

Using the procedure described in Chapter 8 for programming a second-order equation, we may draw an unscaled computer diagram as shown in Fig. 9-6.

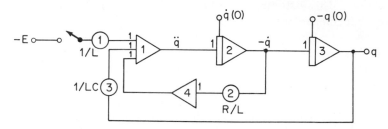

FIGURE 9-6   Unscaled computer diagram for RLC circuit.

To select amplitude scale factors, we must estimate the maximum values of the variables. This may be done by assuming a solution of the form

$$\dot{q} = i = I_m \sin \omega t = \frac{E}{R} \sin \omega t \qquad (9\text{-}12)$$

Using $R = 1$ ohm, I_m is then 1 ampere. Integrating Eq. (9-12) gives an equation for q as

$$q = \int \dot{q} \, dt = \frac{E}{R} \int \sin \omega t \, dt = -\frac{E}{\omega R} \cos \omega t \qquad (9\text{-}13)$$

The maximum value of q occurs when $\cos \omega t = -1$ and is equal to $E/\omega R$. To evaluate q_m, we use the undamped natural frequency ω_n of the circuit as an estimate of ω. Thus

$$\omega \cong \omega_n = \frac{1}{\sqrt{LC}} = 1.414 \text{ rad/s} \qquad (9\text{-}14)$$

Substituting for ω in Eq. (9-13) gives 0.707 coulombs as an estimate for the maximum value of q.

Differentiating Eq. (9-12), we obtain

$$\frac{d\dot{q}}{dt} = \ddot{q} = \frac{\omega E}{R} \cos \omega t \qquad (9\text{-}15)$$

The maximum value of $\ddot{q}$, which occurs when $\cos \omega t = 1$, is 1.414 coulombs per s².

Assuming that the computer has a 10-volt reference, the scale factors may be determined by inserting the estimated maximum values of the variables in Eq. (8-9). However, in order to produce convenient scale factors, the maxima are first rounded off to slightly higher values. The scaling table for the problem is given below.

Problem Variable	Estimated Maximum	Scale Factor	Computer Variable
q	1 coulomb	10 V/coulomb	$(10q)$
$\dot{q}$	1 coulomb/s	10 V/coulomb/s	$(10\dot{q})$
$\ddot{q}$	2 coulombs/s²	5 V/coulomb/s²	$(5\ddot{q})$
E	1 volt	10 V/V	$(10E)$

Since the natural frequency of the circuit is reasonable for computer operation, no change in time scale is necessary and the simulation is performed in "real time."

Substituting the computer variables into Eq. (9-11) while maintaining equality gives the scaled equation

$$\frac{1}{5}(5\ddot{q}) = -\frac{R}{10L}(10\dot{q}) - \frac{1}{10LC}(10q) + \frac{1}{10L}(10E) \qquad (9\text{-}16)$$

Equation (9-16) may be simplified to

$$(5\ddot{q}) = -\frac{R}{2L}(10\dot{q}) - \frac{1}{2LC}(10q) + \frac{1}{2L}(10E) \qquad (9\text{-}17)$$

The gains of the integrators are determined by taking the ratio of the scale factor of the output variable to the scale factor of the input variable. Thus, the gain of integrator 2 is

$$\frac{a_{\dot{q}}}{a_{\ddot{q}}} = \frac{10}{5} = 2$$

and the gain of integrator 3 is

$$\frac{a_q}{a_{\dot{q}}} = \frac{10}{10} = 1$$

The scaled computer diagram is shown in Fig. 9-7. Since there is no initial value of either $\dot{q}$ (current) or q (capacitor charge), no initial-condition voltages are applied to the integrators. The table in Fig. 9-7 shows the settings of potentiometer 2 for the three cases being studied. To obtain settings less than unity, the values of $R/2L$ have been multiplied by 1/10 and the corresponding gain of amplifier 1 increased by a factor of 10.

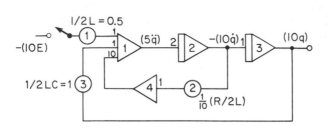

FIGURE 9-7   Scaled computer diagram for *RLC* circuit.

Problem-check voltages for Case I with 1 volt temporarily connected to the initial-condition inputs are given below.

Amplifier Number	Output Voltage	Derivative Voltage
1	2.0	
2	−1.0	−4.0
3	−1.0	1.0
4	0.4	

The currents in the series *RLC* circuit for resistances of 8, 1, and $2\sqrt{2}$ ohms are shown in Figs. 7-5, 7-6, and 7-7 respectively. Since the simulation results should duplicate these curves, they are not repeated here.

9-4 STUDY OF CHEMICAL PROCESSES

Chemical processes convert raw materials into products through chemical reactions. In chemical production, the aim is to obtain from reactions the maximum yield of product at lowest cost. Since side products may also be formed in a chemical reaction, the process must be controlled to maximize the conversion of raw material into product but, at the same time, to minimize its conversion into side products. Many different types of reactors are used to bring about chemical reactions. Reactions may take place in either open or pressurized vessels in which the materials are held and stirred; these are known as *batch reactions*. In other cases, the materials flow continuously through one or more vessels or tubes while the reaction is taking place.

Computer simulation provides a convenient, inexpensive, and danger-free means of studying chemical reactions under varying process conditions. This particular study provides a simple but effective illustration of the analog computer's ability to simulate a chemical reaction involving simultaneous differential equations.

Chemical reactions involve the joining together or the separation of atoms and molecules. One type of simple reaction may be expressed as

$$A + B \longrightarrow C \qquad (9\text{-}18)$$

where elements A and B combine chemically to form a product C. In the reaction

$$A + B \longrightarrow C + D \qquad (9\text{-}19)$$

a defined product C is accompanied by a definite side product D.

A consecutive multi-step reaction involues several elements; the first element proceeds through a reaction to produce a second element which then changes to a third element. This type of reaction is represented by

$$A \longrightarrow B \longrightarrow C \qquad (9\text{-}20)$$

Chemical reactions proceed at rates determined by the reactivity of the elements involved. Rates of reaction may be expressed by differential equations which originate in the theory of reaction kinetics. These equations account for the amount of raw material depleted per unit time, or the amount of product formed per unit time. In one common form of reaction, the rate of change of material is proportional to the quantity of that material present. This is known as a *first-order reaction* and (for a material A) is expressed by the first-order differential equation

$$\frac{dN_A}{dt} = -kN_A \qquad (9\text{-}21)$$

where N_A is the concentration and k is the reaction-rate constant of the material.

For our simulation study, we will assume a two-step reaction which proceeds according to Eq. (9-20). It is carried out in a batch reactor initially charged with the pure material A. The desired component of the reaction mixture is element B, whose concentration passes through a maximum during the course of the reaction. The time and magnitude of the maximum depend on the parameters of the system, namely the reaction-rate constants. Eventually, the reacting mixture becomes pure C.

In order to simplify the problem, we will use normalized concentrations for the elements expressed as

$$n_A = \frac{N_A}{N_o} \qquad n_B = \frac{N_B}{N_o} \qquad n_C = \frac{N_C}{N_o} \qquad (9\text{-}22)$$

where n_A, n_B, and n_C are dimensionless concentrations varying between zero and unity, and N_o is the initial concentration of material A. From Eq. (9-21), the differential equations expressing the change of concentration of each of the three materials with time may be written

$$\frac{dn_A}{dt} = -k_1 n_A \quad \text{(rate of depletion of } A) \tag{9-23}$$

$$\frac{dn_B}{dt} = k_1 n_A - k_2 n_B \quad \text{(net rate of formation of } B) \tag{9-24}$$

$$\frac{dn_C}{dt} = k_2 n_B \quad \text{(rate of formation of } C) \tag{9-25}$$

For our example, we will assume that the reaction constants k_1 and k_2 have values of 0.1 per minute and 0.025 per minute, respectively. The normalized concentrations at $t = 0$ are $n_A(0) = 1.0$, $n_B(0) = 0$, and $n_C(0) = 0$.

Using the circuits for a first-order equation derived in Section 8-2, the unscaled computer diagram for the system is shown in Fig. 9-8.

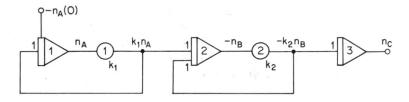

FIGURE 9-8   Unscaled computer diagram for chemical reaction.

The magnitude scaling for the problem using a ± 10-volt computer reference is summarized in the following table. As previously mentioned, the quantities n_A, n_B, and n_C are dimensionless, and their maximum values are unity, based on the conservation of matter.

Problem Variable	Estimated Maximum	Scale Factor (volts/dim. unit)	Computer Variable
n_A	1.0	10	$(10n_A)$
n_B	1.0	10	$(10n_B)$
n_C	1.0	10	$(10n_C)$

Substituting the computer variables into the unscaled equations, the scaled equations are:

$$\frac{d(10n_A)}{dt} = -k_1(10n_A) \tag{9-26}$$

$$\frac{d(10n_B)}{dt} = k_1(10n_A) - k_2(10n_B) \tag{9-27}$$

$$\frac{d(10n_C)}{dt} = k_2(10n_B) \tag{9-28}$$

We next come to the matter of choosing a suitable time scale for the simulation. The analog computer is designed to integrate with respect to time in units of seconds, whereas the rate constants k_1 and k_2 are in units of amount per minute. Hence, it will be convenient to define one second of computing time as corresponding to one minute of problem time. In this case, we can interpret k_1 and k_2 as being 0.1 per second and 0.025 per second, respectively. Nonetheless, with these magnitudes for the rate constants, we can anticipate a solution time of several hundred seconds. Hence, it would appear desirable to speed the solution up by a factor of 10. Thus, the computer time τ is defined by $\tau = \beta t = t/10$, from which

$$t = 10\tau \quad \text{and} \quad dt = 10d\tau \tag{9-29}$$

Introducing this time-scale charge, the scaled equations become

$$\frac{d(10n_A)}{10d\tau} = -k_1(10n_A)$$

or

$$\frac{d(10n_A)}{d\tau} = -10k_1(10n_A) \tag{9-30}$$

Likewise

$$\frac{d(10n_B)}{d\tau} = 10k_1(10n_A) - 10k_2(10n_B) \tag{9-31}$$

$$\frac{d(10n_C)}{d\tau} = 10k_2(10n_B) \tag{9-32}$$

The scaled computer diagram for the reaction simulation is shown in Fig. 9-9. The initial-condition voltage of -10 volts applied to integrator 1 corresponds to the value of $n_A(0)$.

Figure 9-10 shows the computer solution of the problem for $k_1 = 0.1$

and $k_2 = 0.025$. The curves show the normalized concentration versus problem time for each of the three elements of the mixture. The concentration of A decreases exponentially as A reacts to form B. The concentration of B, the desired product, increases to a maximum and then decreases to zero as B is converted to C. The by–product C increases continuously and, if the reaction is allowed to continue to its completion, the concentration of C becomes unity as all of the material is converted to C. For maximum product yield, we should terminate the reaction after about 18 minutes.

The shape of the concentration–time profiles depends on the values of the reaction-rate coefficients. A different choice of k_1 and k_2 may produce curves completely different from those shown in Fig. 9-10.

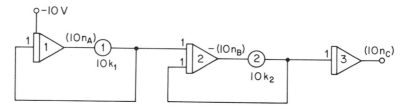

FIGURE 9-9   Scaled computer diagram for chemical reaction.

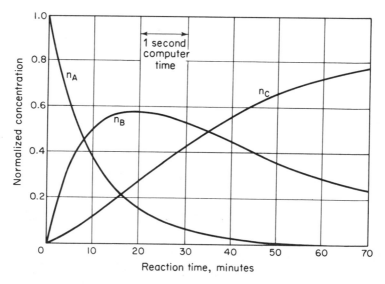

FIGURE 9-10   Material concentrations for first-order chemical reactions.

9-5 SIMULATION OF AUTOMOBILE
SUSPENSION SYSTEMS

In Section 8-5 we showed the computer solution of simultaneous differential equations that describe a coupled system. As an illustration of the simulation of a coupled mechanical system, consider the problem of designing a suitable suspension system for an automobile. In particular, assume that we wish to investigate the effect of various degrees of shock-absorber damping on the response of the car to irregularities in the road surface.

A complete representation of a suspension system is too complex for our purposes. Hence we will consider a simplified model that ignores the influence of forward speed and car steering and further assumes that the tires are idealized as resilient springs.* Figure 9-11 shows one wheel of the simplified system.

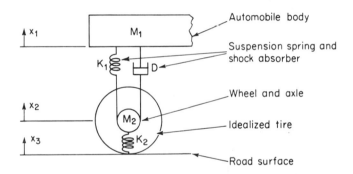

FIGURE 9-11   Simplified representation of automobile suspension system.

The following quantities are included in the model.

$M_1 = \frac{1}{4}$ mass of automobile

$M_2 =$ mass of wheel $+\frac{1}{2}$ mass of axle

$K_1 =$ spring constant of suspension spring

$D =$ damping coefficient of shock absorber

$K_2 =$ spring constant of tire

$x_1 =$ displacement of the body of the automobile

$x_2 =$ displacement of the wheel

$x_3 = x(t) =$ forcing function describing profile of road surface

---

*From *Applications Reference Library*, 7.6.13a. Electronic Associates, Inc.: Long Branch, New Jersey, September, 1968.

The differential equations of motion of the system are obtained by summing the forces acting on each mass. Thus we have

$$M_1\ddot{x}_1 + D(\dot{x}_1 - \dot{x}_2) + K_1(x_1 - x_2) = 0 \tag{9-33}$$

$$M_2\ddot{x}_2 + D(\dot{x}_2 - \dot{x}_1) + K_1(x_2 - x_1) + K_2(x_2 - x_3) = 0 \tag{9-34}$$

Solving these equations for the highest-order derivatives gives

$$-\ddot{x}_1 = \frac{D}{M_1}(\dot{x}_1 - \dot{x}_2) + \frac{K_1}{M_1}(x_1 - x_2) \tag{9-35}$$

$$\ddot{x}_2 = \frac{D}{M_2}(\dot{x}_1 - \dot{x}_2) + \frac{K_1}{M_2}(x_1 - x_2) + \frac{K_2}{M_2}(x_3 - x_2) \tag{9-36}$$

Note that Eq. (9-36) has been multiplied by -1; this simplifies the programming since common variables appear in both equations. Figure 9-12 is an unscaled programming diagram for solution of these equations.

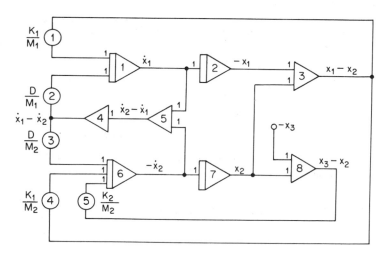

FIGURE 9-12   Unscaled computer diagram for automobile suspension system.

The magnitudes of the parameters are assumed to be as follows:

$$M_1 = 25 \text{ slugs} \qquad K_1 = 1000 \text{ lb/ft}$$
$$M_2 = 2 \text{ slugs} \qquad K_2 = 5000 \text{ lb/ft}$$
$$0 \leq D \leq 200 \text{ lb/ft/s}$$

From our knowledge of the problem, we will estimate the maximum value of the displacements x_1, x_2, and x_3 to be one foot. Since the displacements may occur in either direction from the equilibrium point, the maximum value of $|x_1 - x_2|$ is two feet.

We next estimate the maximum values of the other variables using Eq. (8-19). Neglecting the coupling terms in the system, the undamped natural frequency of the main mass is

$$\omega_{n_1} = \sqrt{K_1/M_1} = 6.32 \text{ rad/s} \tag{9-37}$$

and the undamped natural frequency of the wheel and axle is

$$\omega_{n_2} = \sqrt{(K_1 + K_2)/M_2} = 54.8 \text{ rad/s} \tag{9-38}$$

For convenience we will use $\omega_{n_1} = 5$ rad/s and $\omega_{n_2} = 50$ rad/s. The scaling table for the problem, based on a 10-volt computer reference, is given below.

Problem Variable	Estimated Maximum	Scale Factor	Computer Variable
x_1	1 ft	10V/ft	$(10x_1)$
$\dot{x}_1$	5 ft/s	2V/ft/s	$(2\dot{x}_1)$
x_2	1 ft	10V/ft	$(10x_2)$
$\dot{x}_2$	50 ft/s	0.2V/ft/s	$(0.2\dot{x}_2)$
$x_1 - x_2$	2 ft	5V/ft	$[5(x_1 - x_2)]$
$\dot{x}_1 - \dot{x}_2$	50 ft/s	0.2V/ft/s	$[0.2(\dot{x}_1 - \dot{x}_2)]$
$x_2 - x_3$	2 ft	5V/ft	$[5(x_2 - x_3)]$
$\ddot{x}_1$	25	0.4V/ft/s²	$(0.4\ddot{x}_1)$
$\ddot{x}_2$	2500	0.004V/ft/s²	$(0.004\ddot{x}_2)$
x_3	1 ft	10V/ft	$(10x_3)$

With the above scale factors, integrators 1 and 2 in Fig. 9-12 must provide gains of 5 and integrators 6 and 7 gains of 50. Since the latter gains are rather high, a change in time scale should be considered. If the problem is slowed down by a factor of 10, the gains become 0.5 and 5, which are reasonable values, and the maximum frequency in the simulation is about 5 rad/s, which is suitable for electromechanical recording equipment.

Substituting the computer variables into Eqs. (9-35) and (9-36) gives the scaled equations

$$-(0.4\ddot{x}_1) = \frac{2D}{M_1}[0.2(\dot{x}_1 - \dot{x}_2)] + \frac{2K_1}{25M_1}[5(x_1 - x_2)] \tag{9-39}$$

$$(0.004\ddot{x}_2) = \frac{D}{50M_2}[0.2(\dot{x}_1 - \dot{x}_2)] + \frac{K_1}{1250M_2}[5(x_1 - x_2)]$$

$$+ \frac{K_2}{1250M_2}[5(x_3 - x_2)] \tag{9-40}$$

Figure 9-13 shows the final scaled simulation. The time-scale change is incorporated into the settings of the integrator coefficient potentiometers. Note that the integrator inputs and potentiometer ratios have been selected so that the latter will be less than unity. The table of problem-check voltages for this simulation was previously given in Example 8-10.

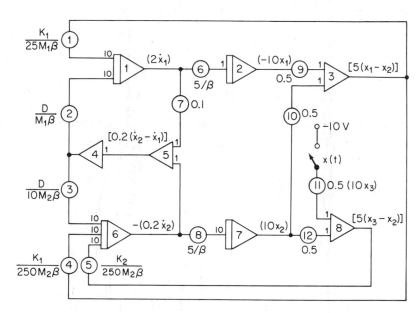

FIGURE 9-13   Scaled computer diagram for automobile suspension system.

Various "road" functions may be introduced into the simulation by providing an appropriate excitation voltage for $x(t)$. For example, a sinus-

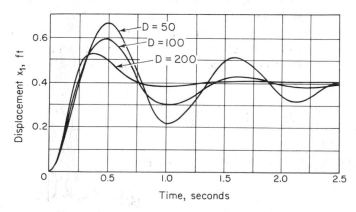

FIGURE 9-14   Response of car body to step input.

oidal input of varying frequency would simulate traveling over a "washboard" surface at different speeds. For simplicity, we will assume a step-input forcing function, as would be encountered by an automobile riding over a curb whose height, in this case, is 5 inches. Figure 9-14 shows the response of the car body with shock-absorber damping at 50, 100, and 200 lb/ft/s. We note that less damping introduces more "bounce"; conversely, increased damping produces a stiffer response, which would display a "jolting" characteristic.

PROBLEMS FOR CHAPTER 9

The following problems are intended to further illustrate the use of the analog computer in simulating physical systems. In each problem a completely scaled computer diagram should be developed using a 10-volt reference. The diagram should show each signal, the setting of each coefficient potentiometer, and the value of each initial-condition voltage. Assume that the specified outputs are to be recorded so that the solution frequencies should be in the range of approximately 0.1 to 1.0 Hz.

If a small analog computer (6–10 operational amplifiers) is available, the problems may be programmed and solved on the computer as laboratory exercises.

1. The rate of decay of a radioactive isotope is expressed by the equation

$$\frac{da}{dt} = -\lambda a$$

where a is the quantity of isotope present and λ is the disintegration-rate constant, equal to 0.693 divided by the half-life of the isotope (half-life is the time in which one-half of the remaining atoms of the isotope disintegrate). Develop a simulation to show the decay of 100 grams of the zirconium isotope Zr^{95} which has a half-life of 60 days.

2. Newton's Law of Cooling states that the rate of change of temperature of a body is proportional to the difference between the temperature of the body and the temperature of the surrounding medium. The constant of proportionality is called the heat-transfer coefficient and its value depends upon the material and size of the body. For uniform temperature throughout the body, its cooling is given by the equation

$$\frac{dT}{dt} = -k(T - T_A)$$

where T is the temperature of the body, T_A is the temperature of the surrounding medium and k is the heat-transfer coefficient. Develop a simulation for the cooling of a body whose initial temperature is 100°C. Assume that T_A remains constant at 25°C and $k = 0.2$.

3. Certain chemical processes are reversible. In a particular reversible reaction

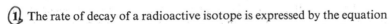
$$A \underset{K_2}{\overset{K_1}{\rightleftarrows}} B$$

The differential equations expressing the change of concentration of each of the materials are

$$\frac{dN_A}{dt} = -K_1 N_A + K_2 N_B$$

$$\frac{dN_B}{dt} = K_1 N_A - K_2 N_B$$

where N_A and N_B are the concentrations and K_1 and K_2 are the reaction-rate constants. Develop a simulation for the reaction assuming the normalized concentrations of A and B are unity and zero respectively at $t = 0$, and that $K_1 = 0.5/\text{hr}$ and $K_2 = 0.2/\text{hr}$.

4. In the circuit below, switch 1 is closed for a sufficient time to establish a steady-state current through the inductor. Develop a simulation to show the inductor current after switch 2 is closed.

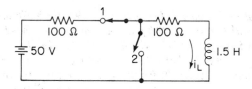

5. The tank shown below is a vertical cylinder having a cross section of 10 ft.^{2} It initially contains 50 ft.^{3} of water. Water is flowing in at the rate of 5 ft.^{3}/min and out at the rate of 10 ft.^{3}/min. Develop a computer simulation which shows the water level H as a function of time. (*Hint:* Write an equation for dH/dt.)

6. A water tank contains 2000 lb of water at an initial temperature of 60°F. Water at 100°F flows into the tank at the rate of 500 lb/min and the outflow is regulated so that the content of the tank is held constant. The rate of change of temperature in the tank is defined by the equation

$$\frac{dT}{dt} = \frac{W_i}{M} T_i - \frac{W_o}{M} T$$

where W is the flow rate and M the weight of the water in the tank. Develop a simulation for the temperature of the stored fluid.

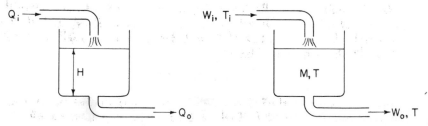

7. A second inlet is added to the tank in Problem 6 which introduces water at a temperature of 120°F at a rate of 100 lb/min. Assuming the tank content is again held constant, modify the simulation to include the second input stream.

8. Develop a simulation for the vibrating spring system shown in Fig. 7-8 (page 209), using the parameters and initial conditions given in Example 7-21 (page 212).

9. The solution of the second-order equation

$$\frac{d^2x}{dt^2} + \omega^2 x = 0$$

is an undamped sine wave having a frequency of ω rad/s. Develop a computer circuit which can serve as a sine-wave generator whose frequency can be conveniently varied between 1 and 100 Hz and whose peak amplitude is 10 volts.

10. The equation of motion of the simple pendulum shown below is

$$\frac{d^2\theta}{dt^2} + \frac{g}{L} \sin \theta = 0$$

where g is the constant of gravitational acceleration and θ is the angular displacement measured in radians. If θ is kept small (20° or less), then sin $\theta \cong \theta$ and a linear equation

$$\frac{d^2\theta}{dt^2} + \frac{g}{L}\theta = 0$$

is obtained. Develop a simulation which gives θ as a function of time for $L = 8$ inches, $\theta_o = 0.1$ radian, and $\dot{\theta}_o = 0$ radians/second.

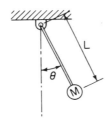

11. The switch in the circuit below is closed at $t = 0$. Develop a computer simulation to obtain e_o as a function of time. Assume that there is no energy stored in the circuit prior to closing the switch.

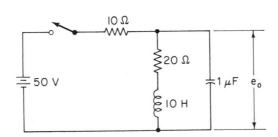

12. The system shown overleaf is initially at rest. At time $t = 0$ the cord connecting the two masses is cut. Develop a computer simulation which shows the motion x of W_1.

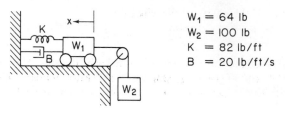

$$W_1 = 64 \text{ lb}$$
$$W_2 = 100 \text{ lb}$$
$$K = 82 \text{ lb/ft}$$
$$B = 20 \text{ lb/ft/s}$$

13. Develop a computer simulation for the coupled mechanical system shown in the figure below.

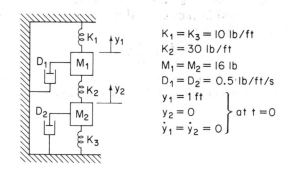

$$K_1 = K_3 = 10 \text{ lb/ft}$$
$$K_2 = 30 \text{ lb/ft}$$
$$M_1 = M_2 = 16 \text{ lb}$$
$$D_1 = D_2 = 0.5 \text{ lb/ft/s}$$
$$y_1 = 1 \text{ ft}$$
$$y_2 = 0 \qquad \Big\} \text{ at } t = 0$$
$$\dot{y}_1 = \dot{y}_2 = 0$$

CHAPTER 2

1. $e_o = 0.305\text{V}, \Delta e_o = -0.045\text{V}$
5. $\beta = 0.333, \quad A\beta = 667,$
   $e_o = 5.991\text{V}, \varepsilon = 0.15\%$
7. $R_i = 100 \text{ k}\Omega, R_i = 10\text{k}\Omega$
12. $k = 0.685$
14. $\alpha = 0.500$
16. (a) $z = -(x + 10y),$
    (c) $z = -(10ax + by/10),$
    (e) $z = -(1.25x + 0.35y)$

18. $e_o = -\left(\dfrac{1-k}{k}\right)e_i$

20. (a) $e_o = -\displaystyle\int (10e_1 + 5e_2)\, dt,$

    (c) $z = -\displaystyle\int (10x_1 + x_2)\, dt - Z_o$

22. $e_o = 15t - 100$
25. (a) $z = 60\text{V}$, (c) $z = 19\text{V}$,
    (e) $z = -10\text{V}$

27. $e_o = -\dfrac{C_1}{C_2}e_i$

28. (a) $G(j\omega) = -\dfrac{1 + j\omega CR_2}{j\omega CR_1}$

29. (a) $e_o = 10 \cos 100t$

CHAPTER 3

1. $e_o = -0.9978\text{V}, \varepsilon = 0.32\%$
3. $\Delta A = +0.02\%$ and -0.03%
5. (a) $e_o = 11.1\text{mV},$
   (c) $e_o = 0.4\text{mV/s}$
6. $\Delta e_o = 0.25\%$
8. $f_c = 10{,}700\text{Hz}$
9. $f_c = 2.5 \text{ MHz},$
   gain $= 0.999 \angle -2.3°$
11. $R_1 = 233\text{k}\Omega$
15. gain $= 140\text{dB}$
16. $e_o = 70\mu\text{V}$

ANSWERS TO SELECTED PROBLEMS

CHAPTER 4

6. (a) $e_1 = \dfrac{xy}{100}$, $e_2 = \dfrac{-xz}{100}$, $e_3 = \dfrac{xu}{10}$

10. (b) $\frac{1}{3}V = 1$ unit $f(x)$

(c)

Tap	Voltage	Tap	Voltage
End	−1.67	6	−9.66
1	−4.67	7	−8.66
2	−7.00	8	−7.00
3	−8.66	9	−4.67
4	−9.66	End	−1.67
5	−10.00		

CHAPTER 5

1.

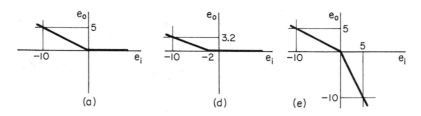

3.

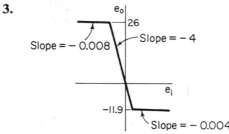

5. $k_1 = 0.5$, $k_2 = 0.6$

7.

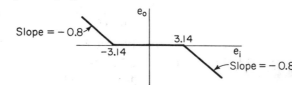

13. $e_o = -3.5V$, $e_o = -0.35V$

15. One possible set of values is $R_1 = 100\text{k}\Omega$, $R_2 = 2\text{k}\Omega$, $R_3 = 10\Omega$.

CHAPTER 6

9. $e_o = 0.99\text{V}$

14. $E_R = 10\text{V}$

CHAPTER 7

13. $y = \dfrac{x^2}{2} + C$

15. $y = \dfrac{t^4}{4} + C$

17. $y = \sqrt{x^2 + C}$

19. $y = C\sqrt[3]{x^4}$

21. $\ln(xy) + y - x = C$

23. $y = \dfrac{x}{2} + C$

25. $y = x^2 + 4x + 3$

27. $y = e^{-x} + 10$

29. $q = 2t^3$

31. $x = 2$ inches

33. $n = 272$

35. $v_C = E(1 - e^{-t/RC})$

37. $v = 100(1 - e^{-0.1t})$

39. $y = C_1 e^{1.707t} + C_2 e^{0.293t}$

41. $y = C_1 e^x + C_2 e^{2x} + C_3 x e^{2x}$

43. $y = C_1 e^x \cos x + C_2 e^x \sin x$

45. $y = C_1 e^{0.5t} \sin \tfrac{1}{2}\sqrt{3}\,t + C_2 e^{0.5t} \cos \tfrac{1}{2}\sqrt{3}\,t$

47. $y = 3e^{-2x} + 2e^{3x}$

49. $y = 3e^{-x} \sin x$

51. $x = -3 \cos 16t$ inches

53. $b = 12$

55. $i = 45e^{-1000t} + 84.8 \sin(628t - 0.561)\ mA$

57. $\theta = \theta_o \cos \sqrt{k/J}\,t + (\omega_o/\sqrt{k/J}) \sin \sqrt{k/J}\,t$

CHAPTER 8

1.

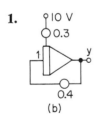

(b)

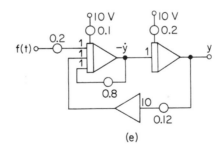

(e)

2. (a) $\dot{x} + 0.7x = 0,\ x(0) = -2$

3.

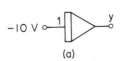

(a)

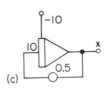

(c)

6. $(10\ddot{x}) + 6.25\,(4\dot{x}) + 25(2x) = 0$

7. Scaled equation $(2\dot{v}) + 0.8(0.1v) = 0$

8. Scaled equation $(0.01\ddot{x}) + 0.32(0.05\dot{x}) + 0.8\,(0.2x) = 0$

9. Scaled equation $(0.0005\ddot{q}) + (0.02\dot{q}) + 0.625\,(2q) = 0$

12.

Amplifier number	Output voltage	Derivative voltage
1	10	2
2	−10	4
3	10	5
4	−10	
5	−10	
6	−8	

The following references provide an introduction to analog computers at an elementary level.

Truitt, T. D., and Rogers, A. E., *Basics of Analog Computers*. New York: John Rider, Inc., 1960.

Computer Basics: Volume I, *Introduction to Analog Computers*, and Volume II, *Analog Computers: Mathematics and Circuitry*. Indianapolis, Indiana: Howard W. Sams and Co., 1962.

Jacobowitz, H., *Electronic Computers*. Garden City, New York: Doubleday and Co., 1963.

Stice, J. E., and Swanson, B. S., *Electronic Analog Computer Primer*. New York: Blaisdell Publishing Co., 1965.

The following references are written at an engineering level and emphasize analog computing circuits and techniques.

Scott, N. R., *Analog and Digital Computer Technology*. New York: McGraw Hill Book Co., 1960.

Johnson, C. L., *Analog Computer Techniques*. New York: McGraw-Hill Book Company, 1963.

Korn, G. A. and T. M., *Electronic Analog and Hybrid Computers*. New York: McGraw-Hill Book Co., 1964.

Handbook of Analog Computation. Princeton, N. J.: Electronics Associates, Inc., 1967.

The following references emphasize the application of analog computers to the solution of engineering problems. They assume a knowledge of differential equations.

BIBLIOGRAPHY

Fifer, S., *Analog Computation*. New York: McGraw-Hill Book Company, 1960.

Ashley, J. R., *Introduction to Analog Computation*. New York: John Wiley and Sons, Inc., 1963.

James, M. L., Smith, G. M., and Wolford, J. C., *Analog Computer Simulation of Engineering Systems*. Scranton, Pa.: International Textbook Co., 1966.

Peterson, G. R., *Basic Analog Computation*. New York: Macmillan Company, 1967.

Handbook of Analog Computation. Concord, Calif.: Systron-Donner Corp., 1967.

Moyle, M. P., *Introduction to Computers for Engineers*. New York: John Wiley and Sons, Inc., 1967.

Applications Reference Library and Educator's Demonstration Series. Long Branch, N. J.: Electronics Associates, Inc. (index available on request).

The following references describe the characteristics and applications of operational amplifiers.

Handbook of Operational Amplifier Applications. Tucson, Arizona: Burr-Brown Research Corporation, 1963.

Handbook of Operational Amplifier Active R C Networks. Tucson, Arizona: Burr-Brown Research Corporation, 1966.

Applications Manual for Computing Amplifiers. Dedham, Mass.: Philbrick Researches, Inc., 1966.

APPENDIXES

APPENDIX A-1: TABLE OF SIMPLE DERIVATIVES

In this table, u and v represent functions of x; a, n, and e represent constants (e = 2.718 . . .); and all angles are measured in radians.

$\frac{d}{dx}(a) = 0$	$\frac{d}{dx}(x) = 1$
$\frac{d}{dx}(ax) = a$	$\frac{d}{dx}(au) = a\frac{du}{dx}$
$\frac{d}{dx}(x^n) = nx^{n-1}$	$\frac{d}{dx}(u^n) = nu^{n-1}\frac{du}{dx}$
$\frac{d}{dx}(\sin x) = \cos x$	$\frac{d}{dx}(\sin u) = \cos u\frac{du}{dx}$
$\frac{d}{dx}(\cos x) = -\sin x$	$\frac{d}{dx}(\cos u) = -\sin u\frac{du}{dx}$
$\frac{d}{dx}(\ln u) = \frac{1}{u}\frac{du}{dx}$	$\frac{d}{dx}(\log u) = \frac{0.4343}{u}\frac{du}{dx}$
$\frac{d}{dx}(e^u) = e^u\frac{du}{dx}$	$\frac{d}{dx}(a^u) = a^u \ln a\frac{du}{dx}$
$\frac{d}{dx}(u \pm v \pm \cdots) = \frac{du}{dx} \pm \frac{dv}{dx} \pm \cdots$	$\frac{d}{dx}\left(\frac{u}{v}\right) = \frac{v(du/dx) - u(dv/dx)}{v^2}$
$\frac{d}{dx}(uv) = u\frac{dv}{dx} + v\frac{du}{dx}$	

APPENDIX A-2: TABLE OF SIMPLE INTEGRALS

In this table, a, n, and e represent constants; C denotes the constant of integration; and all angles are measured in radians.

$\int du = u + C$	$\int a\,du = au + C$
$\int (du \pm dv) = \int du \pm \int dv$	$\int u^n\,du = \frac{u^{n+1}}{n+1} + C \qquad n \neq -1$
$\int \frac{du}{u} = \ln u + C$	$\int e^u\,du = e^u + C$
$\int a^u du = \frac{a^u}{\ln a} + C$	$\int \sin u\,du = -\cos u + C$
$\int \cos u\,du = \sin u + C$	$\int \ln u\,du = u \ln u - u + C$

APPENDIX B: TABLE OF PROGRAMMING SYMBOLS

Element	Symbol	Function
Operational amplifier (without feedback)	$x \circ\!\!-\!\!\left[-A \right]\!\!-\!\!\circ z$	$z = -Ax$
Inverter	$x \circ\!\!-\!\!^{1}\!\!\left[\triangleright \right]\!\!-\!\!\circ z$	$z = -x$
Summer	$x \circ\!\!-\!\!^{1} \quad y \circ\!\!-\!\!^{10} \left[\triangleright \right]\!\!-\!\!\circ z$	$z = -(x + 10y)$
Coefficient potentiometer (grounded)	$x \circ\!\!-\!\!\bigcirc_{k}\!\!-\!\!\circ z$	$z = kx$
Coefficient potentiometer (ungrounded)	$H \circ \quad {}^{\circ x} \bigcirc_{k} \; z \quad {}_{\circ y}$	$z = k(x-y) + y$
Integrator	$x \circ\!\!-\!\!^{1} \; {}^{\circ z(0)} \; y \circ\!\!-\!\!^{10} \left[\triangleright \right]\!\!-\!\!\circ z$	$z = -\int (x + 10y)dt - z(0)$
Servomultiplier	$x \circ\!\!-\!\!\boxed{N} \quad {}^{\circ y}\bigcirc_{\circ -y}\!\!-\!\!\circ z$	$z = \dfrac{xy}{E_R}$
Servo function generator	$x \circ\!\!-\!\!\boxed{N} \quad {}^{E_R}\!\!\!\!\curvearrowright\!\!-\!\!z \quad {}_{-E_R}$	$z = f(x)$
Servo resolver	$\theta \circ\!\!-\!\!\boxed{R} \quad {}^{\circ r}\!\!\!\curvearrowright\!\!\circ y \;\; \circ z \quad {}_{\circ -r}$	$y = r \sin \theta$ $z = r \cos \theta$
Multiplier (general)	$x \circ\!\!-\!\! y \circ\!\!-\!\!\boxtimes\!\!-\!\!\circ z$	$z = \dfrac{xy}{E_R}$
Multiplier (quarter–square with amplifier)	$x \circ\!\!-\!\! -x \circ\!\!-\!\!\boxtimes \; {}^{y \; -y}\!\!\left[\triangleright \right]\!\!-\!\!\circ z$	$z = \dfrac{-xy}{E_R}$
Variable function generator	$x \circ\!\!-\!\!\left[f \right]\!\!-\!\!\circ z$	$z = f(x)$

APPENDIX C: TABLE OF TRANSFER IMPEDANCES

Network	Transfer Impedance
	R
	$\dfrac{1}{j\omega C}$
	$\dfrac{R}{1+j\omega RC}$
	$R+\dfrac{1}{j\omega C}$
	$2R+j\omega RC$
	$\dfrac{1}{j\omega C}\left(\dfrac{1+j\omega 2RC}{j\omega RC}\right)$
	$R_1\left[\dfrac{1+j\omega 2R_2C}{1+j\omega(R_1+R_2)C}\right]$
	$\dfrac{1}{j\omega C_1}\left[\dfrac{1+j\omega R(C_1+C_2)}{1+j\omega RC_2}\right]$
	$2R_1\left[\dfrac{1+j\omega(R_2+R_1/2)C}{1+j\omega R_2C}\right]$
	$2R_1\left(\dfrac{1+j\omega 2R_2C_2}{1-\omega^2 2R_1R_2C_2^2}\right)$

$R_1C_1=4R_2C_2$

282

INDEX

Abacus, 1
Absolute-value circuit, 139–140
Accuracy:
    analog computer, 12–13
    digital computer, 6
Addition (*see* Summation)
Airpax Electronics, Inc., 91
Alarm, overload, 171–173
Amplifier:
    bistable, 138
    chopper stabilized, 86–98
    differential, 76–86
    drift-stabilized, 86–98
    operational (*see* Operational
        amplifier)
    servo, 110–113
    stabilizer, 88–90, 98
Amplitude scaling (*see* Magnitude
    scaling)
Analog:
    mathematical, 7
    physical, 7
Analog computer:
    comparison with digital computer, 13
    general description, 9–12, 164
    time limitations, 240–241
Analog principle, 3
Analog simulation, 7–9
Arbitrary functions, 119–120
Attenuator (*see* Coefficient
    potentiometer)
Automatic balancing (*see* Drift
    stabilization)
Automatic gain control, 126
Automobile suspension system,
    265–269
Auxiliary equation, 195

Babbage, Charles, 2
BALANCE mode, 170
Balancing, of dc amplifiers, 76, 85, 87,
    97

Ball and disc integrator, 3–4
Bistable amplifier, 138
Bootstrap technique, 224
Boundary conditions, 184
Breakpoint, 131, 141
Bush, Vannevar, 3

Capacitor, computing, 102–103
Checking, computer programming,
    245–248
CHECK mode, 169
Chemical reaction, 260–264
Chopper, 88
    electromechanical, 90–92, 113
    FET, 93–94
    photo, 94–95
    summary of characteristics, 95
    transistor, 92–93
Chopper stabilization (*see* Drift
    stabilization)
Clevite Corp., Brush Instruments Div.,
    174
Coefficient potentiometer:
    description, 34–35
    grounded, unloaded, 35–37
    grounded, with load, 37–39
    setting methods, 34, 39–40
    ungrounded, 36–37
    use with operational amplifier,
        43–46
Common-mode rejection, 79
Comparator, 138
Compensating network, 72
COMPUTE mode, 168
Computer:
    analog (*see* Analog computer)
    digital (*see* Digital computer)
    general definition of, 1
    history of, 1–5
    hybrid, 13–15
    programming (*see* Programming)
Computer variable, 8, 233

284